ILLUSTRATOR 9

in easy steps

ROBERT SHUFFLEBOTHAM

COMPUTER STEP

In easy steps is an imprint of Computer Step
Southfield Road . Southam
Warwickshire CV47 OFB . England

http://www.ineasysteps.com

Notice of Liability
Every effort has been made to ensure that this book contains accurate and current information. However, Computer Step and the author shall not be liable for any loss or damage suffered by readers as a result of any information contained herein.

Trademarks
Adobe® and Illustrator® are registered trademarks of Adobe Systems Incorporated. All other trademarks are acknowledged as belonging to their respective companies.

Printed and bound in the United Kingdom

ISBN 1-84078-121-1

Table Of Contents

The Working Environment

Chapter One

Adobe Illustrator is a powerful drawing application that you can use to produce anything from the simplest of logos through to the most complex of maps, diagrams or illustrations. Illustrator provides a rich array of tools and commands for creating compelling, distinctive graphics for print, presentations and the Web.

This chapter introduces the fundamentals of the working environment. It covers page setup, the Toolbox, the Macintosh and Windows working environments, and a number of conventions and techniques that will help you to work efficiently in Adobe Illustrator.

Covers

Vector v Bitmap

Adobe Illustrator is an object-oriented, vector based drawing application.

Object-oriented means that each shape you create in Illustrator exists as a complete, distinct entity. (Even if an object is completely obscured by another object it still exists and is part of the file.)

Vector based means that the shapes or paths you create in Illustrator are defined by mathematical formulae. One significant advantage of this is that if you import an EPS created in Illustrator into a page layout application such as Adobe PageMaker, Adobe InDesign or QuarkXPress, you can enlarge it without losing any quality – lines and curves will still print smoothly and crisply. Illustrations created in Illustrator are termed 'resolution-independent'.

Vector illustration at actual size

This is what makes Adobe Illustrator good for creating artwork consisting of clear-cut, well defined shapes and type effects as you often find in logos and diagrams.

In contrast, applications such as Adobe Photoshop are pixel based applications. Images scanned into Photoshop, or created from scratch within Photoshop, consist of a rectangular grid of pixels. So, for example, in Photoshop a circle is not an independent, separate, complete shape – it is the pixels in that area of the grid coloured to look like a circle.

Bitmap images are resolution dependent. This means if you scale them up they tend to create jagged, 'blocky' output.

Bitmap images are best for images which represent subtle transitions of shade and colour as you find in continuous tone images such as photographs.

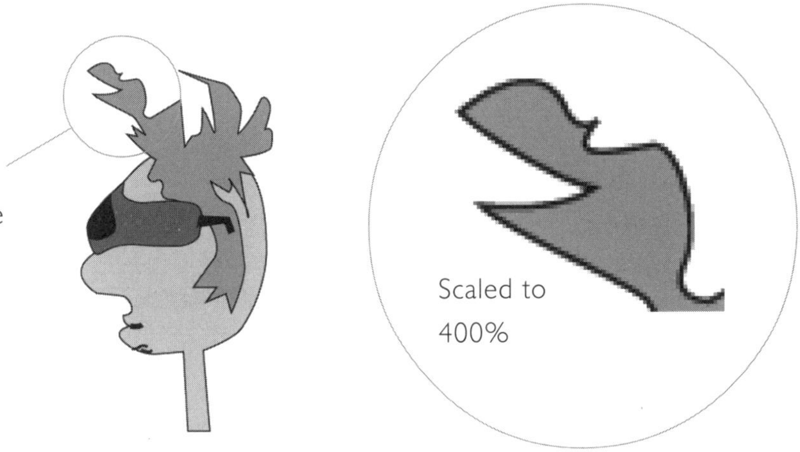

200ppi (pixels per inch) bitmap image at actual size

The Illustrator Screen Environment

When you launch Adobe Illustrator for the first time, your first Illustrator page appears in the centre of the Illustrator window.

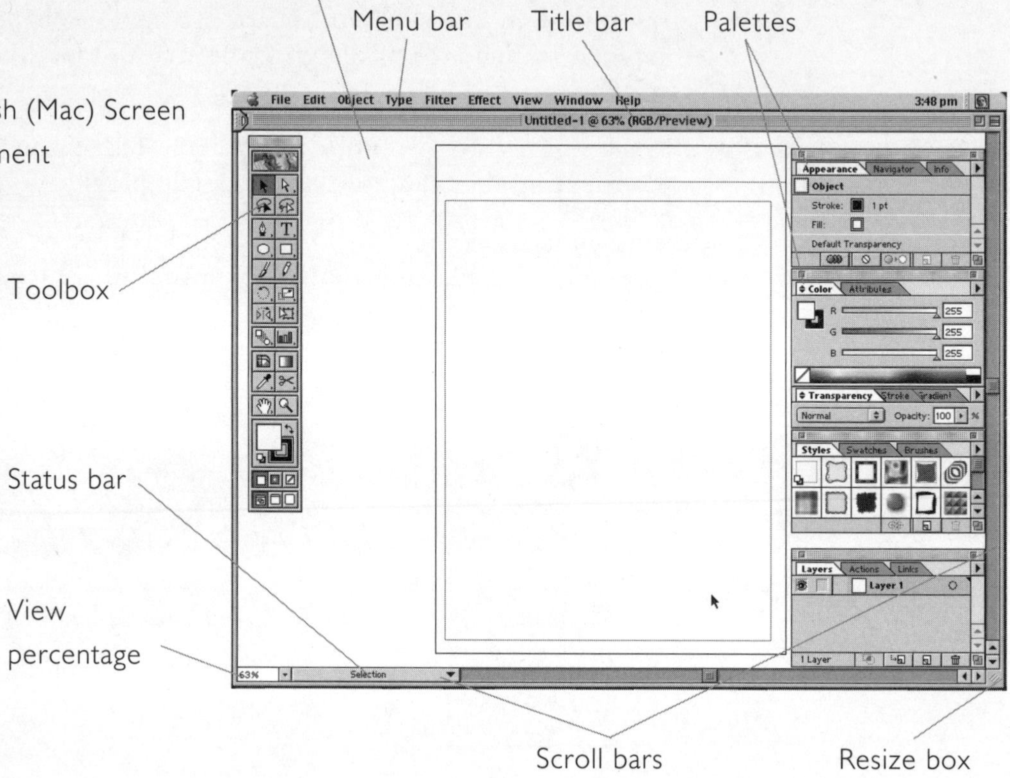

Macintosh (Mac) Screen Environment

Command (often referred to as 'Apple') on the Mac and Ctrl, for Windows users, and Alt (Mac) and Alt (Windows) are used identically as modifier keys. Shift is standard on both platforms.

Along the right-hand side of the window the various Illustrator palettes are arranged in their default positions. The Toolbox appears in its default position along the left edge of the window.

Mac v Windows

This book uses a mixture of Macintosh and Windows screen shots and the instructions given apply equally to both platforms. The functionality of Adobe Illustrator on the Macintosh and Windows platforms is virtually identical as an examination of both application windows shows and as you will see from a comparison of various Mac and Windows dialogue boxes throughout the book.

Windows Screen Environment

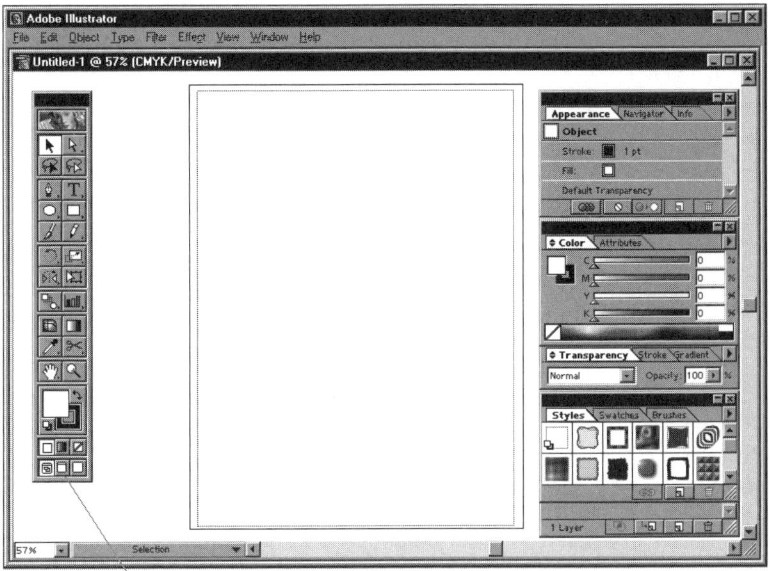

At the very bottom of the Toolbox are three icons that allow you to control the overall appearance of the Illustrator window:

Windows users can use the right mouse button to access context sensitive menus; Mac users can hold down the Ctrl key and press their single mouse button.

1. To change the Screen Mode, click the Full Screen mode with Menu Bar button to go to Full Screen mode. Here you see a full screen window with a menu bar, but no title bar or scroll bars.

2. Click the Full Screen Mode button to go to Full Screen mode. Here you see a full screen window, but with no title bar, menu bar or scroll bars.

3. Click the Standard Screen mode button to go to Standard Screen mode. Here you see a standard window with a menu bar along the top and scroll bars along the right and bottom edges. Standard Screen mode is the default view shown in these screen shots.

Toolbox Techniques

There are a number of useful general techniques that relate to choosing tools in the Toolbox, including those from the expanded range of hidden tool pop-ups.

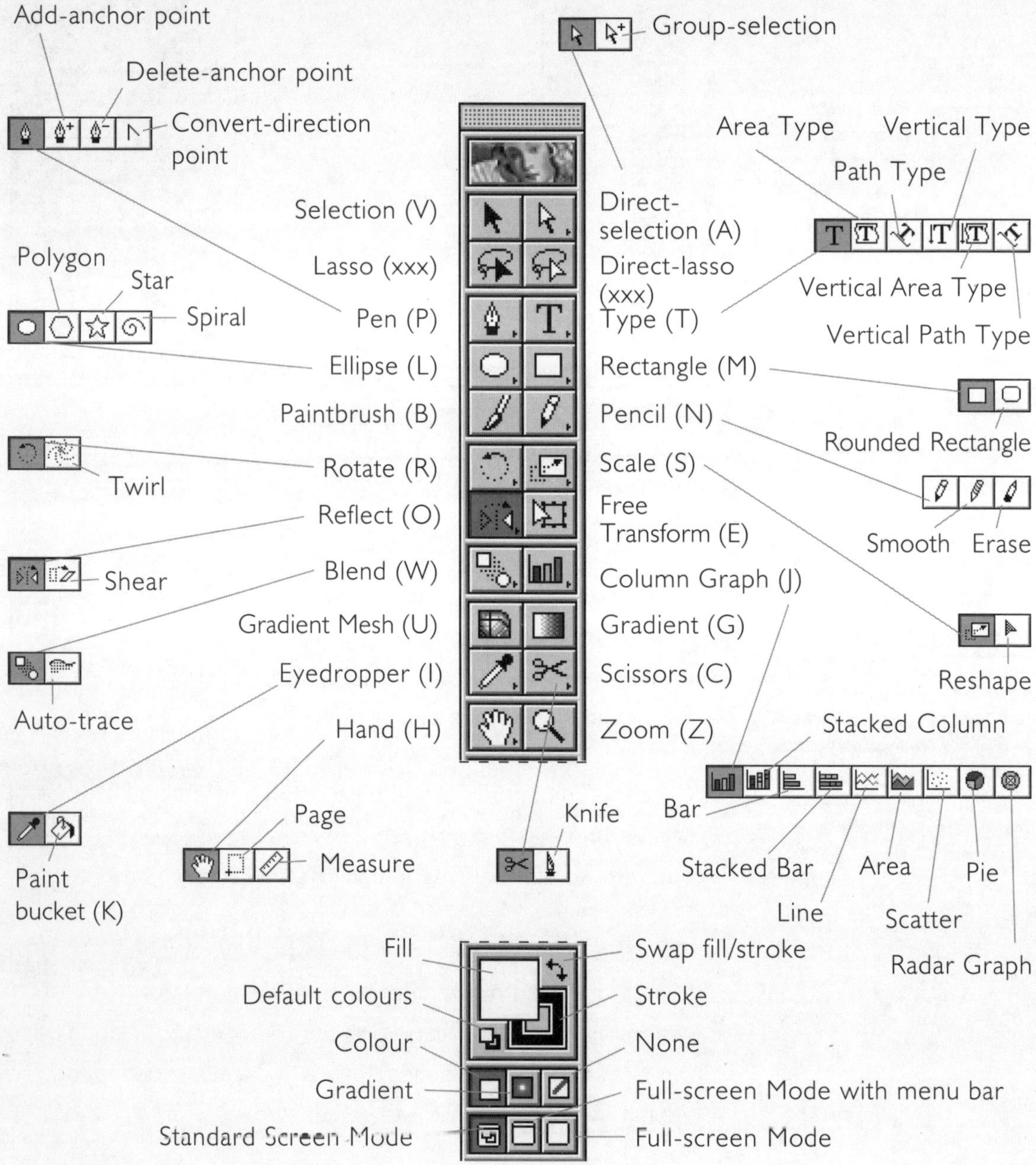

1 To choose a tool, click on the tool to select it. The tool highlights. When you position your cursor on the page the cursor icon changes to indicate the tool you selected.

Rest your cursor on a tool for a few seconds to see the tool tip label which tells you the name of the tool and its keyboard shortcut.

2 A small triangle in the bottom right corner of a tool icon indicates that there are additional tools available in the tool group. To access additional tools, press and hold on the default tool to show the tool pop-up. Move your cursor onto one of the additional tools then release to select that tool. The tool you select becomes the default tool and appears in the main Toolbox until you make another choice from the tool group.

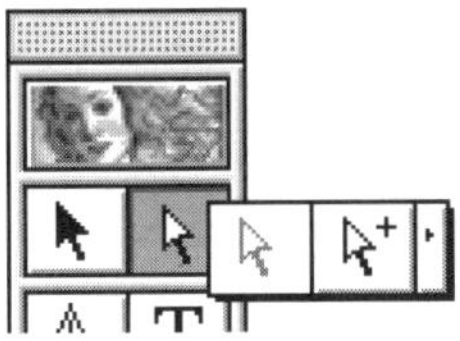

3 Press the keyboard shortcut key on the keyboard to access a tool. To cycle through the additional tools in a tool group, hold down Shift and press the keyboard shortcut key until you reach the tool you want.

Even when you have created a tear-off palette, you can still access all the tools from the main Toolbox if you want to.

4 You can create a tear-off palette for any of the tool groups. Press and hold on a tool group, move your cursor onto the small triangle in the bar that appears to the right of the tool group. Drag this bar to create a separate tear-off palette of the tools. Reposition this palette as you would for any other palette. Click the Close box or button in the tear-off palette to close the tear-off.

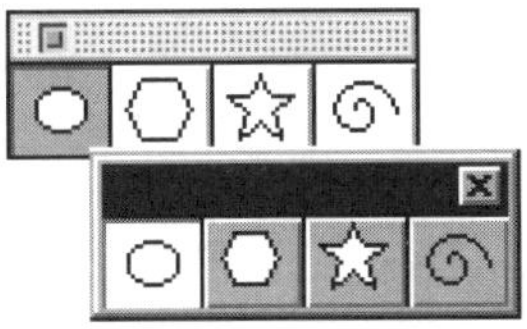

New Document Setup

Once you've launched Illustrator, you can set up a new document. You use the New Document dialogue box to define the artboard size, and to choose either CMYK or RGB colour as the colour mode in which you want to work. You can also suggest a name for the file.

The maximum artboard size is 227" x 227".

1 Choose File > New. Enter a name for the new document in the Name field. This is optional at this stage. You can create the new document, then do a Save as to name the file and specify where you want to save it.

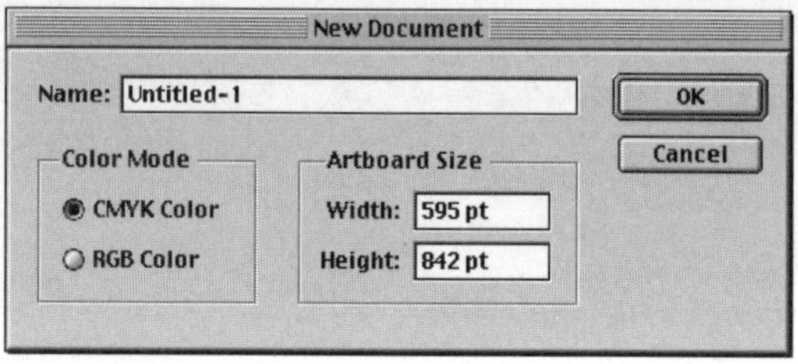

Choose CMYK colour if you intend your artwork to be colour separated and printed on a commercial printing press using process (CMYK) inks. Choose RGB if you intend your artwork to be used on the World Wide Web or in other screen-based presentations.

2 Choose a Colour Mode. Use CMYK Colour if your final artwork file is destined for commercial printing using process inks. Choose RGB Colour for images that are destined for the Web or screen based presentation.

3 Enter Width and Height values to define the size of the Artboard. The Artboard is the overall working area for your document. It is not necessarily the page size of the document, and can be larger than the physical paper size on which you intend to print. OK the dialogue box. The solid black rectangle that appears in the centre of your screen area represents the size of the artboard. The dotted, inner rectangle defines the printer margin, depending on the current, default printer.

Most printers cannot print right to the very edge of the paper. The area that cannot be printed to is called the printer margin, or the non-imageable area.

You can click the Page Setup button in the Document Setup dialogue box to access the Page Setup dialogue box.

4 To make changes to the artboard size, choose File > Document Setup. Use the Size pop-up to change the artboard size. Select the Use Page/Print Setup option to match the artboard to the paper size and orientation selected in the Page/Print Setup dialogue box.

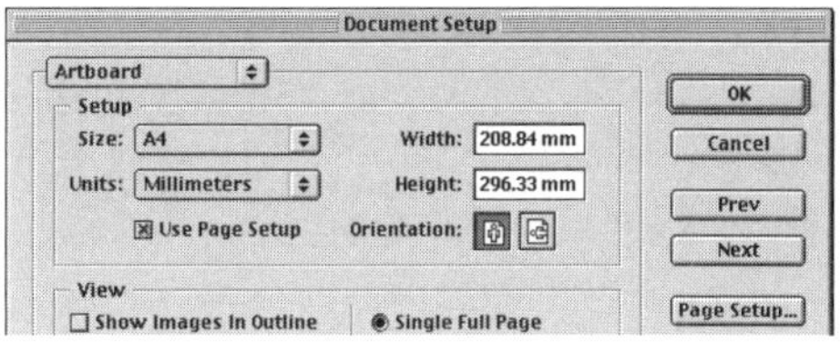

5 Use the Measurements pop-up to choose the unit of measurement for the document. (To change the unit of measurement for all subsequently created Illustrator files, choose Edit > Preferences > Units & Undos.)

You can choose File > Page Setup to access the Page Setup dialogue box without going through the Document Setup dialogue box.

6 Click the Page/Print Setup button to access the Page/Print Setup dialogue box. The appearance will vary depending on the currently set default printer. Create settings as required. Refer to your printer manual for detailed information on the options available. If Use Page/Print Setup is selected in the Document Setup dialogue box, changes to paper size and orientation in the Page/Print Setup dialogue box are immediately reflected in the Document Setup dialogue box.

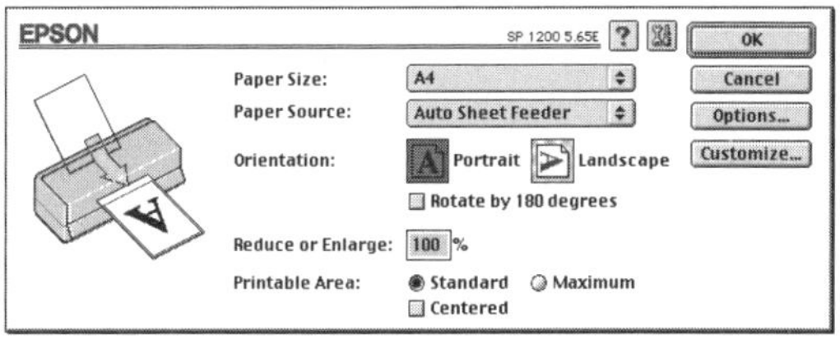

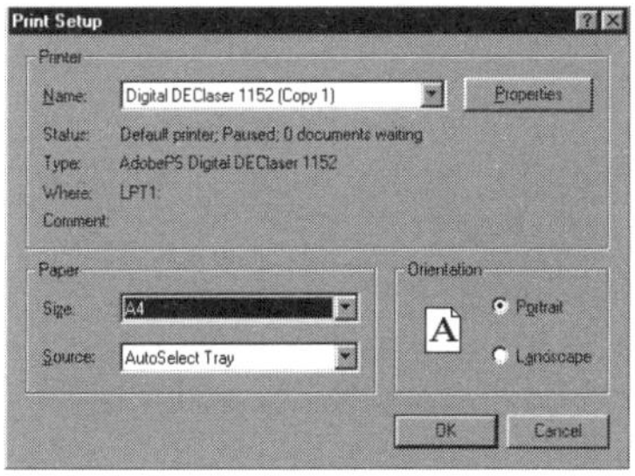

The area outside the artboard is referred to as the Scratch area. This extends from the edge of the artboard to the edge of the maximum 227" x 227" dimensions. Objects placed on the scratch area are visible on screen, but do not print.

Magnification and Scrolling

The Navigator palette, Zoom tool (Z), Hand tool (H) and the Scroll Bars let you move precisely to any part of your illustration and to zoom in and out on different portions:

1 Choose Window > Show Navigator to show the Navigator palette. Double-click the zoom % entry field to highlight the existing figure, enter a new value (4–6400%), then press Return/Enter to specify a zoom level. Alternatively, drag the zoom slider to the right to zoom in, to the left to zoom out. You can also click the small/large mountain buttons to change the zoom level in preset increments.

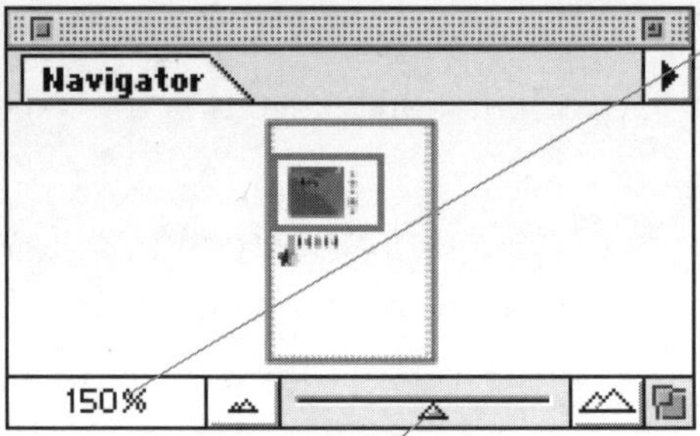

2 Each time you change the zoom level, the size of the Proxy Preview box updates to indicate the area of the illustration that you have zoomed in on. Position your cursor in the red Proxy box, then drag the box to move quickly to different parts of the page, maintaining the same zoom level.

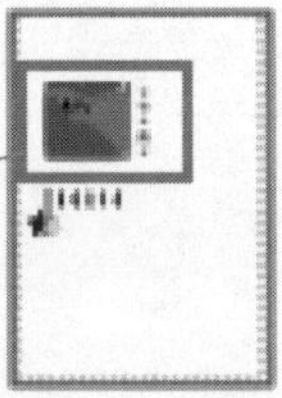

3 To use the Zoom tool, select it, position your cursor on the image and click to zoom in on the area around where you clicked, in preset increments. With the zoom tool selected, hold down Alt. The cursor changes to the zoom out cursor. Click to zoom out in preset increments.

With any tool, other than the Zoom tool selected, hold down Spacebar+Command/Ctrl to temporarily access the Zoom tool. Add Alt to the above combination to zoom out.

4 Another extremely useful technique. With the Zoom tool selected, position your cursor on the illustration, then press and drag to define the area you want to zoom in on. The smaller the zoom area you define, the greater the resulting magnification.

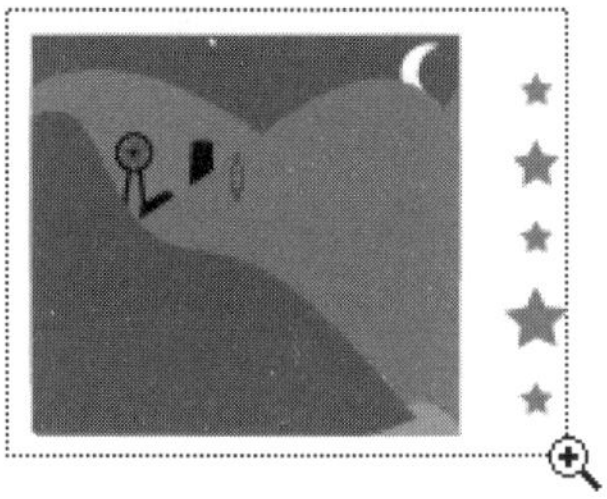

5 The View menu offers four standard options for changing the magnification of the page. The keyboard shortcut is listed with each option.

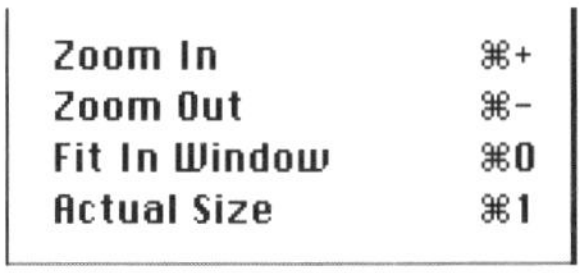

6 Use the pop-up menu in the bottom left corner of the Illustrator screen to access the magnification pop-up. Choose a magnification from the list.

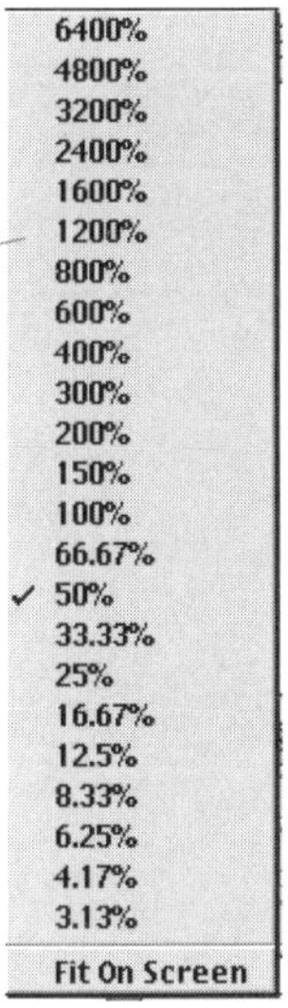

With any tool other than the Hand tool selected, hold down Spacebar to temporarily access the Hand tool.

7 In addition to using standard scroll bar techniques to see different parts of an illustration, you can use the Hand tool. Select the Hand tool, position your cursor in the illustration, then press and drag to change the view.

Palette Techniques

There are a number of floating palettes available in Adobe Illustrator. These moveable palettes appear in front of the artwork you create on your Illustrator page. Most of the palettes are initially organised into different groups. You can customise palette groupings to suit our own needs. Use the following techniques to work effectively with palettes.

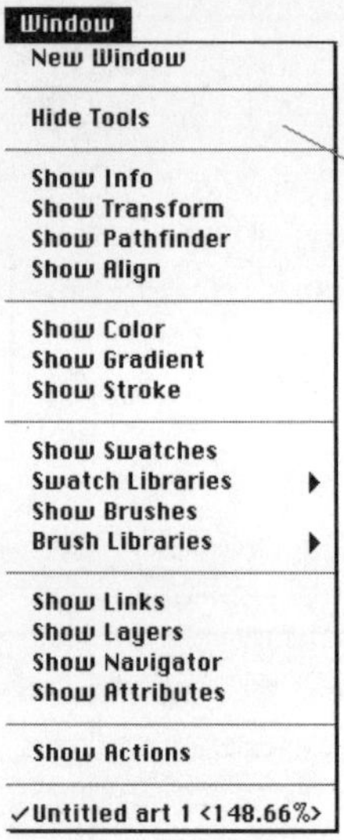

This section uses Macintosh and Windows screen shots to indicate the identical functionality of the application on both platforms.

1 Use the Window menu to show any palette not already showing. Choosing a particular palette shows the palette along with any other palettes initially grouped with it.

2 To close a palette either use the Window menu and select the appropriate hide palette command, or click the Close box (Mac)/Close button (Windows) in the title bar of each palette.

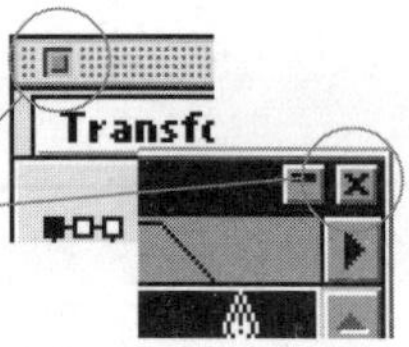

3 To move a palette, position your cursor in the title bar, then press and drag.

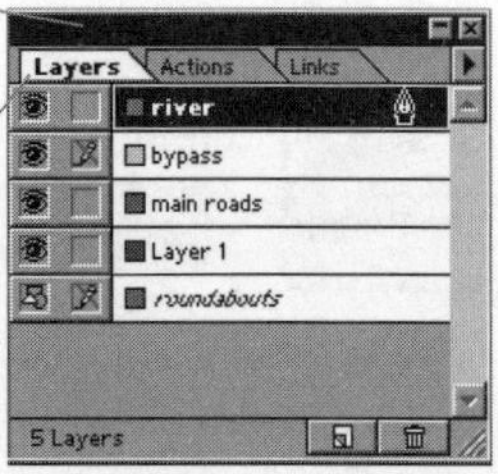

4 To make a particular palette active, click the appropriate tab just below the title bar.

5 Drag a tab out of the palette to convert the palette into a standalone palette.

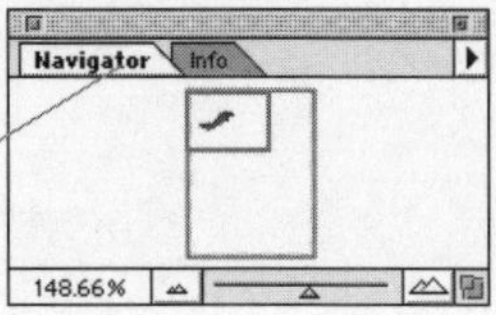

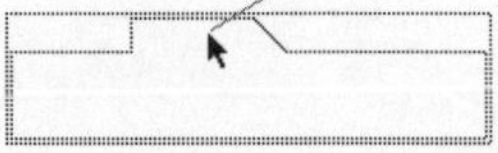

6 Drag a tab into another palette group or individual palette to create a new custom palette group.

7 To make the most of your available screen space you can shrink and roll up palettes. Click the Zoom box (Mac) or the Minimise button (Windows) in the title bar of the palette. Click the same button to restore the palette to its original size. Click twice on the Zoom/ Minimise button if the palette has been resized.

8 Double-click a tab to collapse a default size palette (one that has not been resized) to show title bar and tabs only. Double-click a tab to restore a resized palette to its original size.

9 You can use standard Mac and Windows techniques to resize some of the palettes (e.g. Swatches palette). Press and drag the resize icon for the palette.

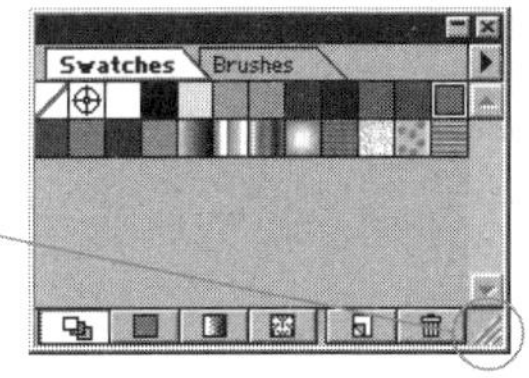

Press the Tab key to hide/show all currently visible palettes including the Toolbox. Hold down Shift, then press Tab to hide/ show all currently visible palettes except the Toolbox.

10 Most of the palettes have a pop-up menu for accessing a range of commands and options relevant to the active palette. Press and hold on the triangle (Mac), or Click on the triangle (Windows).

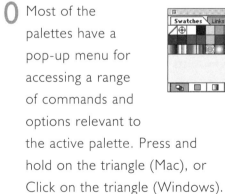

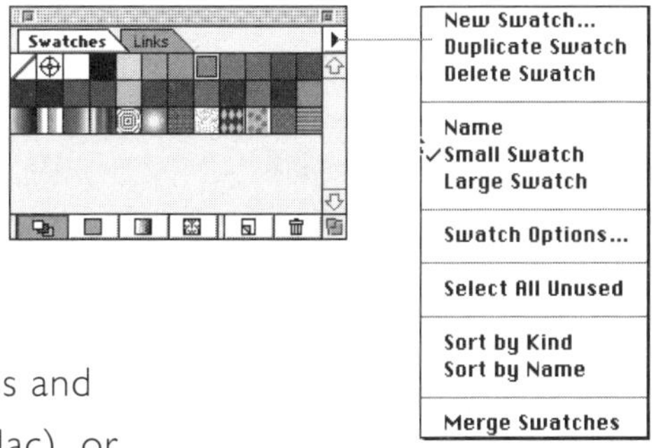

Ruler Guides

Ruler Guides are non-printing guides that enable you to align elements in an illustration accurately and precisely. Make sure that you have page rulers showing in order to create ruler guides. Choose View > Show Rulers (Command/Ctrl+R) if the rulers are not already showing.

Ruler Guides are light blue and they are locked by default. They do not print.

Drawing tool cursors will snap to guides when they come within 2 pixels of a guide. This helps ensure that you create objects precisely and accurately. Also, when you move an object, when the Move cursor comes within 2 pixels of a guide it snaps onto it. The cursor turns hollow to indicate that it has snapped to the guide.

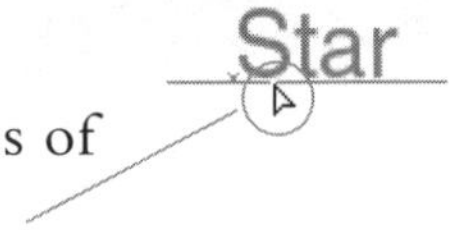

1 To create a ruler guide, position your cursor in either the top or left ruler, then press and drag onto your page. Release the mouse button.

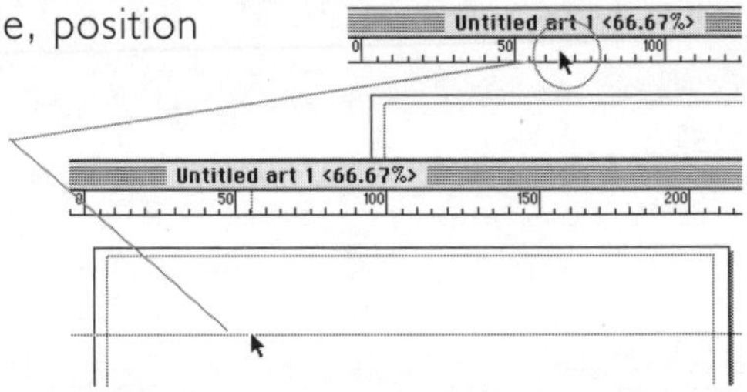

2 As a default, ruler guides are locked as soon as you create them. To reposition a guide, choose View > Guides > Lock Guides (Command/Ctrl+Alt+;). The tick mark indicates that Lock Guides is on. By selecting the option you are switching off Lock Guides. Position your cursor on the guide, then press and drag.

When you use the Lock Guides command you are locking/unlocking all ruler guides in the document.

3 To remove a guide, make sure that the guides are unlocked, then drag the guide back into the ruler from which it came.

4 To temporarily hide ruler guides, choose View > Guides > Hide Guides (Command/Ctrl+;). Choose View > Guides > Show Guides to redisplay hidden guides. To remove all ruler guides, choose View > Guides > Clear Guides.

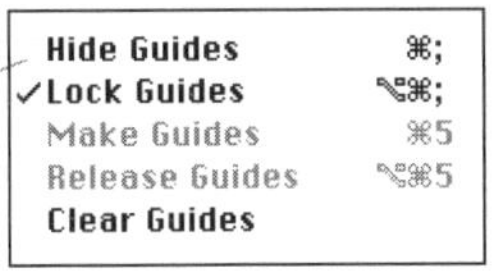

5 Be very careful if you have unlocked guides, then use a marquee select technique to select objects that are positioned next to ruler guides. Unlocked ruler guides can be selected along with the objects you marquee. If you then reposition or delete the selected objects, the guides are also affected. This can sometimes be desirable, sometimes not.

Use the keyboard shortcut, Command/Ctrl+5, to make an object into a guide; Command/Ctrl+Alt+5 to release a guide.

6 You can turn any path into a guide. Select an object you want to convert into a guide. Choose View > Guides > Make Guide.

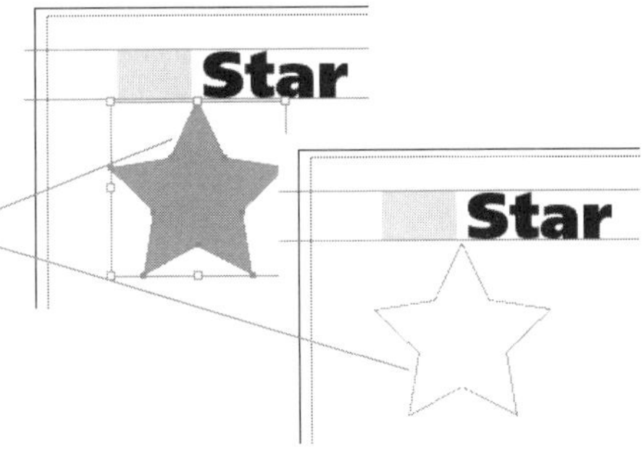

7 To release the guide so that it reverts to an object, unlock guides, click on the guide then choose View > Guides > Release Guides. Original fill/stroke attributes are restored.

8 To set preferences for the appearance and colour of Ruler Guides choose Edit > Preferences > Guides and Grid.

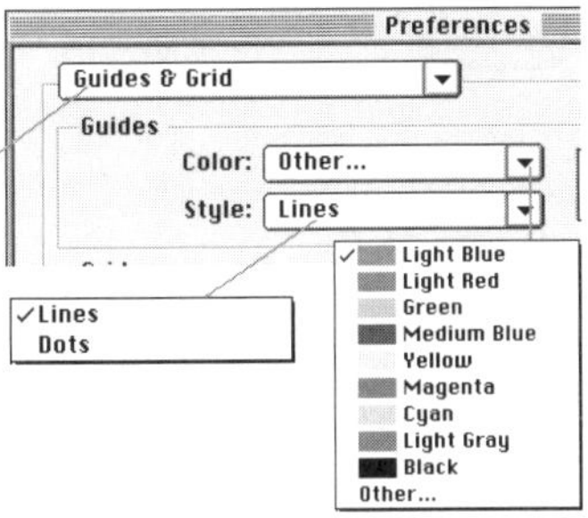

Paths, Points and Selection Tools

There are three selection tools in Adobe Illustrator – the Selection tool, the Direct-selection tool and the Group-selection tool. An important part of understanding Adobe Illustrator is to understand how and why to use each tool.

This section provides an overview of the functionality of each tool and indicates where you can find further information and practical examples of using the tools.

Equally fundamental is understanding paths and points. Chapter Eleven covers working with Paths and Points in detail. But a brief introduction is necessary at the outset.

Paths

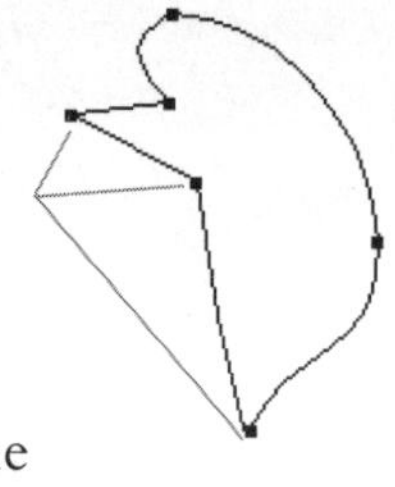

Every object that you create in Adobe Illustrator, with the exception of type, has a path. A path can be open or closed and consists of at least two anchor points, joined together by either straight line segments or curve segments, or a combination of both. The path defines the shape of the object.

You can fill paths with a colour, a gradient or pattern and you can also stroke the path. A stroke is a colour and thickness applied to the path itself and acts as an outline on the path.

The Selection tool

Use the Selection tool when you want to select complete objects or groups. For example, you might want to move or transform them in some way. Also use the Selection tool when you want to select multiple objects (see page 42 for information on selecting multiple objects).

Existing Illustrator users may not like the bounding box. To switch off the bounding box choose File > Preferences > General. Deselect the Use Bounding Box option.

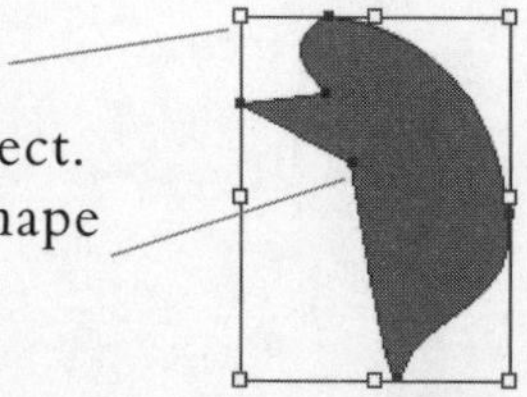

When you click on an object with the Selection tool a bounding box with eight selection handles appears around the object. Also, the anchor points that define the shape of the path appear as solid squares.

The Direct-selection tool

Use the Direct-selection tool when you want to select individual anchor points or path segments

To deselect an object, with any of the selection tools selected, click on some empty space. The bounding box around the previously selected object disappears. Alternatively, you can choose Edit > Deselect All (Command/Ctrl+Shift+A).

that help define the shape of an object in order to edit them. You can also select multiple points (see page 153 for information on selecting and editing points). When you select an individual point it appears as a solid square. Non-selected points appear as hollow squares.

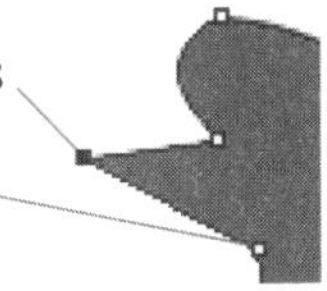

You have to be very precise about the way you use the Direct-selection tool. If a shape was previously selected with the selection tool, it is not enough just to select the Direct-selection tool in order to edit the points. When a shape was previously selected you need to select the Direct-selection tool, click on some empty space to deselect the shape, then click on the edge of the object (its path) to reselect the shape as an editable path. Beware, even when using the Direct-selection tool, if you click in the middle of a filled object, it will select as if you are using the Selection tool.

The Group-selection tool

Use the Group-selection tool to select one, or all, of the objects in a group. The Group-selection tool also enables you to work with groups grouped with other groups in a grouping hierarchy (see page 76 for further information). Illustrator graphs are initially created as a hierarchy of groups and the Group-selection tool is an important tool if you want to be able to continue to edit the data used to create the chart (see Chapter Thirteen).

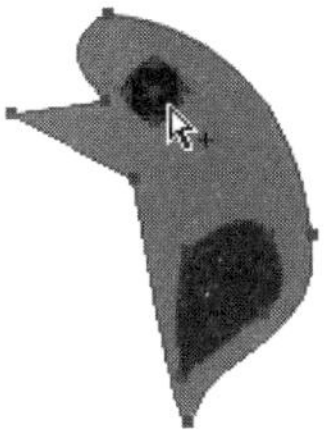

Selected anchor points appear as solid squares, unselected anchor points are hollow.

Lasso Selection Tools

The Lasso selection tools allow you to drag in a freeform manner to create an irregular selection area. Use the Lasso tool to select complete objects and lines (see page 44). Use the Direct-lasso tool to select anchor points or segments (see page 150).

Preview and Outline

Most of the time as you build an illustration you will work in Preview mode. In Preview you see objects partially or fully according to their stacking order and with their fill colour and stroke attributes. In Outline mode, you see a wireframe view of all the paths in the illustration.

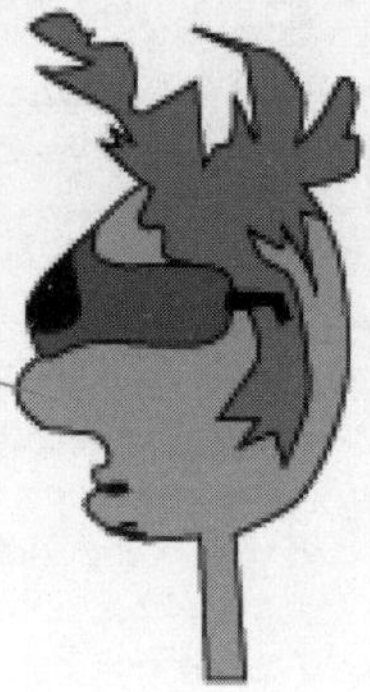

As illustrations become increasingly complex, Outline mode can be very useful to select objects that are difficult to select in Preview and to troubleshoot problems which are difficult to identify in Preview mode. Screen redraw is also quicker in Outline mode, especially when working with complex illustrations.

1. To change from Preview to Outline and vice versa, choose View > Outline/ Preview (Command/Ctrl+Y).

2. To Preview selected objects only, choose View > Preview Selection (Command/Ctrl+Shift+Y).

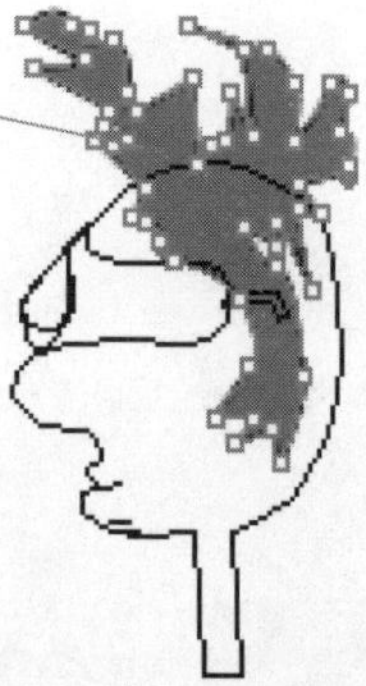

Saving Views

If you need to return to a particular part of an illustration at a particular zoom level, you can create a New View. When you want to return to that particular view you simply use the View menu and choose the view you want.

1. To create a New View, use any of the magnification and scroll techniques to get to a view of your illustration that you want to be able to return to quickly and easily.

2. Choose View > New View. Enter a name for the view, and OK the dialogue box.

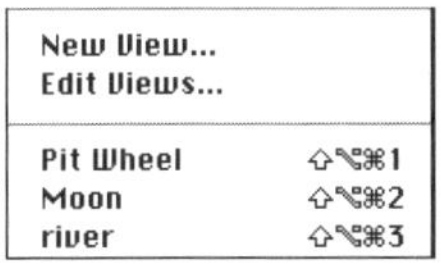

3. To return to exactly the same view, choose View > Name of View.

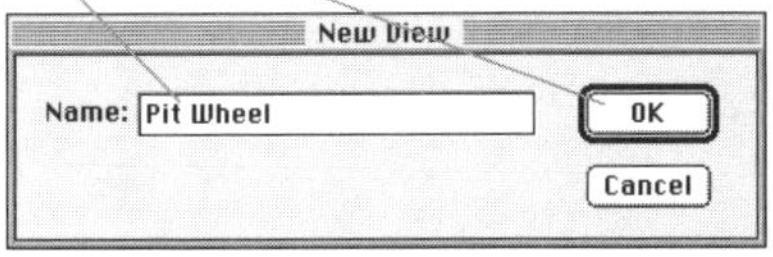

4. To edit a view, choose View > Edit View. Click on the view you want to edit. Either change the name of the view in the Name entry field, or click the Delete button to delete the view.

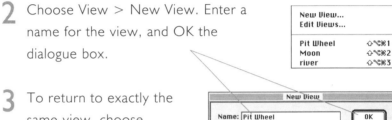

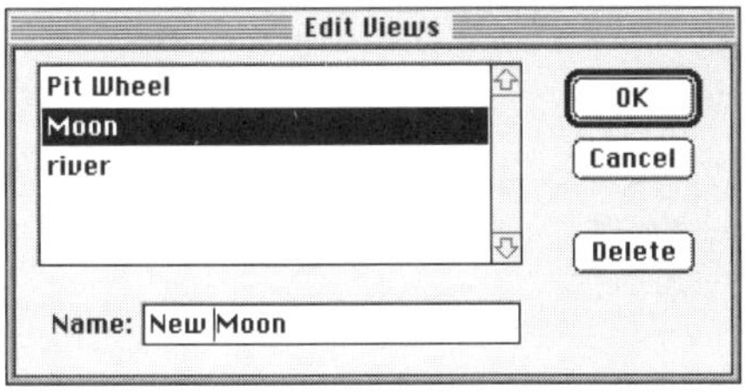

Undoing Mistakes

One of the most essential techniques in Adobe Illustrator is undoing a mistake – when something goes wrong and you need to step back one or two moves.

The number of undos you can perform is unlimited, being restricted only by the amount of memory (RAM) available on your system. You can choose Number of Undos from the pop-up in the Status bar (bottom-left of the Illustrator window) to get a read-out of the Undo/Redo status.

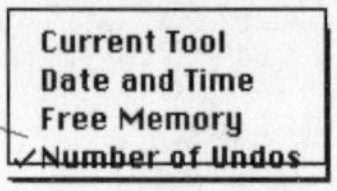

The Undo command will work even after you have used the Save command.

1 To correct a mistake, choose Edit > Undo (Command/Ctrl+Z). The Undo command is dimmed if you cannot undo an operation.

2 Choose Edit > Redo (Command/Ctrl+Shift+Z) to reverse through any undos.

3 To set a minimum number of undo levels, choose File > Preferences > Units and Undo. Enter a value in the Minimum Undo Levels. OK the dialogue box.

4 To revert to the last saved version of a file, choose File > Revert. Confirm 'Revert' in the warning dialogue box. The file reverts to the stage it was at when you last used the Save command. This can sometimes be more efficient than using repeated undo commands.

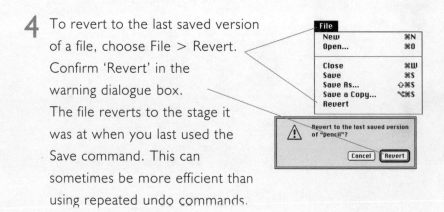

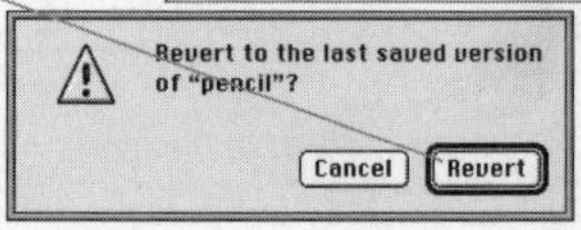

Opening, Placing and Saving Files

Chapter Two

Adobe Illustrator can open files created in Illustrator itself as well as from a wide variety of other applications. You can also place or import files into an existing Illustrator file. Placed files can be either linked (the file remains external to the Illustrator file and Illustrator remembers a link to the file) or embedded (the complete file information for the placed file is included in the Illustrator file).

This chapter also covers saving files in Illustrator EPS format and using the Save for Web dialogue box.

Covers

Opening Files in Adobe Illustrator

If you do not see the file name in the open dialogue box the file is saved in a format that Illustrator cannot read.

Note that graphics file formats you can open include the following:

- *Adobe Illustrator*
- *EPS*
- *Adobe Photoshop*
- *CorelDRAW (v5–8)*
- *FreeHand (v4–8)*
- *GIF*
- *JPEG*
- *Adobe PDF*
- *WMF/EMF (Windows)*
- *DXF (release 13, 14, 2000)*
- *CMX*
- *CGM (v1–3)*
- *SVG*

Note that text file formats you can open include the following:

- *Plain Text (ASCII)*
- *MS RTF*
- *MS Word 6 or later*

Illustrator offers a wide variety of options for opening files. You can open Illustrator files saved in Illustrator format, Illustrator EPS format and Adobe PDF format.

You can also open files created in other applications such as Adobe Photoshop and Macromedia FreeHand. When you open a file created by another application it is converted into a new Adobe Illustrator file. Vector artwork in the file you open is converted into Illustrator paths. Bitmap images remain in bitmap format.

PDF (Portable Document Format) files can be opened as Adobe Illustrator documents. You can edit artwork with Illustrator tools and commands.

1. To open a file, choose File > Open.

2. Use standard Windows/ Macintosh dialogue boxes to navigate to the location of the file you want to open.

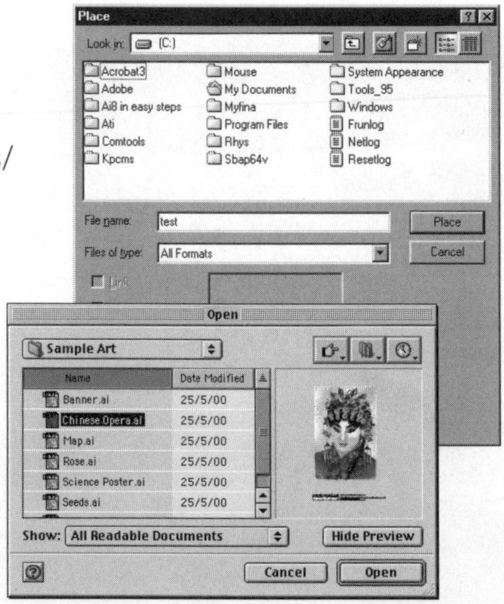

3. Click on the file name to select it. Click the Open button. Alternatively, double-click the file name.

4. Or choose File > Open Recent Files, then select a file from the list of recently opened files.

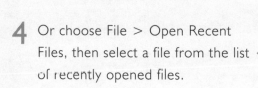

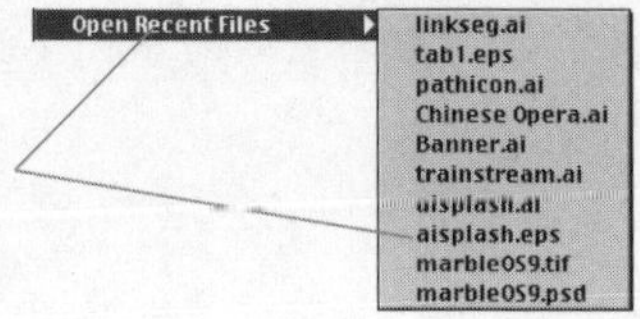

Saving in Illustrator Format

Save a file in Illustrator format when you want to open the file in Adobe Illustrator, place the file into an application which accepts Illustrator format, (such as Adobe Photoshop and Adobe InDesign), or to create an Illustrator file that is compatible with earlier versions of Illustrator.

As with any other software application, it is good practice to save a new, untitled file at an early stage. Use the Save as command to specify where you want to save the file and to give it a name.

1 To save an untitled file, choose File > Save as.

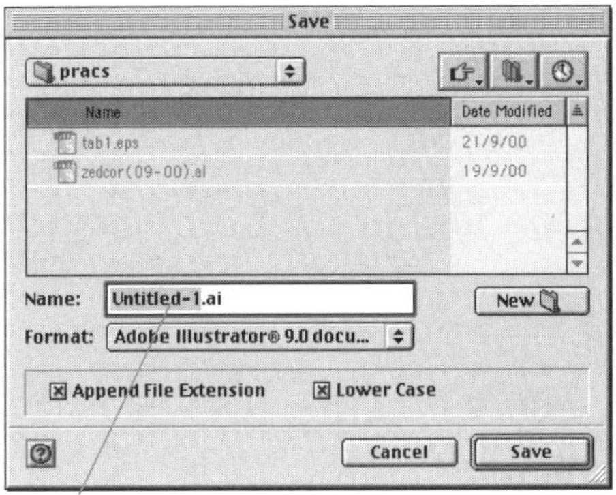

2 Use standard Macintosh/ Windows dialogue boxes to specify the folder into which you want to save the file.

HOT TIP

Leave the Append File Extension and Lower Case options selected. This is especially useful and important if your artwork is likely to be used on the World Wide Web.

3 Make sure that the Name field is highlighted. Drag across the existing text, if necessary, to highlight it. Enter a name for the file. Be careful not to overwrite the .ai file extension.

4 The default format is set to Illustrator. Click the Save button.

5 In the Illustrator Native Format dialogue box use the Compatibility pop-up to choose a compatibility option. Leave

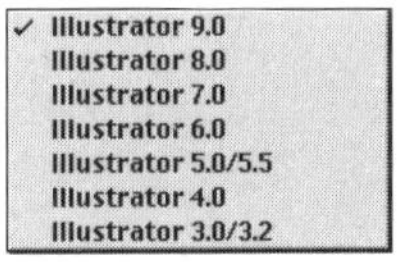

compatibility set to version 9 unless you want to make the file compatible with earlier versions of Illustrator. If you choose to make the file compatible with earlier versions of Illustrator, new features, not available in the earlier version, are not retained. For example, Gradient Mesh objects cannot be saved in Illustrator v5 format.

Use the Save command (Command/ Ctrl+S) regularly to save changes you make to the illustration. Then, if there is any kind of system failure or crash, you can restart your computer and reopen the file at the stage it was at when you did your last save.

6 Select Embed All Fonts to include fonts used in the artwork as part of the file. This increases the size of the file. Choose the Subset Fonts option to save partial font information only. In other words the complete set of font information does not become part of the Illustrator file. Enter a % threshold value to specify when a font subset is created. When the percentage of font characters exceeds the threshold value you enter, the complete font information is saved with the file.

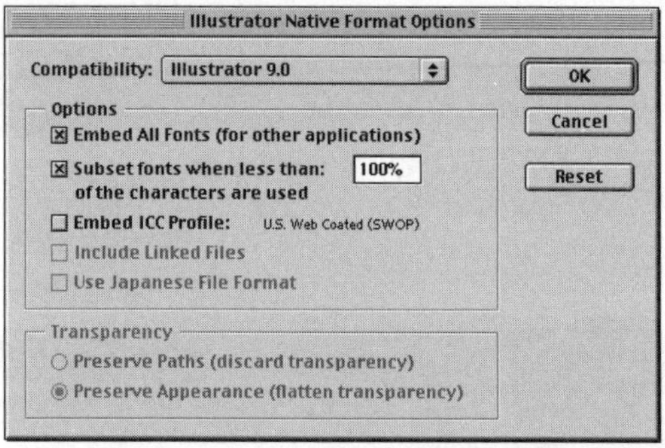

Use the File > Save a Copy command to save a copy of the current file (Illustrator automatically adds the word 'copy' to the file name), leaving the original file as the active file, which you can then continue to work with.

7 If you want to embed linked images you have placed within the file you are saving, select the Include Linked Files option. This option is only available if you have placed files in the illustration (see page 35).

8 See page 32 for information on setting transparency options when you are saving a file using a compatibility setting for an earlier version of Illustrator.

Saving in Illustrator EPS Format

Save a file in Illustrator EPS (Encapsulated PostScript) format when you want to place it into another application such as QuarkXPress, Adobe InDesign or Adobe PageMaker. The majority of page layout, word-processing and graphics applications allow you to import or place EPS files, making this a very versatile format.

1 Follow steps 1–3, Saving in Illustrator Format (page 29).

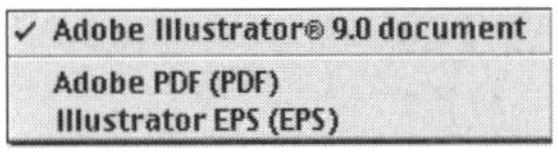

2 Choose Illustrator EPS from the Format pop-up (Mac), or Type pop-up (Windows). When you save a file in EPS format in Windows, the .eps file extension is automatically added to the file name. Click the Save button.

3 Choose a compatibility option if necessary (see Step 5 on page 29).

4 Choose a Preview option. Preview refers to the on-screen preview of the EPS file that you see when you import it into another application. The 8-bit options give the best preview, but increase the overall size of the EPS file. Choose an IBM PC or Macintosh preview depending on which platform you will use the file on. Transparent/Opaque options become available when you choose an 8-bit colour TIFF preview. Select Transparent to create a transparent background for the preview image when it is placed in another application. Opaque gives a solid background.

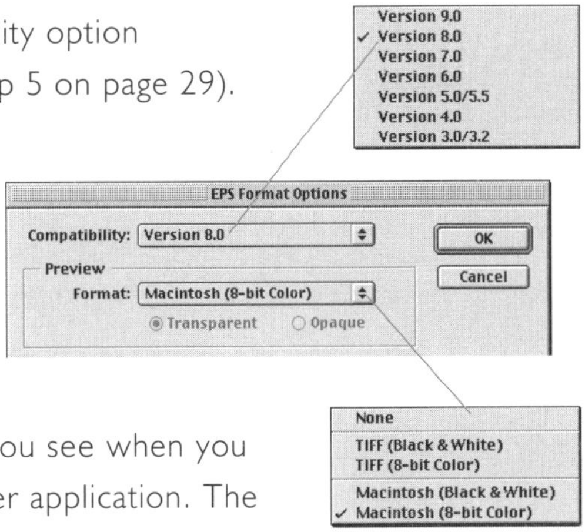

Choose Opaque as the background option for an 8-bit TIFF preview if the EPS is to be placed in a Microsoft Office application.

5 Select the Include Linked Files option to embed placed images linked to the file you are saving. Selecting this option increases the size of the EPS file.

6 Select the Include Document Thumbnails option if you want to see a preview of the file in Illustrator's Open dialogue box.

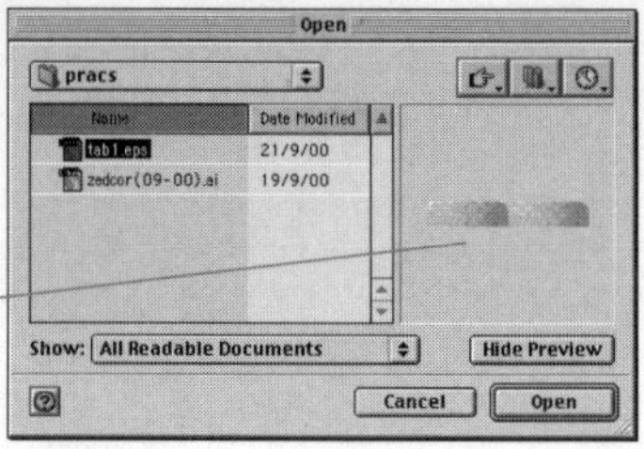

7 Select Include Document Fonts to save any fonts used in the file with the EPS. This can increase the size of the file.

8 Select the CMYK PostScript option to convert RGB colours used in the file to their CMYK equivalents. This option allows you to print the EPS from an application which does not support RGB output.

9 Use the PostScript pop-up to specify the PostScript format for the file. Make sure you choose PostScript 3 if you have included gradient mesh objects in the file and you are printing to a PostScript Level 3 printer. This helps ensure efficient printing for such objects.

10 Select Preserve Paths (discard transparency) to reset all transparency values to 100%, effectively preventing transparent effects from exporting with the file. Select Preserve Appearance to retain transparent effects in the file. The artwork is flattened to achieve this result.

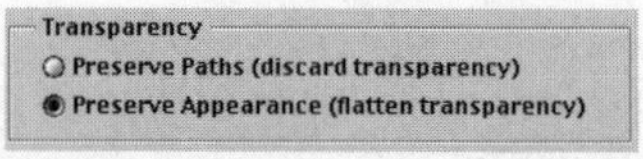

Save for Web

Click the 4-Up tab to see representations of the Original image, the Optimized image and two other, lower quality variations of the current optimisation settings.

The Save for Web dialogue box enables you to save vector artwork created in Illustrator in a bitmap file format (.gif, .jpg and .png) suitable for use on the World Wide Web or other on-screen presentations. Establishing an optimal balance between file size and image quality – optimisation – is the central issue when saving files for such purposes.

1 Choose File > Save to save any changes to the original Illustrator artwork. Then choose File > Save for Web.

2 Click the 2-Up tab to see the original image side by side with the image as it appears with the current optimisation settings applied to it. The annotations area at the bottom of the palette displays useful information, including file format, size and approximate download time for the image.

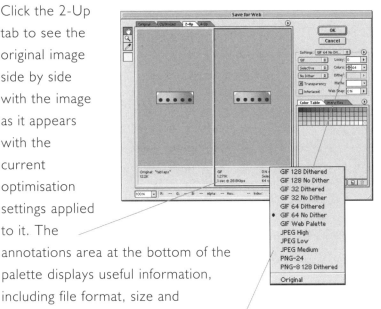

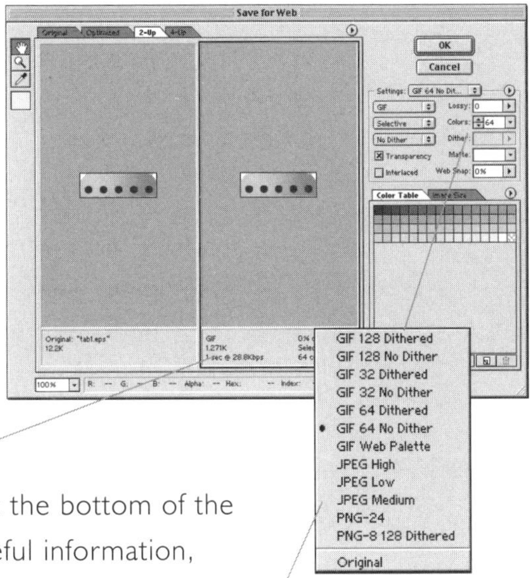

If you click into an optimisation pane, the pane becomes active, indicated by a black border on the pane. When you OK the dialogue box, the version of the image in the active pane is saved.

3 Choose a preset optimisation setting from those available in the Settings pop-up. The fields in the Optimization area of the dialogue box update automatically, as does the preview in the Optimized image pane.

4 Use the Download pop-up menu to choose a modem speed. The estimated download time in the annotations area changes depending on the speed you choose.

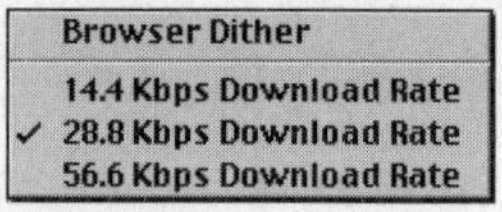

5 Click OK when you are satisfied. Use the Save Optimized As dialogue box to specify a name and location for the file. The file extension is added automatically and depends on the optimisation setting chosen. Be careful not to delete the file extension if you change the name of the file.

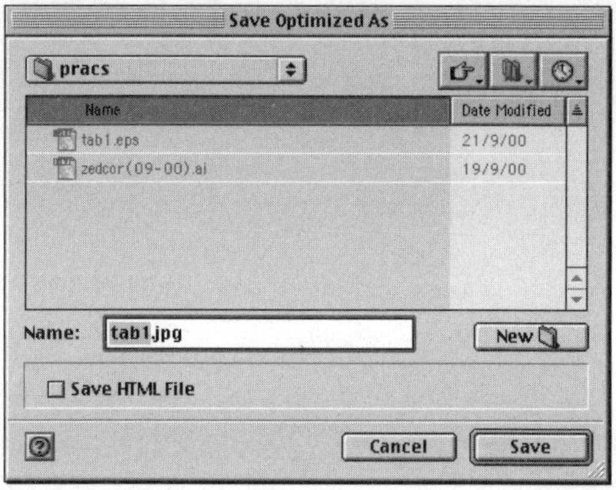

6 Select the Save HTML file option if you want Illustrator to generate an additional HTML file with the image. You can open the HTML file in your browser to evaluate the results of the settings you have specified. The file is named automatically and saved into the same folder as the optimised image.

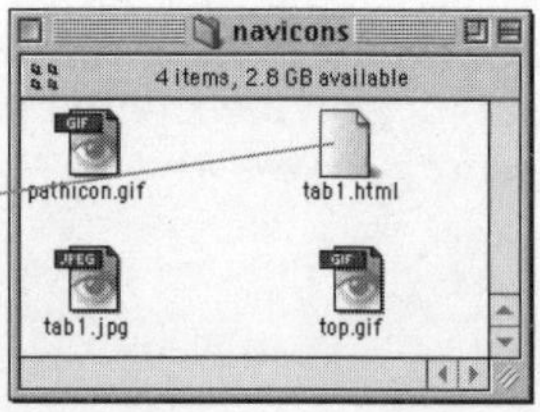

Placing Files

You can place, or import, files created in other applications that you want to become part of your Adobe Illustrator artwork. Such placed files can either be linked (the file remains external to the Illustrator file and Illustrator remembers the link), or embedded (the full information for the placed file is included in the Illustrator file).

Note that graphics file formats you can place include the following:

- *EPS*
- *Adobe Photoshop*
- *TIFF*
- *Kodak PhotoCD*
- *FreeHand (v4–8)*
- *GIF 89a*
- *JPEG*
- *Adobe PDF*
- *WMF/EMF (Windows)*
- *DXF (release 13, 14, 2000)*
- *CMX*
- *CGM (v1–3)*
- *SVG*

Text Formats include:

- *Plain Text (ASCII)*
- *MS RTF*
- *MS Word*

1 To place a file, choose File > Place. Use standard Macintosh/Windows dialogue boxes to navigate to the file you want to place.

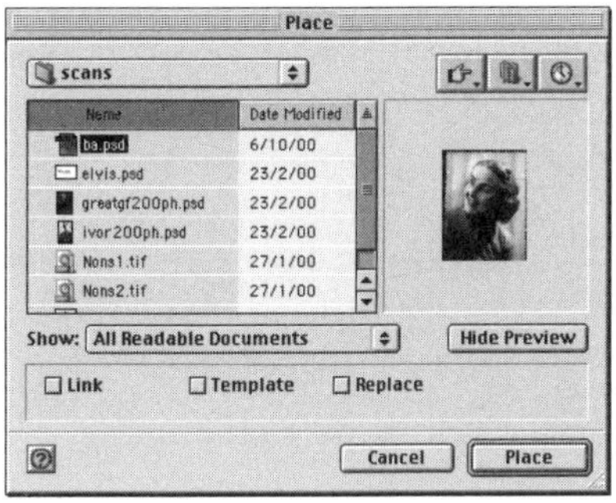

2 Click on a file name to select it. If available, a preview appears to the right of the dialogue box.

3 Click the Hide Preview button if you do not want to see the thumbnail preview of files.

4 Select the Template option to place a file on a new, non-printing layer. The image will appear dimmed. You will not be able to select, move or otherwise manipulate it without first unlocking the layer.

Deselect the Link option when you are placing an EPS file that you want to be able to edit and change from within Illustrator.

5 If you deselect the Link option, the information in the placed file will be included in the Illustrator file. This will add to the file size of the Illustrator document. Select the Link option to create a link between the image and the Illustrator file. The image will not be

Choose File > Document Setup and click the Show Images in Outline option if you want to see a preview of placed files in Outline view. Otherwise, placed images will display as a bounding box with a cross through it in Outline view.

embedded in the Illustrator file, it remains independent. Use this option to keep the actual file size of the Illustrator document smaller.

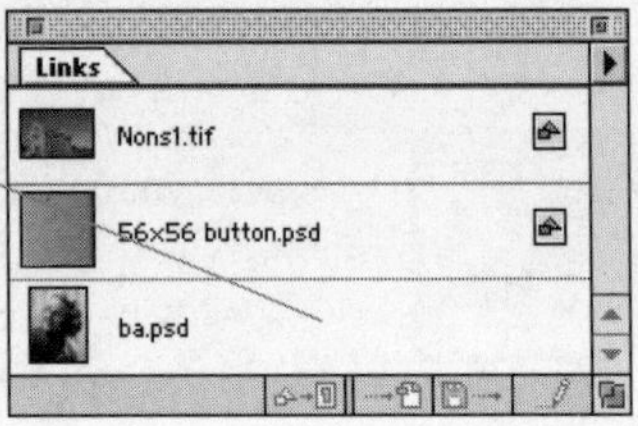

A link must remain intact so that the full information in the linked file can be accessed when you print the Illustrator file. If this link is broken, a low resolution screen preview will be used to print the illustration. Illustrator will automatically update the placed file if any changes are made to it. Use the Links palette to monitor and update the status of placed and embedded files.

6 The Replace option is only available when you have selected a placed image in your Illustrator document before choosing File > Place. The selected file will be replaced by the new image you place.

When you place some formats, such as PDF, a supplementary dialogue box allows you to make choices specific to that format

7 Click the Place button when you are satisfied with the options you have selected. The image is placed into Illustrator and is initially selected. Provided that the placed file was saved with an appropriate preview, the placed image file always displays in Preview view.

Managing Links

When working with linked files within your Illustrator file you can use the Links palette to manage the links. For example, you can relink to a linked file if the original file has been moved to another folder since it was placed. When you show the Links palette (Window > Show Links), all linked and embedded images are listed.

Linked files appear as a thumbnail and name. A question mark icon next to a linked image indicates that the original file has been moved or is missing. An embedded file is indicated by the generic objects icon.

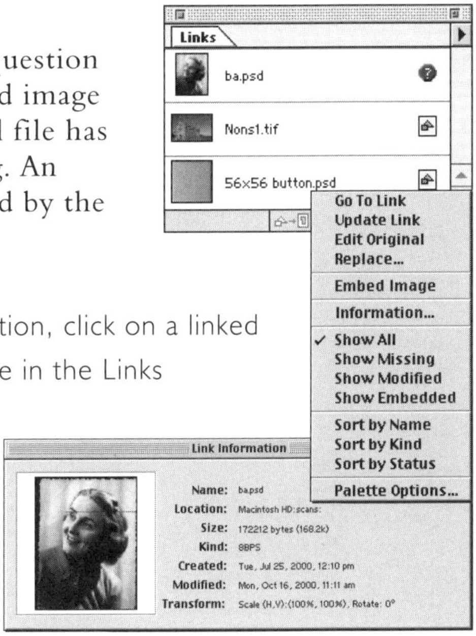

1 To display link information, click on a linked file or an embedded file in the Links palette, then choose Information from the pop-up menu. You can also double-click a placed file name in the Links palette.

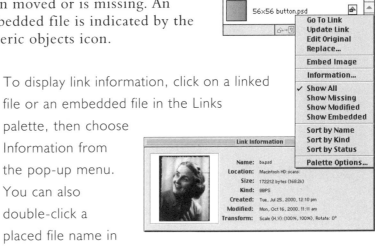

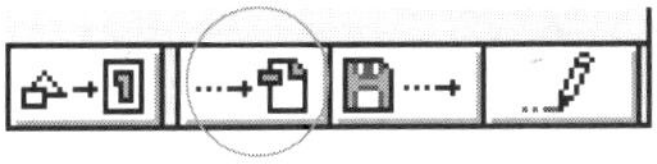

2 To move to a linked file, click on a placed file in the Links palette to select it. Either click the Go to Link button, or choose Go to Link from the pop-up menu. This moves you to the page where the placed file is located and the object is selected.

3. To update a link, select a Linked file that has been modified since it was placed. Either click the Update Link button, or choose Update Link from the pop-up menu.

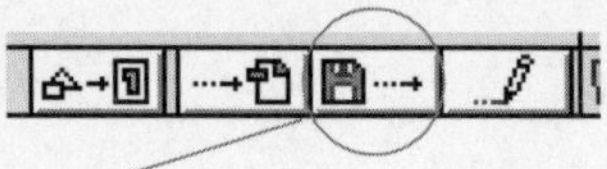

4. To embed a linked file within the Illustrator file, click on the linked file to select it. Choose Embed Image from the pop-up menu in the Links palette. This will increase the file size of the Illustrator file.

5. To replace a linked file with another file, click on the linked file that you want to replace.

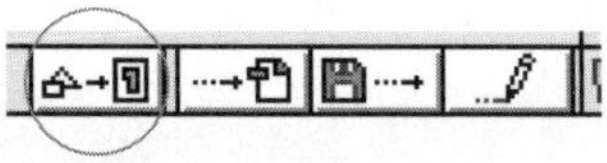

Either, click the Replace Link button, or choose Replace Link from the pop-up menu. Use standard Windows/Macintosh dialogue boxes to locate the file you want. Click on the file name to select it, then click Place. The position and any scaling or other transformations are applied to the replacement image.

If a linked file is missing, when you print the file only a low resolution screen preview will print. Illustrator must be able to access the full image information in a linked file in order to print it correctly.

6. If a linked file is moved from its current location on the hard disk, when you next open your Illustrator file a Warning box indicates that the link is missing.

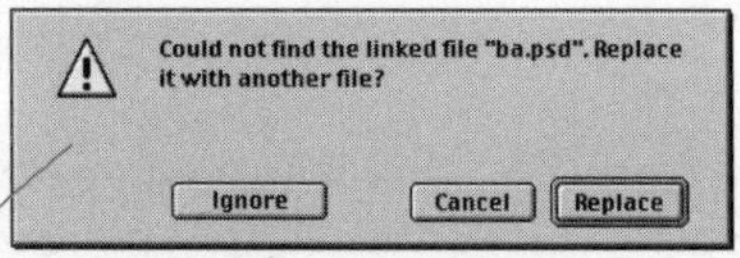

Click the Replace button, then navigate to the file if you want to relink to it. Click the Ignore button to open the Illustrator file without relinking to the missing file. A question mark icon indicates that the file is missing.

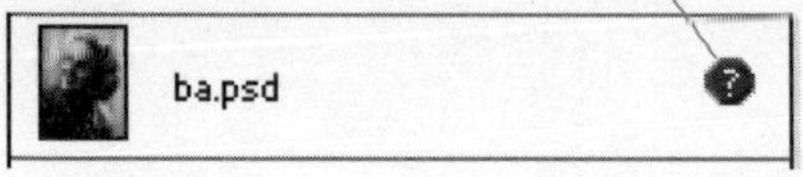

Basic Shapes

Basic shapes such as rectangles and squares, ovals and circles, stars, polygons and lines form the staple of most illustrations created in Adobe Illustrator. This chapter looks at various techniques for creating these basic shapes, and at other basic but essential techniques such as selecting, deselecting, scaling, moving and deleting objects.

Covers

Chapter Three

Drawing Basic Shapes

The following drawing techniques can be used with the tools below.

In the middle of drawing a basic shape, in other words, before you release the mouse button, hold down the Spacebar if you want to reposition the shape as you draw it.

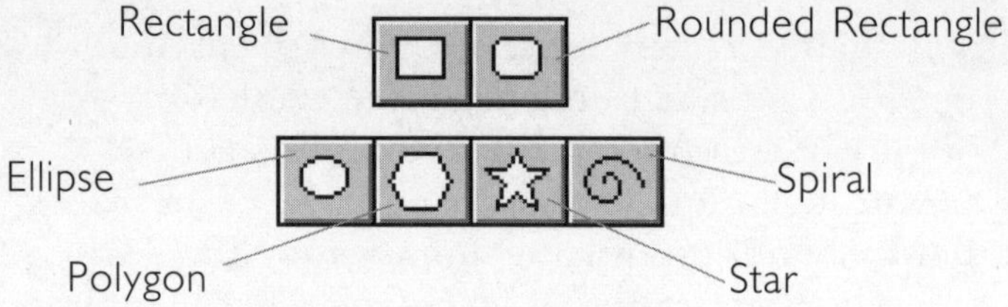

By default, objects drawn using the Rectangle tools and the Ellipse tools grow outward from the point at which you start to drag. Objects drawn with the Polygon, Spiral and Star tools grow from their centre point outward.

1. To draw basic shapes, select one of the above tools. Position your cursor on the page. The cursor changes to the standard drawing cursor. Press and drag. You can drag in any direction away from the start point. Typically you will drag down and to the right.

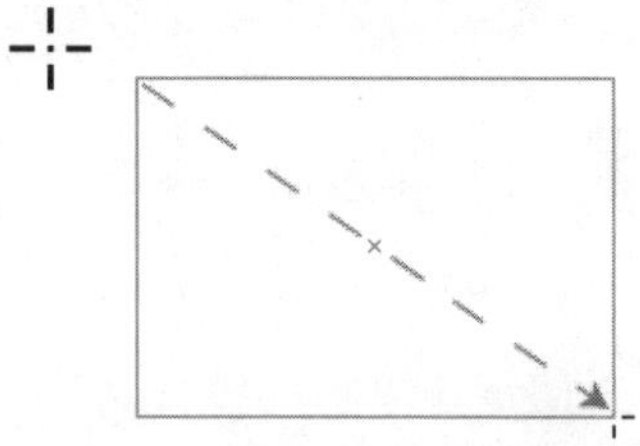

When you use the Shift key as a constraint, make sure that you release the mouse button before you release the Shift key, otherwise the constraint effect will be lost.

2. To draw squares and circles, select the Rectangle tool or the Ellipse tool. Position your cursor on the page. Hold down Shift, then press and drag. The shape is constrained to square or circular proportions as long as you hold down the Shift key. Release the mouse button before you release the Shift key.

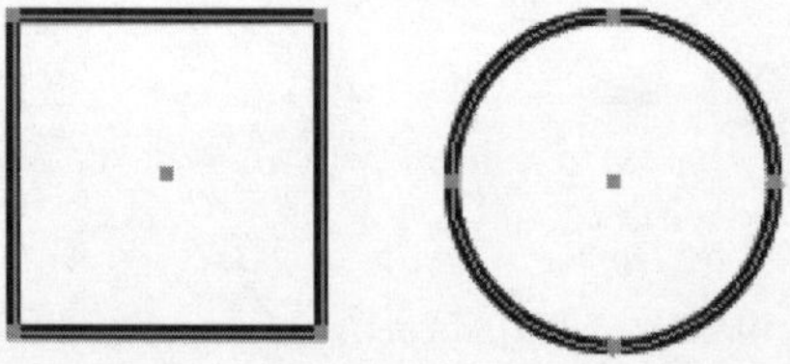

To draw a square or a circle from the centre out, hold down Shift+Alt as you drag.

3 To constrain Polygons and Stars, select either the Polygon or Star drawing tool. Position your cursor on the page. Hold down Shift, then press and drag to create the shape. Holding down Shift in this instance ensures that you keep the base of the polygon, or the 'legs' of the star, level. Release the mouse button before you release the Shift key.

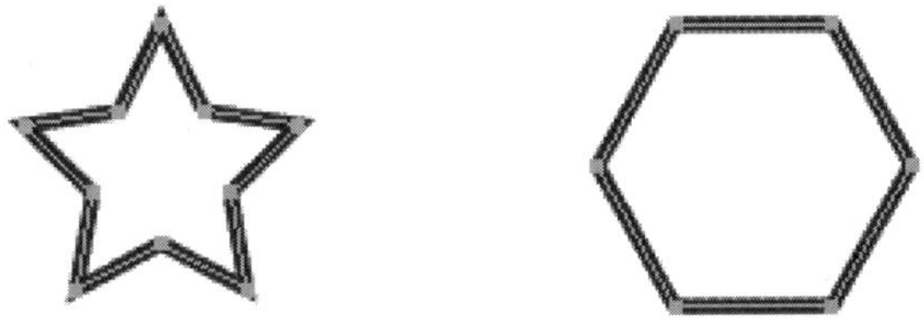

After you draw a basic shape, the object remains selected - indicated by the solid anchor points that define the shape of the path. The current fill and stroke attributes are automatically applied to the object. Click away from the object if you want to deselect it. If you select the Selection tool, a bounding box with 8 selection handles also appears around the object.

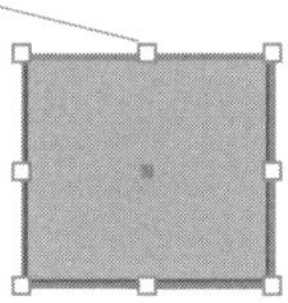

4 To draw rectangles and ellipses from the centre out, select a Rectangle or Ellipse drawing tool. Position your cursor on the page. Hold down Alt. The cursor changes to the 'centre out' drawing cursor. Press and drag to create the shape. Release the mouse button before you release the Alt key.

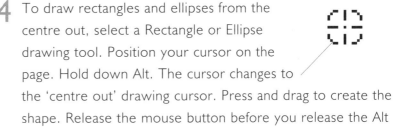

5 To delete an object, make sure the object is selected, using the Selection tool, or the Group-selection tool, then choose Edit > Clear, or press the backspace/delete key.

Dialogue Box Method

When you need precise control over the size of an object, you can use a dialogue to create shapes to exact dimensions.

1 To create a shape to precise dimensions, select the basic shape drawing tool you want to use.

2 Position your cursor on the page. Click (do not press and drag). The appropriate dialogue box appears.

3 Enter values for Width and Height for rectangles and circles, and a corner radius value for rectangles with rounded corners.

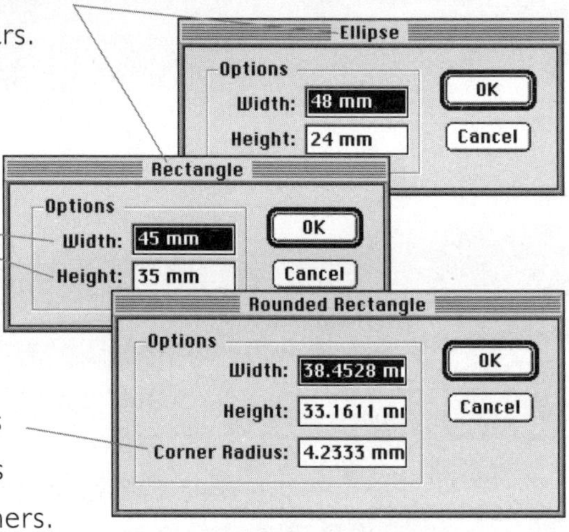

4 For a polygon enter a Radius value. The Radius is the distance form the centre point to the end point of each segment that constitutes the polygon. Enter a value for number of sides, or use the increment arrows to increase/decrease the number of sides.

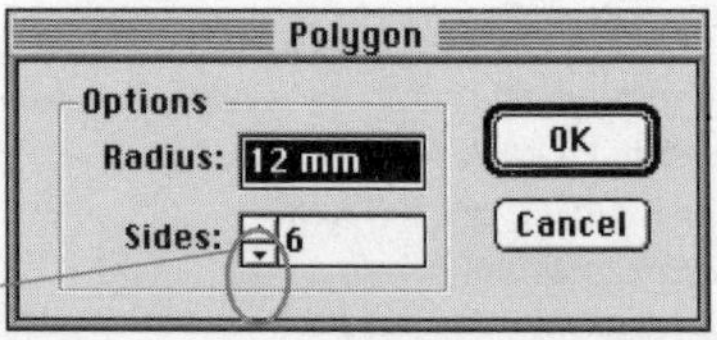

When you use a drawing tool dialogue box, the values initially displayed are those used to create the last shape you drew with that tool.

5 For a star enter Radius 1 and Radius 2 values. The radius 1 value describes the radius of a circle that defines the inner points in the star; the radius 2 describes the radius of a circle that defines the position of the outer points of a star. Click the increment arrows to increase or decrease the number of points in the star, or enter a value in the Points entry box.

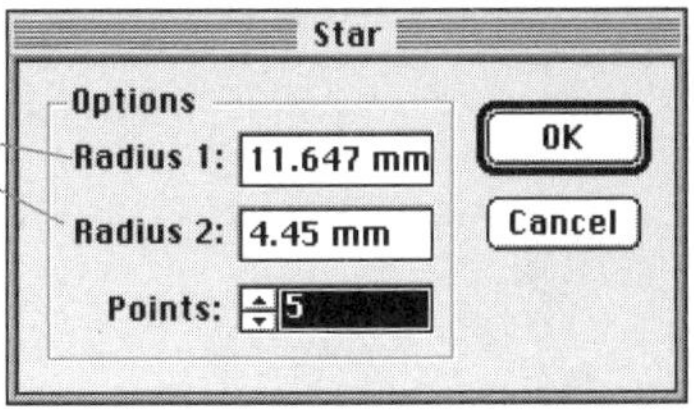

6 For spirals enter a radius value. This is the distance from the centre point to the outermost point in the spiral. Enter a decay rate. Decay rate determines the rate of expansion of each successive wind of the spiral. (A wind is one complete turn of the spiral e.g. from the 12 o'clock to 12 o'clock position). Enter a value for segments. Illustrator uses 4 segments to create one complete wind of the spiral. Click the clockwise or anticlockwise radio button to determine the direction of the spiral.

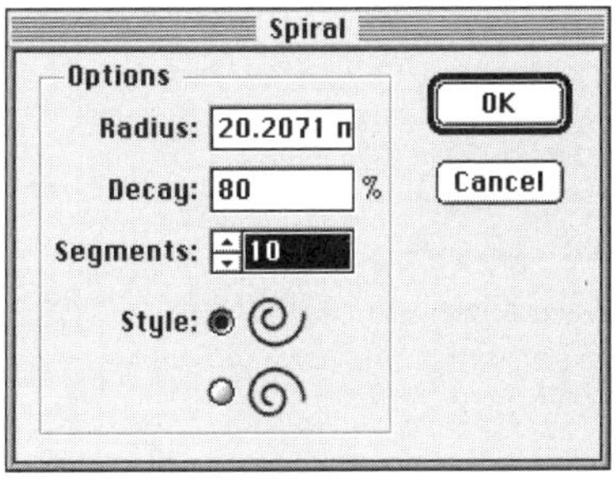

Decay = 70

Decay = 80

Decay = 90

Selecting Multiple Objects

Objects selected using the following techniques form a temporary grouping – moving one object moves all the selected objects whilst maintaining their exact position relative to each other. As soon as you click away, this temporary grouping is lost.

Once you have multiple objects selected you can move, fill, transform and manipulate them using any editing tool.

There are three essential techniques for selecting multiple objects. Use the Selection tool (solid arrow) or the Lasso Selection tool when selecting complete objects.

Selecting all objects

1 Working with the Selection tool, choose Edit > Select all to select all objects in the illustration. This includes objects on the pasteboard, but not any locked or hidden objects.

Selecting multiple objects with the Shift key

1 Select the Selection tool. Click on the first object you want to select. Hold down the Shift key, then click on other objects that you want to add to the initial selection.

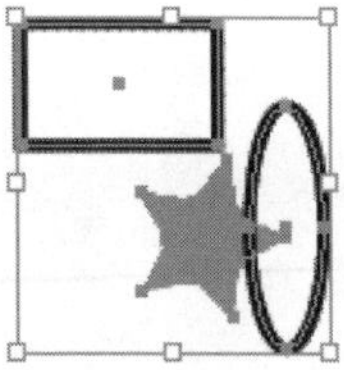

To 'marquee' select multiple objects

1 Make sure you have the Selection tool selected if you want to select complete objects. Position your cursor so that it is not on top of any existing objects. Press and drag. A dotted marquee box appears as you drag the mouse. Whatever this dotted rectangle touches will be selected when you release the mouse button. This is an extremely powerful selection technique and is worth practising if it is new to you.

2 Use the Lasso Selection tool to create a freeform, non-rectangular selection around objects. This tool can create complex, more precise selections than the previous, but takes longer.

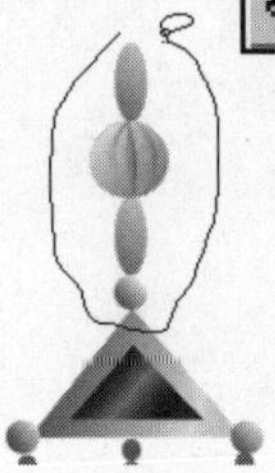

Resizing Objects

Once you have drawn a basic shape you can resize it manually using the Selection tool. You can also similarly resize groups, open paths, brush strokes and text.

If an object does not have a fill, you must click on its path (the edge) to select it - it will not select if you click inside the shape.

1 To resize a basic shape, select the Selection tool. Select the object or group you want to resize. A bounding box with 8 selection handles appears around the object or group.

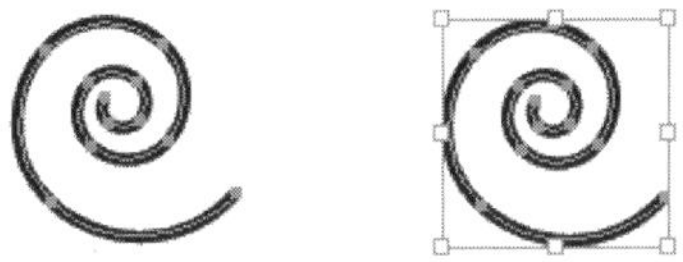

To select an individual object, select either the Section tool or the Group-selection tool, then click on the object. A bounding box with 8 selection handles appears around the object.

2 Drag the centre left /right handle to increase/decrease the width only of the object. Drag the centre top/bottom handle to resize the height only. Drag a corner handle to resize width and height simultaneously. As you resize an object Illustrator creates a preview of the new size of the object, indicated by a thin blue preview line. Release.

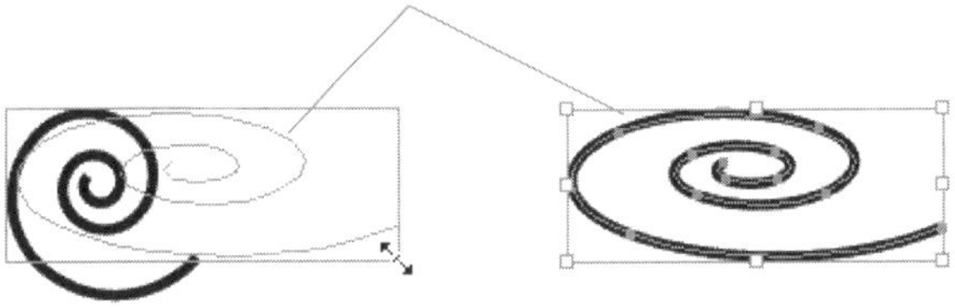

3 To maintain the proportions of an object or group, hold down Shift then drag a selection handle.

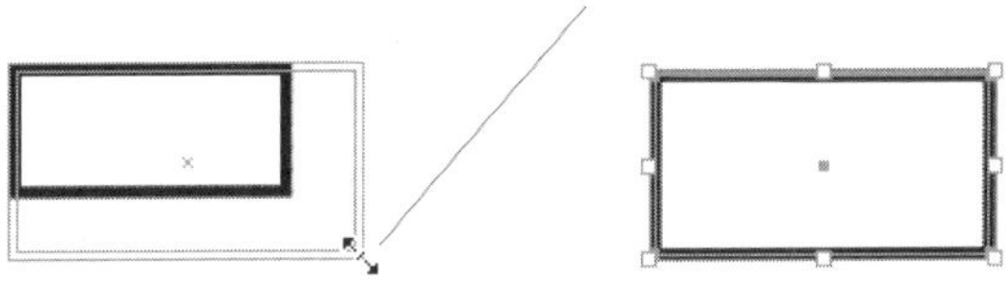

4 To scale an object around its centre point, hold down Alt then drag a selection handle.

Moving Objects

Depending on your requirements you can move objects visually using the mouse, or precise distances using the Move dialogue box or the keyboard.

Start to drag the object(s), then hold down Shift to constrain the movement of the object(s) horizontally, vertically, or to increments of 45 degrees.

1. To move an object visually, select the Selection tool. Click on an object to select it.

2. For an object with no fill, position your cursor on the path. For an object with a fill you can position your cursor inside the object. Do not position your cursor on one of the selection handles.

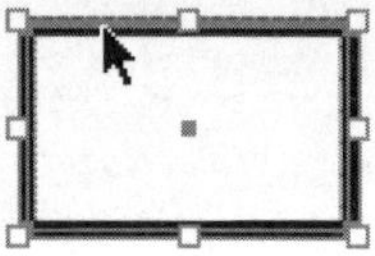

3. Press and drag to move the object to a new position. Release the mouse button when the preview, indicated by a blue bounding box, is where you want it.

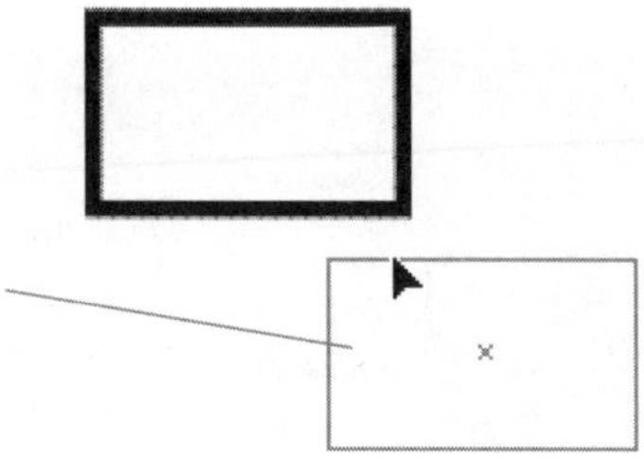

Moving objects in increments

1. Using the Selection tool, click on an object(s) to select it. Press the up, down, left or right arrow keys on the keyboard to move the object in 1 point increments.

2. To change the cursor increment, choose Edit > Preferences > General. Enter a new value in the Keyboard Increment entry box.

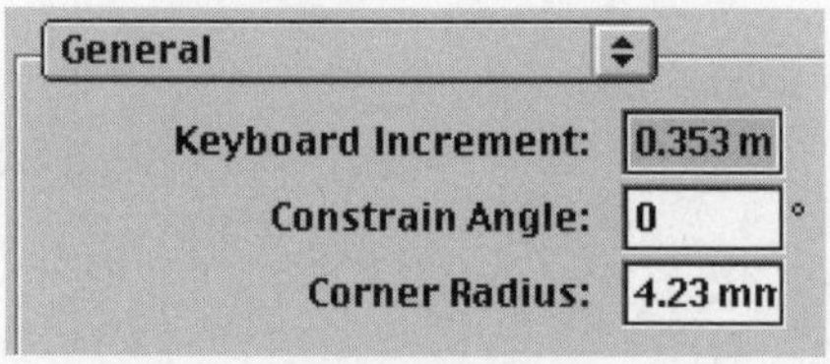

Moving objects precise distances

1. Using the Selection tool, select an object(s). Choose Object > Transform > Move.

Enter positive Horizontal values to move an object to the right. Enter a negative Horizontal value to move an object to the left. Enter a positive Vertical value to move an object upward. Enter a negative Vertical value to move an object downward.

2. In the Move dialogue box, either enter values for Horizontal and Vertical, or enter values for Distance and Angle. If you enter values for Horizontal and Vertical, the Distance and Angle values update and vice versa.

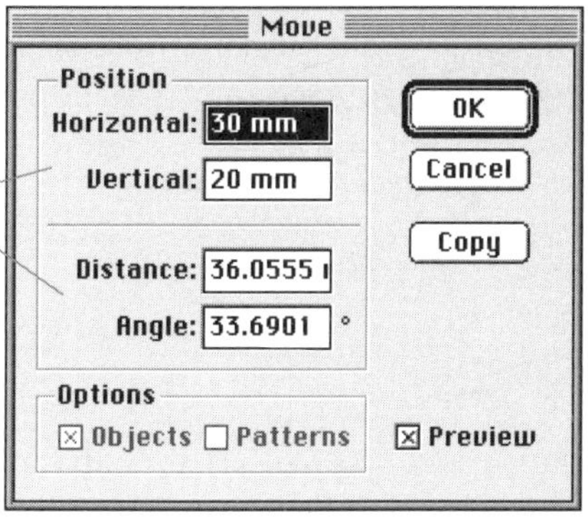

3. Click the Preview button to see a preview of the move before you OK the dialogue box.

4. Click the Copy button if you want to move a copy of the object(s). The original remains in place and a copy of the object(s) is moved to the new position specified.

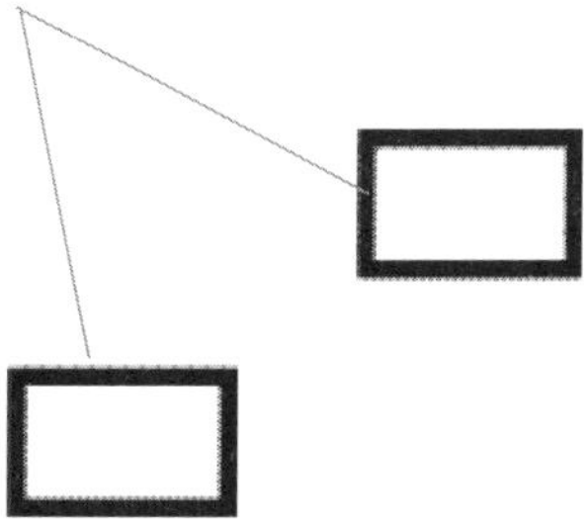

Cut, Copy, Paste, Clear

Use the Clipboard as a temporary storage area only. If you cut something important to the Clipboard, paste it back into the document as soon as possible to minimise the risk of accidentally overwriting it with another cut or copy action.

The Cut/Copy/Paste commands use the Clipboard as a temporary storage area for objects you create in Illustrator as well as for placed objects. The Clipboard can only hold the results of one cut or copy at a time. For example, if you copy some text to the Clipboard, then at a later stage, cut an object to the Clipboard, the object you cut overwrites the previous contents of the Clipboard - the text. After you cut or copy an object to the Clipboard, you can paste it into the active Illustrator file as many times as you like.

The Copy command leaves the original on the page and places a copy of the selected object onto the Clipboard. The Cut command removes whatever is selected from the page and places it on the Clipboard.

You can use the Clipboard to cut/copy information from one Illustrator document and then paste it into another.

The contents of the Clipboard are not saved when you close Adobe Illustrator.

1. To cut or copy an object to the Clipboard, first select the object using the Selection tool or the Group-selection tool. Choose Edit > Cut/Copy.

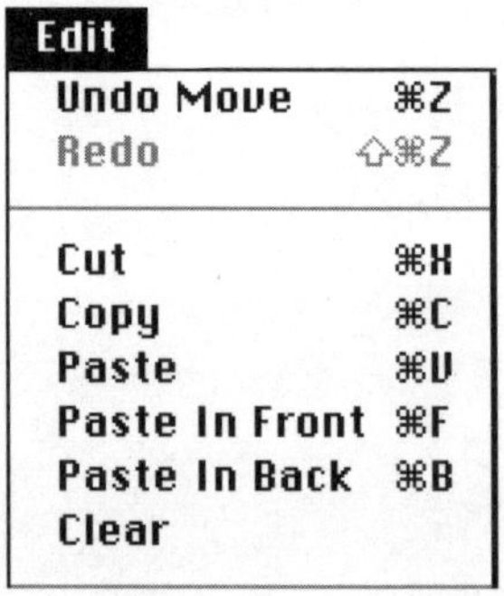

2. To paste an item from the Clipboard, make sure that you have the Selection tool selected, then choose Edit > Paste. The object is pasted into the middle of your screen display.

3. Select an object using the Selection tool or the Group-selection tool, then choose Edit > Clear to remove the object from the document. The Clear command does not use the Clipboard and therefore does not overwrite any existing objects on the Clipboard.

Pencil and Paintbrush Tools

Chapter Four

The Pencil tool and the Paintbrush tool can be used to create open or closed paths. They both work in a freeform manner as you drag the mouse. They can be very useful for sketching lines and shapes quickly when precision is not necessary.

There are three Pencil tools. The Paintbrush tool works in conjunction with the Brushes palette.

Covers

The Pencil Tool

Paths do not have to be selected before you use the Erase and Smooth tools, just drag the tool near an existing path for the path to be affected.

There are three tools in the Pencil tool group – the Pencil tool, the Smooth tool, and the Erase tool. Use the Pencil tool to draw freeform paths, like sketching with a pencil; the Smooth tool to create a smoother version of an existing path; and the Erase tool to erase portions of an existing path.

1 To draw an open path, select the Pencil tool. Position your cursor on the page. The cursor changes to the Pencil tool cursor.

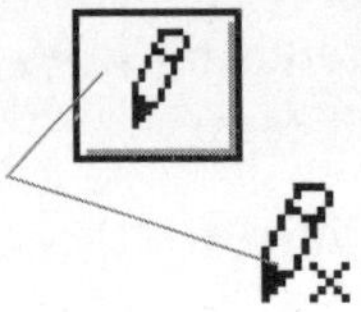

2 Press and drag to create the path. A dotted line appears on screen to represent the shape of the path.

The current settings for fill and stroke colour and stroke weight are applied to the path after you finish drawing it. (See Chapter Six for more information on setting stroke colour and weight.)

3 Release when you have finished drawing the path. The path remains selected. Illustrator automatically sets anchor points along the path to define its shape.

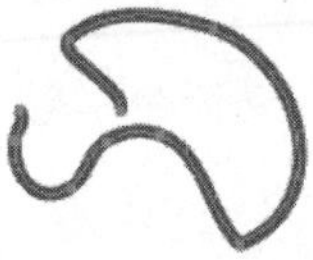

4 To add to an existing path, make sure the path is selected. Click on the Pencil tool to select it. Position your cursor on one of the end points of the selected path, then press and drag.

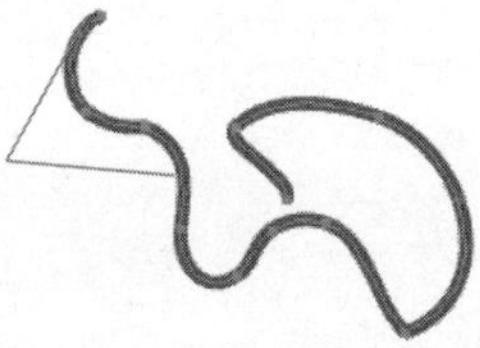

Drawing Closed Paths

Press N on the keyboard to select the currently visible Pencil tool. Hold down Shift and press N to cycle through the tools in the group.

1 To draw a closed path, select the Pencil tool.

2 Position your cursor on the page. Press and drag to begin defining the path.

3 Hold down Alt as you drag. A small circle appears next to the Pencil cursor.

If you release the mouse button before your cursor is positioned at the start point, Illustrator creates a straight line segment from the point at which you release to the start of the path.

4 Continue dragging the cursor back to the start point. Release the mouse button, then release the Alt key to close the path.

Redrawing Paths

1 To redraw a path, select the path you want to reshape. Select the Pencil tool and position it on, or very near to, the path you want to reshape. Press and drag to redraw the path.

Setting Pencil Tool Preferences

1 To set preferences for the Pencil, Smooth and Paintbrush tools, double-click the tool.

You can connect a new path to an existing, selected path. With a path selected, select the Pencil tool. Start to drag to define a new path. Hold down Command/Ctrl and drag onto the end point of the existing path.

2 Enter a value for Fidelity, or drag the Fidelity slider to control how may anchor points are used to create the path and how closely the path conforms to the actual movement of the mouse. Higher values create smoother, less complex paths with fewer anchor points. Lower values result in paths that conform more closely to the movement of the mouse. These paths are more complex, with a greater number of anchor points.

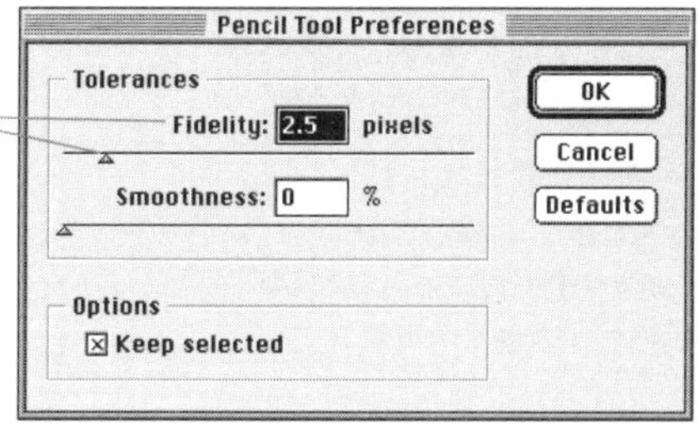

3 Enter a Smoothness value, or drag the Smoothness slider to control the degree to which the path is smoothed as you draw it. Higher values create smoother paths.

The Smooth and Erase Tools

The Smooth tool allows you to smooth entire paths or portions of paths, whilst retaining the overall shape of the path. Depending on the complexity of the original path, the Smooth tool tends to reduce the number of anchor points.

If you have the Pencil tool selected, hold down Alt to gain temporary access to the Smooth tool.

1. To smooth a path, select the path you want to smooth. Select the Smooth tool.

2. Click on the path with the Smooth tool to smooth the entire path.

3. Or press and drag along the section of the path you want to smooth. You may have to do this several times, depending on the preference settings for the tool, to achieve the effect you want.

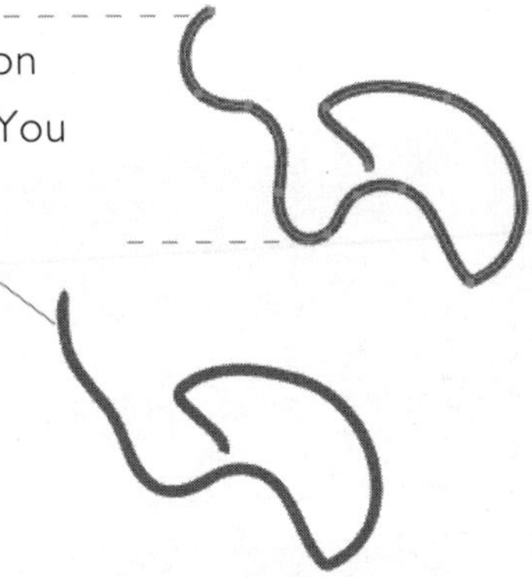

You can double-click the Smooth tool to set Smooth tool preferences. See page 51 for further information on the preference controls.

The Erase tool allows you to erase portions of existing open or closed paths. The Erase tool does not work on text or gradient mesh objects.

1. To erase paths, select the Erase tool.

2. Position your cursor on the path. The cursor changes to the Erase cursor. Press and drag along the path. Anchor points are added to the ends of any new paths that the Erase tool creates.

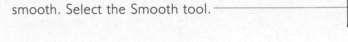

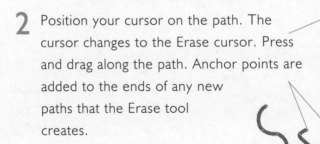

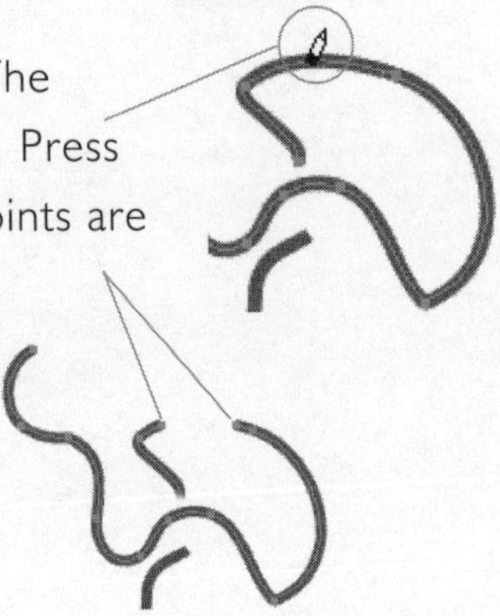

The Paintbrush Tool

The Paintbrush tool can be useful when you want to quickly sketch freeform shapes, where accuracy is not too important. Before using the Paintbrush tool to create 'brush strokes', you must first select a brush from the Brushes palette.

Note that you can choose from the following kinds of brush:

- *Calligraphic*
- *Scatter*
- *Art*
- *Pattern*

1 To draw an open brush stroke, click once on the Paintbrush tool to select it, or press B on the keyboard. Make sure the Brushes palette is showing (Window > Show Brushes).

2 Click on a brush in the Brushes palette to select it. A black highlight box around the brush indicates the currently selected brush.

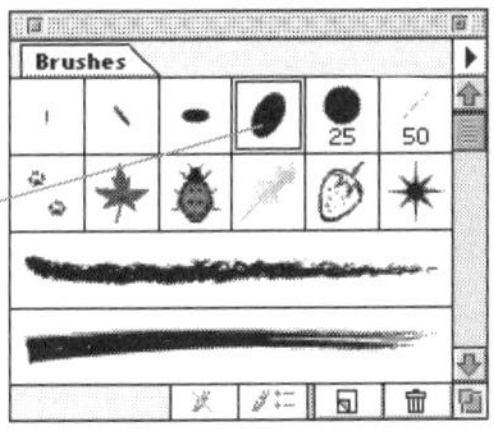

3 Position your cursor on the page then drag to define the brush stroke.

4 To apply a different brush stroke style, select the brush stroke, then click on any other brush in the Brushes palette to apply a different brush style to the path.

You can edit the shape of a brush stroke using the Direct-selection tool. (See Chapter Eleven.)

Drawing Closed Brush Strokes

1 To draw a closed brush stroke, select the Paintbrush tool. Position your cursor on the page. Press and drag to begin defining the brush stroke.

2 Hold down Alt as you drag. A small circle appears next to the Paintbrush cursor.

If you release the mouse button before your cursor is positioned at the start point, Illustrator creates a straight line segment from the point at which you release to the start of the path.

3 Position your cursor at the start point. Release the mouse button, then release the Alt key to close the brush stroke path.

Redrawing Brush Strokes

1 To redraw a brush stroke, select the brush stroke you want to reshape.

2 Select the Paintbrush tool and position it on, or very near to, the brush stroke. Press and drag to redraw the path.

Applying Brush Strokes

1 To apply a brush style to an existing path, create a path using a tool such as the Pen, Pencil, Rectangle or Oval tools.

You can double-click the Paintbrush tool to set Paintbrush Tool preferences. See page 51 for further information on the preference controls.

2 Make sure that the path remains selected and that the Brushes palette is showing.

3 Click on a brush in the Brushes palette to apply the brush characteristics to the path.

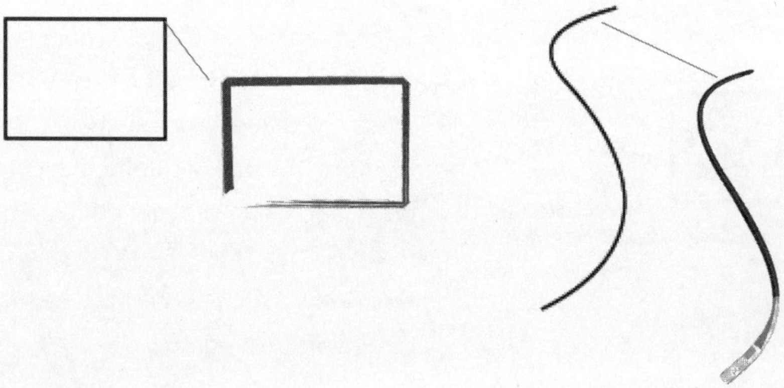

The Brushes Palette

The Brushes palette contains four types of brushes – Calligraphic, Scatter, Art and Pattern. Using the Brushes Palette, you can create your own brushes, edit existing brushes and delete brushes.

The Calligraphic brushes create strokes similar to those drawn by a calligraphic pen.

The Scatter brushes scatter or spray copies of objects along the path.

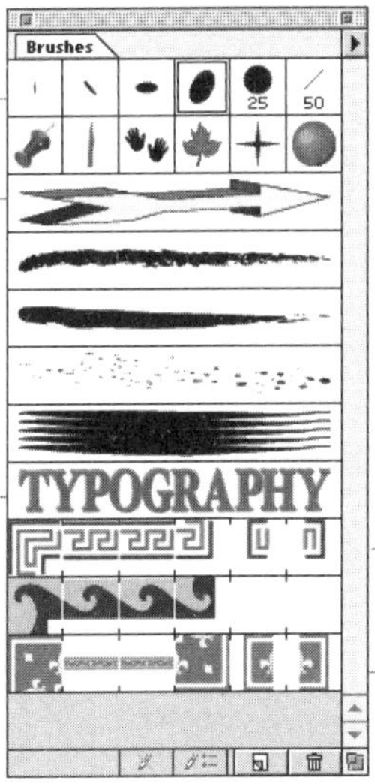

The Art brushes stretch an object, or grouped shapes, drawn in Illustrator along the path.

The Pattern brushes use a repeating tile pattern along the path. Pattern brushes can have up to five tiles – side, inner, corner, beginning and end tiles.

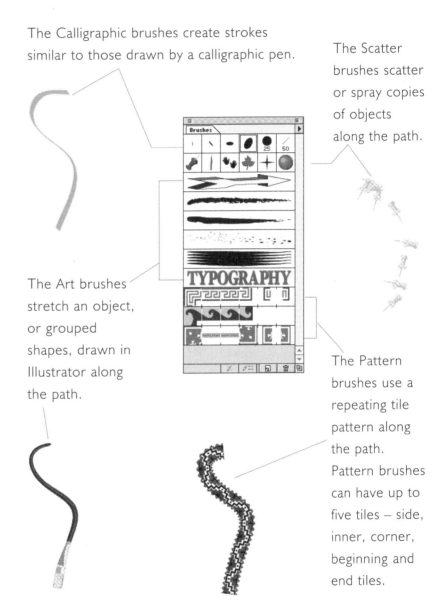

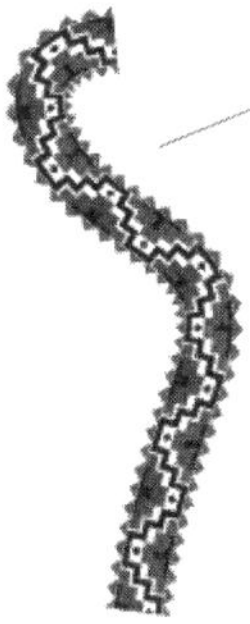

1 With a brush stroke selected, click the Remove Brush button to revert the brushed path back to a standard path.

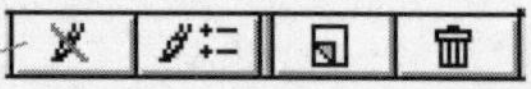

The controls available and the appearance of the Stroke Options dialogue box vary according to the brush you have selected.

2 With a brush stroke object selected, click the Options of Selected Object button. Use the dialogue box to make changes to the attributes of the selected object.

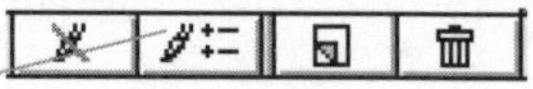

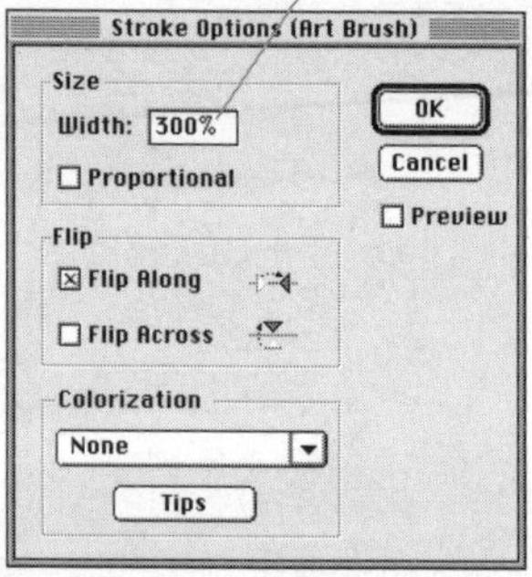

3 Click the New Brush button to create a new brush. (See next page for more information on creating new brushes.) New brushes are saved with the current file.

4 Click on a brush to select it, then Click on the Wastebasket button to delete the brush from the palette. Click Yes in the Warning dialogue box. If you delete one of the default brushes it will reappear as a default tool in new documents after you relaunch Illustrator.

Creating a New Calligraphic Brush

You can create your own Calligraphic, Art, Scatter and Pattern brushes. The following steps show you how to create a new calligraphic brush.

1. To create a calligraphic brush, click the New Brush button at the bottom of the Brushes palette, or choose New Brush from the pop-up menu in the Brushes palette.

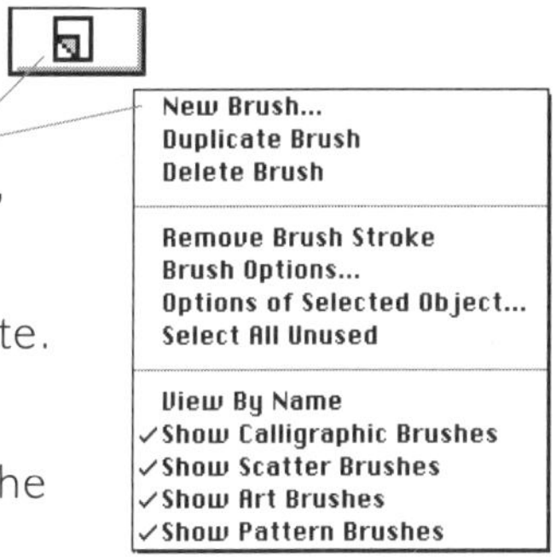

2. Select New Calligraphic Brush in the New Brush dialogue box. OK the dialogue box.

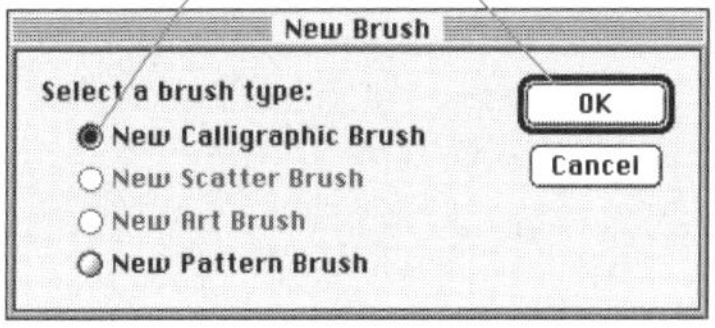

3. Enter a name for the new brush in the Name entry field.

4. Either drag the arrow tip in the Brush Shape Editor to change the angle of the brush, or enter a value in the Angle entry box.

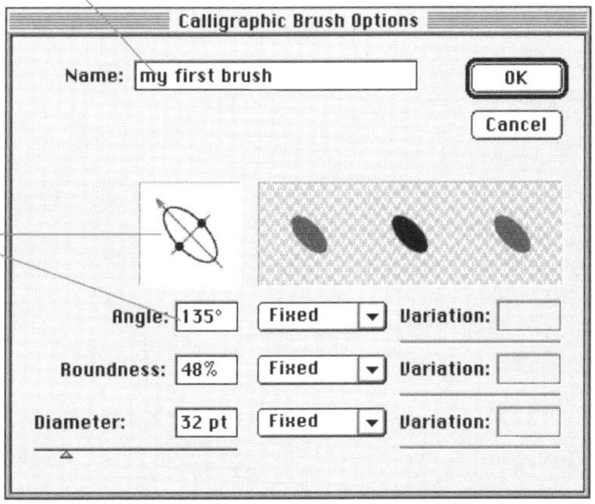

To edit settings for a calligraphic brush, double-click the brush in the palette to go into the Calligraphic Brush Options dialogue box.

5 Either drag the black circles in the Brush Shape Editor, or enter a value in the Roundness field to change the Roundness of the brush.

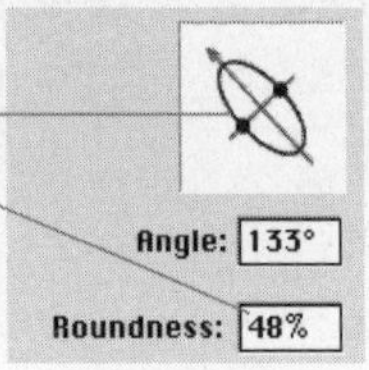

6 Enter a value in the Diameter field or drag the Diameter slider to specify the thickness of the brush.

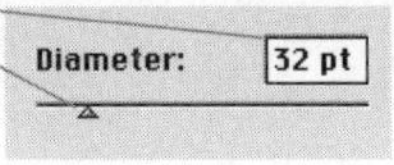

7 If you want to create variable brush strokes, use the pop-ups to the right of the entry fields to change from Fixed to Random. Then, enter a value in the entry field to the right of the pop-ups to specify the range of allowable variation. The brush preview box above these fields gives a visual indication of the variation values you enter.

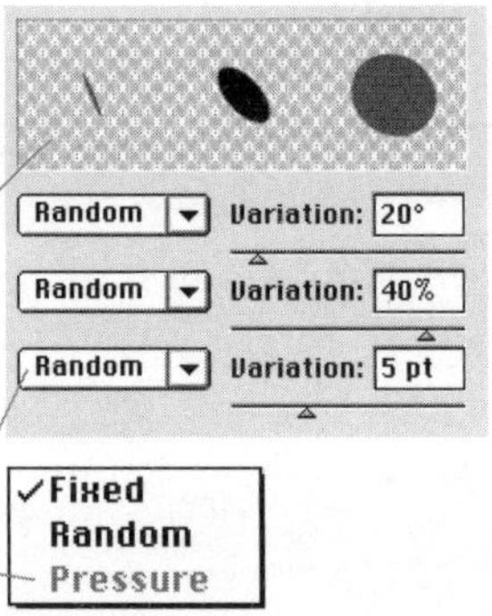

8 Pressure is only available if you are working with a Pressure Sensitive pen.

9 OK the dialogue box. The new brush appears in the Brushes palette and is saved with the current file.

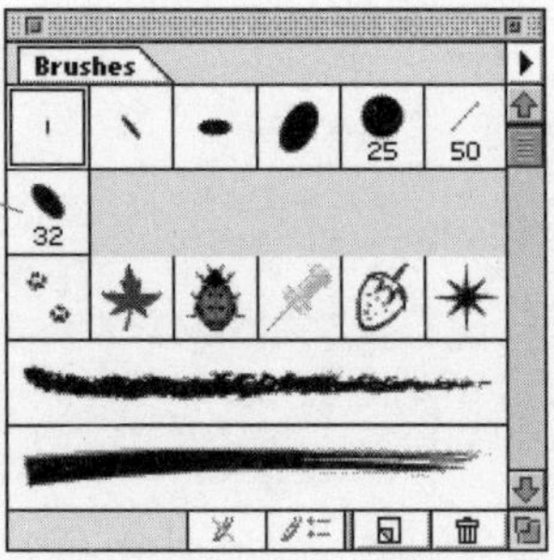

Arranging Objects

Positioning and spacing objects accurately and controlling whether objects appear in front of or behind other objects is critical as soon as you have more than one overlapping object in an illustration. This chapter looks at how you can change the stacking order of objects. It also looks at using the Layers and Alignment palettes, and at working with groups.

Covers

Chapter Five

Stacking Order

The positioning of an object in front of or behind another object is referred to as its stacking order. The order in which you create, paste or place objects in an illustration initially determines their relative stacking order.

Understanding stacking order and the various techniques for controlling it forms a fundamental aspect of working in even the simplest of Illustrator documents.

The basic principle is that the first object you create, paste or place is at the back of the stacking order. Each subsequent object you add to the illustration is placed in front of all the existing objects. The stacking order becomes apparent when objects overlap.

You can send a selected object(s) to the back of the stacking order, bring it to the front, or move it backwards or forwards one object at a time.

1. To bring an object to the front, using the Selection tool, select the object you want to bring to the front of the stacking order. Choose Object > Arrange > Bring To Front.

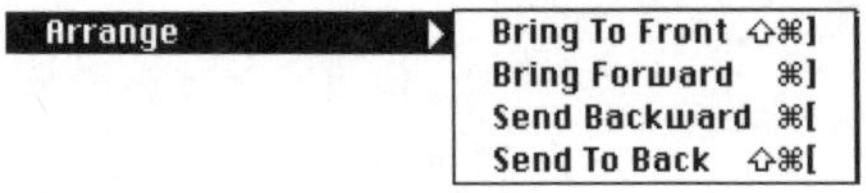

In an illustration with layers, the stacking order works on a layer by layer basis. When working on a layer the Bring to Front/Send to Back commands move an object to the front/back of that particular layer, not to the front/back of the entire illustration.

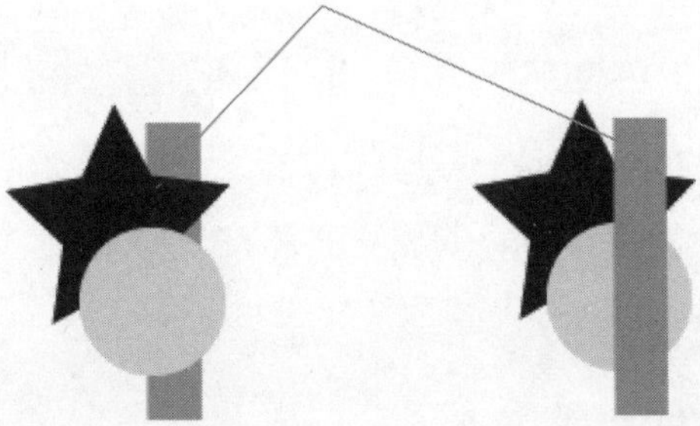

2. To move an object to the back, using the Selection tool, select the object you want to move to the back of the stacking order.

3 Choose Object > Arrange > Send To Back.

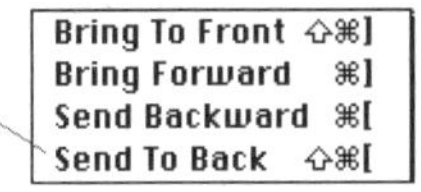

4 To move an object(s) forward or backward, use the Selection tool to select the object(s) you want to move. Choose Object > Arrange > Send Backward or Bring Forward.

5 To select an object that is partially or completely hidden behind other objects, first select one of the frontmost objects then hold down Ctrl then press the mouse button (Mac), or click the right mouse button (Windows), to access the context sensitive menu. Choose Select from the context sensitive menu, then choose an option from the Select sub-menu.

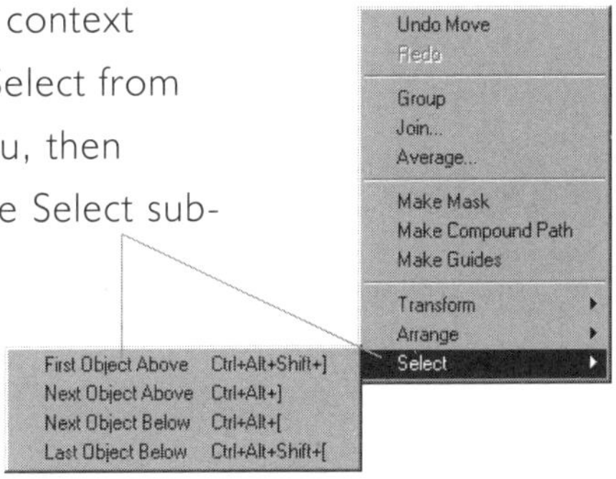

Paste In Front/In Back

When you choose the Paste In Front/In Back command, the objects are pasted at precisely the same position in the illustration from which they were cut. It is only their stacking order that changes.

The Paste In Front/Paste In Back commands allow complete precision when changing the stacking order of objects in complex illustrations, allowing you to move an object to a precise position in the stacking order, without having to use Send Backward/Bring Forward repeatedly.

1. To Paste In Back/In Front, using the Selection tool, select the object(s) you want to paste either directly in front of or directly behind a specific object in the illustration.

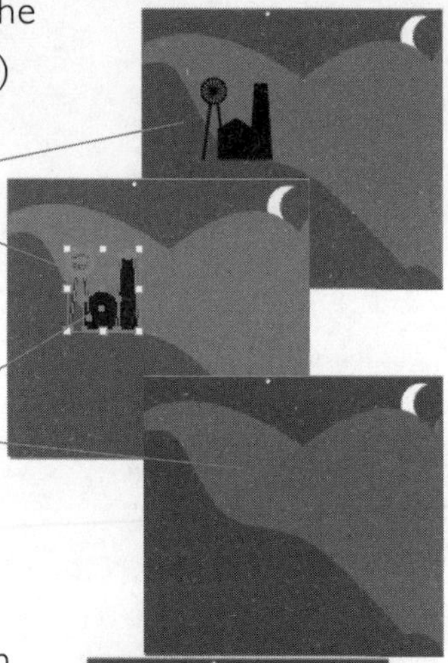

2. Choose Edit > Cut. The object(s) is cut to the clipboard.

3. Select another object behind or in front of which you want the cut object to be placed. If you forget to select an object before you choose Paste In Front/In Back the object will be pasted at the back of all other objects, or in front of all other objects – the equivalent of using Send To Back or Bring To Front.

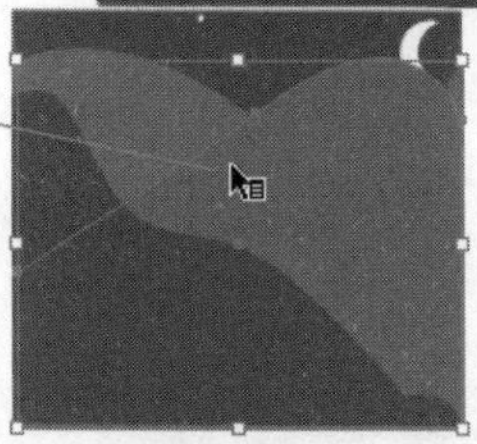

You can use the Group-selection tool to select an object in a group or which is part of a Clipping mask, then use Paste In Front/In Back to add an object (already cut to the Clipboard) to the group or Clipping mask.

4. Choose Edit > Paste In Front/In Back as required.

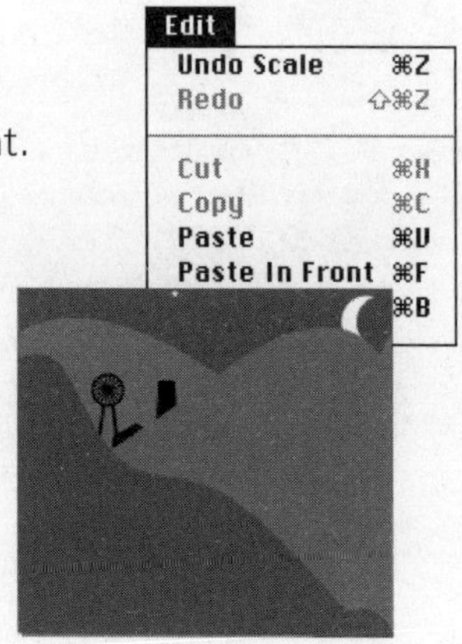

Hide and Lock Commands

Objects that are hidden when you close a file, show automatically when you re-open the file.

In complex illustrations where numerous objects overlap one another, it can be very useful to hide some objects in order to work on other objects unhindered. Hidden objects cannot be selected or edited and do not print.

Lock an object so that it cannot be selected or edited. Again, this can be helpful in complex illustrations when you want to avoid accidentally selecting, moving or otherwise changing certain objects.

Although you can hide individual or multiple objects whenever necessary, you cannot selectively show hidden objects, you have to show all hidden objects.

1 To hide objects, use the Selection tool to select the object(s) you want to hide. Choose Object > Hide Selection. The object is hidden and cannot be selected or manipulated and will not print.

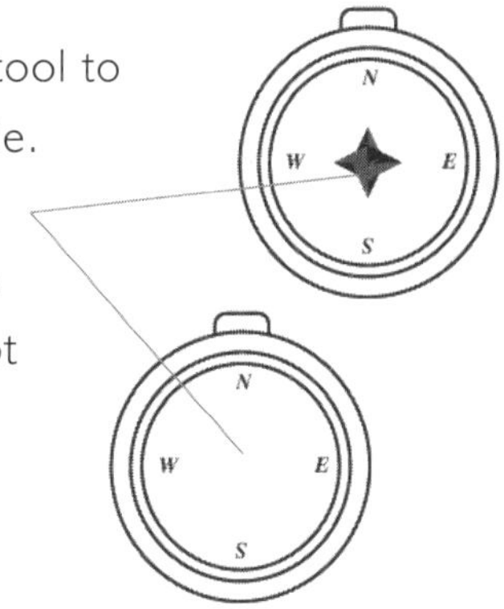

2 To show hidden objects, choose Object > Show All.

3 To Lock objects, use the Selection tool to select the object(s) you want to lock. Choose Object > Lock. Objects that are locked will still print.

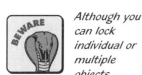

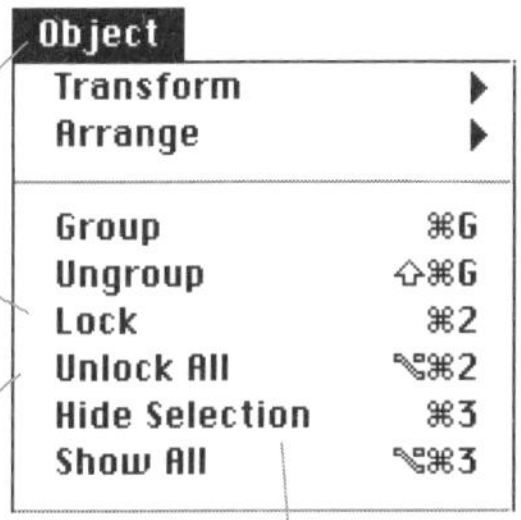

Although you can lock individual or multiple objects sequentially, you cannot selectively unlock objects, you have to unlock all objects.

4 To unlock objects, choose Object > Unlock All.

5 To lock all unselected objects, hold down Alt and then choose Object > Lock.

6 To hide all unselected objects, hold down Shift+Alt then choose Object > Hide Selection

Creating New Layers

Layers provide considerable flexibility in complex illustrations, such as maps and plans, providing an efficient method for managing objects. You can hide and show individual layers, lock and unlock layers, move objects between layers and specify which layers will print.

When you start a new Illustrator document you are automatically working on a layer – Layer 1. This is the default layer. For many straightforward illustrations you only need a single layer. Layers become more and more useful and necessary as illustrations become more and more complex.

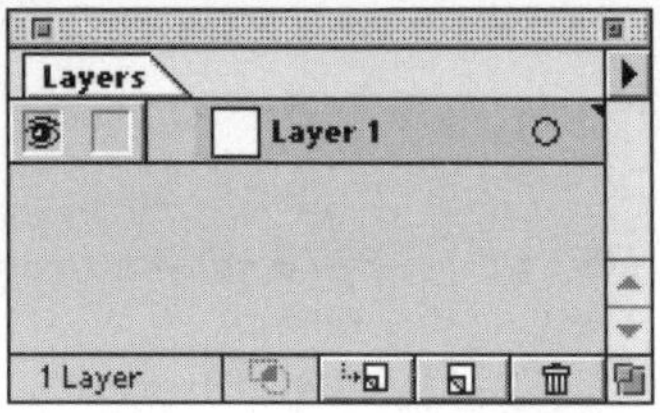

1. To create a new layer, use the pop-up menu in the Layers palette. Choose New Layer.

2. In the Layer Options dialogue box enter a name for the layer.

3. Choose a colour from the Color pop-up menu. The colour you choose is used to highlight selected objects.
This can be extremely helpful when it comes to identifying the layer on which particular objects are positioned.

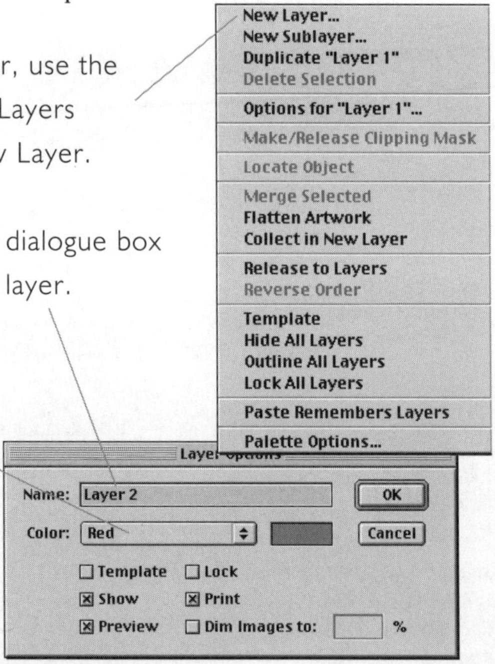

Do not confuse the active layer with visible layers – many layers can be visible, but only one layer is active, indicated by the highlight and the triangle (◥) in the layers palette.

You can now create sub layers within layers. To avoid confusion and over complication, it is best to use this feature only after you are fully confident with basic layer operations.

4 Choose options as required. The options you choose at this stage are not permanent and can be changed at any time when you are working in the document. All the options can be changed after you have created the layer, either using icons in the Layers palette, or by selecting the layer, then choosing Options for 'layer name' from the pop-up menu. Double-clicking a layer also takes you back into the Layer options dialogue box.

Options

'Show' – controls whether a layer is hidden or showing when you create it. You can also use the Eye icon in the Layers palette to hide/show a layer.

'Preview' – leave this option selected if you want the layer to appear in Preview mode. Deselect this and the layer will appear in Artwork mode.

'Lock' – select Lock if you want the layer to be locked when you create it. You can also use the Lock column in the Layers palette to control the lock status of a layer.

'Print' – leave this option selected if you want the layer to print.

When you create an object in a document with more than one layer, the object is placed on the active layer.

'Dim' – select this option for a layer if you intend to place an image (bitmap) on the layer and then manually trace around it. Dimmed images can be easier to trace around as you can see paths more clearly as you create them.

5 Alternatively, click the Create New Layer button at the bottom of the Layers palette. This creates a new layer with a default name and settings. The new layer is placed above the currently active layer.

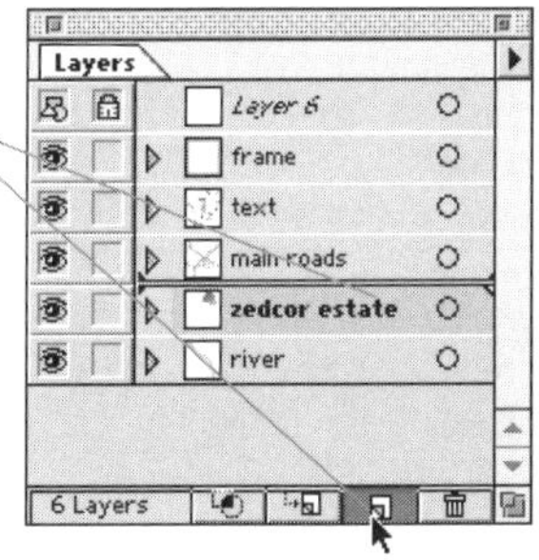

Working with Layers

When you create a new object it is automatically placed on the active layer. The active layer is the layer whose name is highlighted in the Layers palette, and has the triangle (◥) visible to the right of the layer name.

1 To make a layer active, click on the layer name. The layer highlights and a triangle icon appears to the right of the layer.

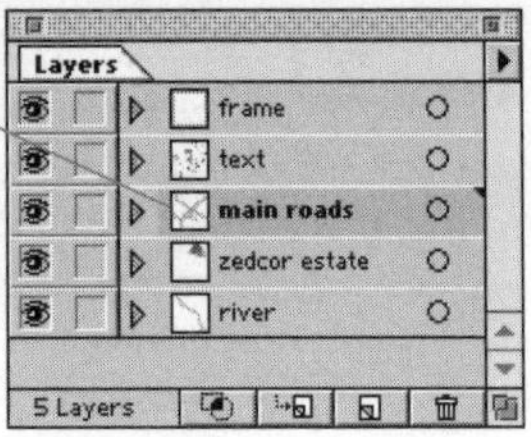

Only one layer can be active at any time.

2 Click on an object with any selection tool to select the object and make the object's layer active. When you select an object on a layer, a small coloured square appears to the right of the layer name.

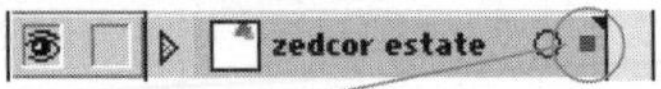

The square indicates the layer the object is on. It also indicates the colour used to highlight objects on that layer. (See Step 3, page 64, for further information on setting this colour.)

To select all objects on a layer, hold down Alt then click the layer name.

4 A template layer has a template objects icon, not an 'eye' icon, to indicate visibility. You can still click on the icon to control visibility of the template layer. Template layers are locked, do not print and do not export.

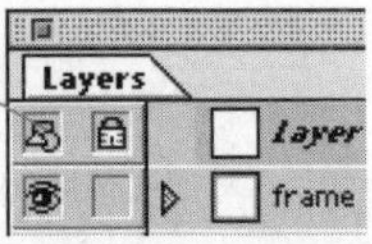

5 To display a layer in Artwork mode, hold down Command/ Ctrl, then click the eye icon for the layer. The eye icon changes to indicate Artwork mode. Repeat the process to bring the layer back into Preview mode.

6 To select all objects on a layer, click to the right of the Target circle. The layer becomes the active layer and the large selection indicator square appears.

Moving Objects Between Layers

The relative stacking order of multiple objects is maintained when objects are moved or pasted onto a different layer. If there are already objects on the layer, objects that you move or paste into the layer are stacked in front of the existing objects.

As you build a complex illustration using layers there will undoubtedly be times when you need to move objects from one layer to another layer.

1 To move an object to another layer, click on the object to select it.

In the Layers palette the object's layer highlights. Notice also to the right of the Target icon a small square dot, which indicates the active layer's selection colour.

To copy an object to a new layer, hold down Alt as you drag the coloured dot to the new layer.

2 Drag the dot to the layer onto which you want to move the object. When you release, the layer you move the object to becomes the active layer. The selection handles and the bounding box highlight around the object change to the highlight colour for that layer. When you move an object to a different layer it becomes the frontmost object on that layer. You can use this technique for multiple selected objects on the same layer, or groups.

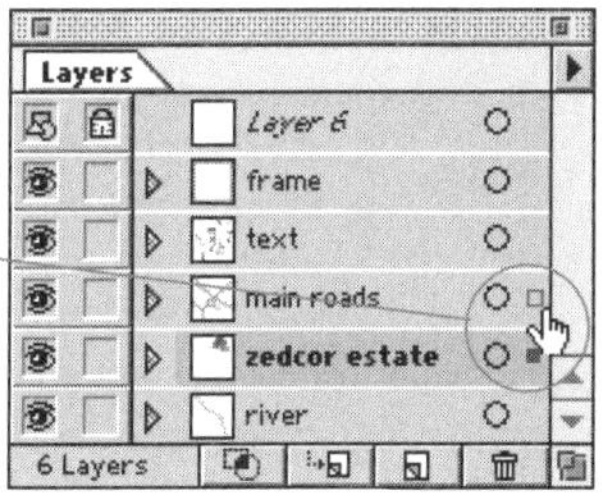

If Paste Remembers Layers is selected, when you paste objects from the Clipboard they are automatically pasted back onto the layer from which they were cut, even if you have clicked on a different layer to make it active.

3 You can also use the Clipboard to move an object to another layer. In the pop-up in the Layers palette ensure the Paste Remembers Layer option is switched off (unticked). Select the object you want to move then choose Edit > Cut to cut the object from its current layer. In the Layers palette, click the name of the layer you want to move the object to. Choose Edit > Paste to paste the object into the active layer.

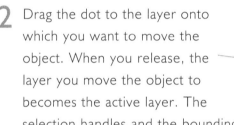

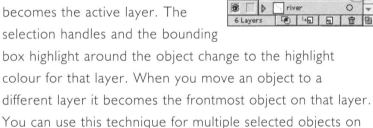

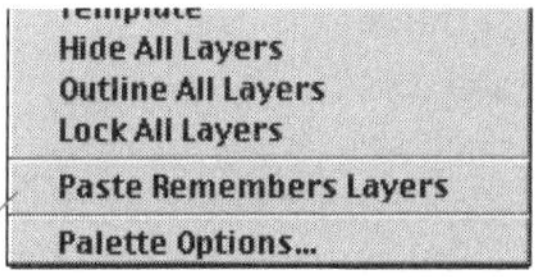

Managing Layers

When re-ordering layers, you do not have to drag the active layer, but when you release the mouse, the moved layer becomes the active layer.

Techniques for managing layers include: deleting, duplicating, changing the order of layers, hiding/showing layers, locking/unlocking layers and changing various layer options. You can also merge layers together to consolidate separate layers into a single layer and you can flatten all layers into a single layer.

1 To change the order of layers, drag the layer you want to move upwards or downward in the Layers palette. As you drag, notice the thick double bar which indicates the position to which the layer will move when you release. Drag a layer upwards to move objects on that layer in front of objects on other layers. Drag a layer downward to move objects behind objects on other layers.

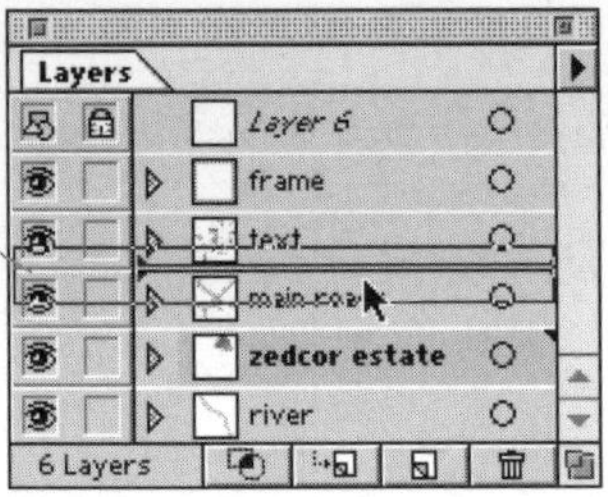

To select non-consecutive layers, select a layer, then hold down Command/Ctrl and click other layer names to add them to the originally selected layer.

2 To duplicate a layer, click on a layer name in the Layers palette to identify it as the layer you want to copy. Choose Duplicate layer from the Layer's pop-up menu.

To select consecutive layers, select the first layer, hold down Shift, then click the last layer name. All layers between the originally selected layer and the layer you Shift-click on are selected.

3 Alternatively, drag the layer you want to copy onto the Create New Layer button at the bottom of the Layers palette.

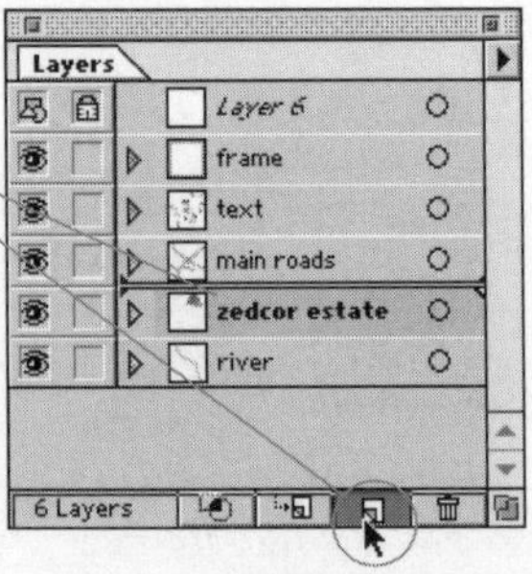

Merging layers

1 Select two or more layers that you want to combine into a single layer.

When reordering layers, if you release the mouse when the cursor is directly on another layer, you create a sub layer, rather than moving the layer to a new position.

2 Choose Merge Selected Layers from the pop-up in the layers palette. The merged layers take the name of the active layer and its position in the layer order.

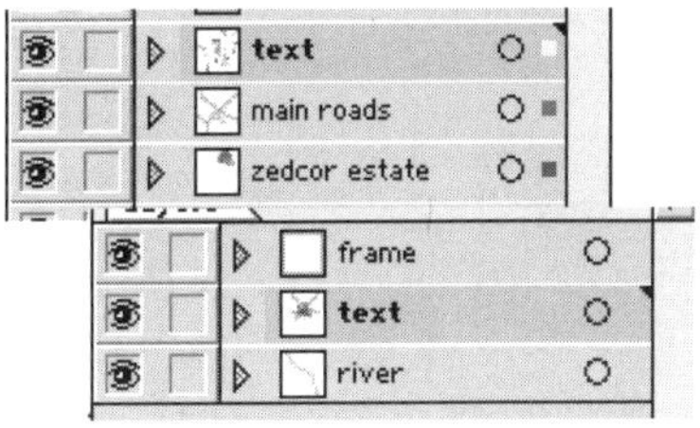

Flattening layers

1 Before you flatten artwork into a single layer, make sure all layers you want included are visible.

2 Choose Flatten Artwork from the Layers palette pop-up menu.

Deleting layers

1 To delete a layer, click on the Layer name you want to delete. Choose Delete Layers from the pop-up in the Layers palette, or click the Wastebasket icon at the bottom of the palette.

2 Alternatively, drag the layer name onto the Wastebasket icon path at the bottom of the palette. Beware, no warning dialogue box appears, even if there are objects on the layer, when you use this technique.

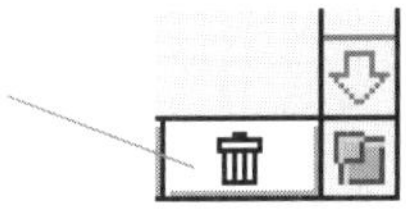

Deleting a layer deletes all objects on that layer. A warning dialogue box appears if there are objects on the layer:

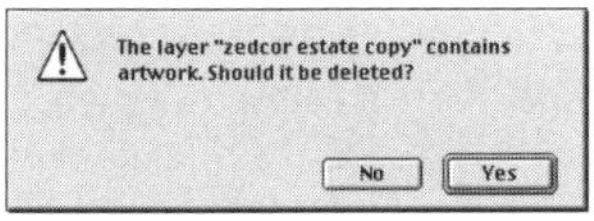

Hiding and Locking Layers

A visible layer has an eye icon in the leftmost column of the layers palette. A locked layer displays a padlock, in the column next to the eye icon.

The option to hide and/or lock layers becomes invaluable as illustrations become more and more complex. Both options can help avoid accidentally making unwanted changes to objects with which you are satisfied.

Hiding Layers

Hiding layers facilitates selecting and manipulating objects in complex illustrations in which objects are overlapped and obscured by other objects on layers higher up in the layer order.

Hidden layers do not print.

1 To hide a visible layer, click on the Eye icon for the layer. The Layer you hide does not have to be the active layer. All objects on the Layer are hidden.

2 To show a layer that is hidden, click in the now empty eye icon column next to the layer you want to show. To show all layers choose Show All Layers from the pop-up menu in the Layers palette.

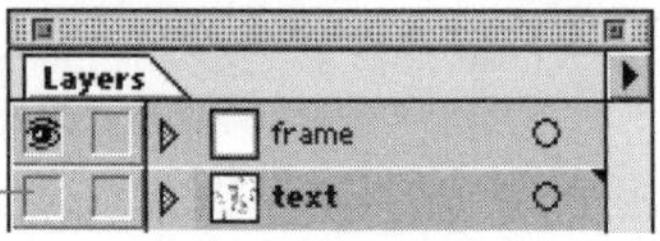

Hold down Alt and click an eye icon to hide all layers except the one on which you click.

Drag through the eye icons column to hide/show a continuous sequence of layers.

Locking Layers

You cannot select or edit any objects on a locked layer. Lock layers when you want to avoid moving, disturbing or otherwise editing objects on the layer.

1 To lock a layer, click in the lock box of the layer you want to lock. A padlock icon appears to indicate that the layer is locked.

2 To unlock a layer, click the padlock icon. The lock column will be empty. To unlock all layers choose Unlock All Layers from the pop-up menu in the Layers palette.

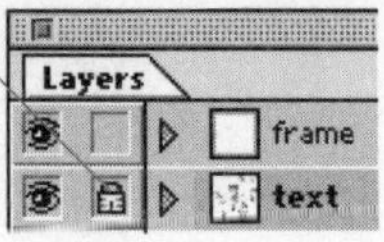

Alt+click on the lock box to lock/unlock all layers except the layer on which you click.

Working with Expanded Layers

A layer containing sub-layers, groups or objects can be expanded to show its contents. This is useful for identifying paths and whether they have Appearance Attributes applied to them (see page 90 for information on Appearance Attributes). Sub-layers and groups can be expanded in turn to show their contents.

See page 72 for information on using the Target icon in the Layers palette.

1 To expand a layer to view its contents, click the grey triangle to the left of the layer thumbnail. To collapse the layer contents, re-click the triangle.

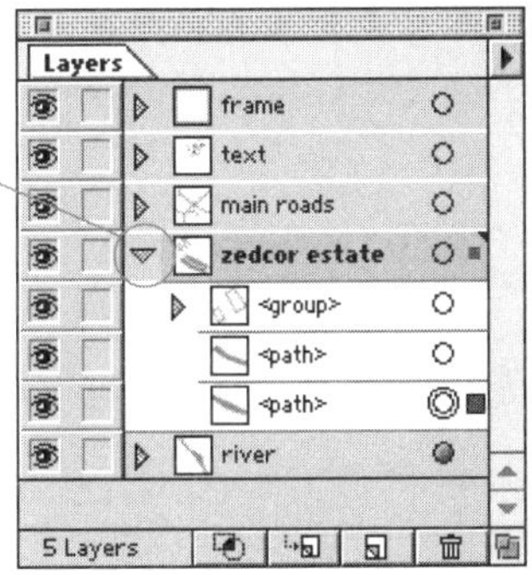

2 To expand a group, first expand the group's layer, then click the grey triangle to the left of the group thumbnail.

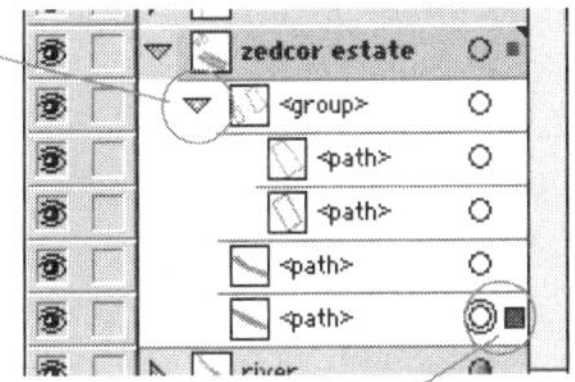

3 When working with expanded layers, click in the selection area to the right of the Target circle to select the object/group in your artwork. The large coloured square that appears indicates that the object/group is selected. A small coloured square to the right of a layers's Target circle indicates that artwork somewhere in the active layer or group is selected.

4 When a layer is expanded and you select an object in your artwork, a large, coloured square appears to the right of the Target circle in the Layers palette. A small coloured square appears to the right of the Target circle for the layer, indicating there is an active selection on the layer.

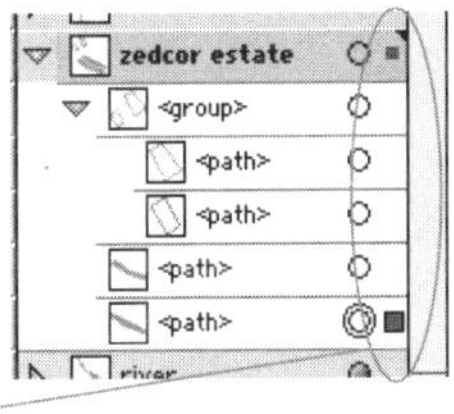

Targeting Layers, Groups and Objects

Using the Target icon (○/●) in the Layers palette you can apply appearance attributes such as Styles, Effects and Transparency to entire layers, groups or individual objects. The Target icon, to the right of the layer palette, changes depending on its status.

If you create an object on, or move or copy an object to, a layer which has appearance attributes applied to it, the object takes on the appearance attributes of that layer.

○ = not targeted, no appearance attributes applied.

● = not targeted, appearance attributes applied.

◎ = targeted, no appearance attributes applied.

◉ = targeted, appearance attributes applied.

1. To target a layer, group or object, click on the Target icon (○/●). You must expand a layer to target a group or an individual object.

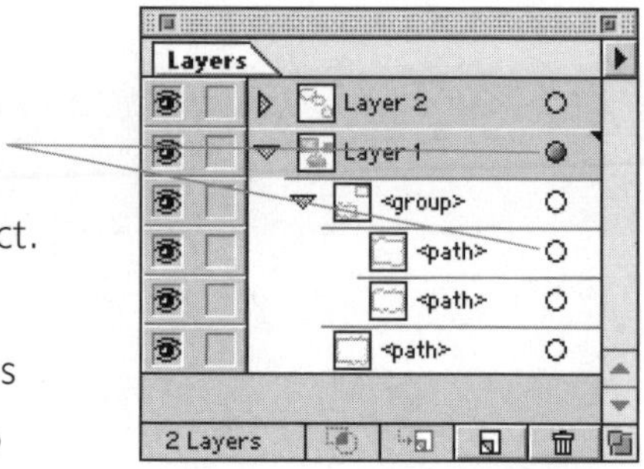

Basic fills and strokes do not count as appearance attributes in the Layers palette.

2. Click on a Style in the Styles palette to apply the style to the targeted layer, group or object.

3. Or choose an effect from the Effects menu to apply an effect. (See page 187)

You can apply combinations of Effect, Style and Transparency attributes to a layer group or object.

4. Or use the Transparency palette to apply transparency settings (see page 92).

5. To delete appearance attributes from a targeted layer, group or object, drag the target with appearance icon (●) into the Wastebasket at the bottom of the palette.

Aligning Objects

You must select two or more objects to use the alignment options.

Illustrator provides flexible controls for aligning objects relative to each other using the Align palette. There are two parts to the Align palette. The top row of buttons is for horizontal and vertical alignment of objects. The bottom row of buttons allows you to space objects evenly, either vertically or horizontally, by distributing the space between them.

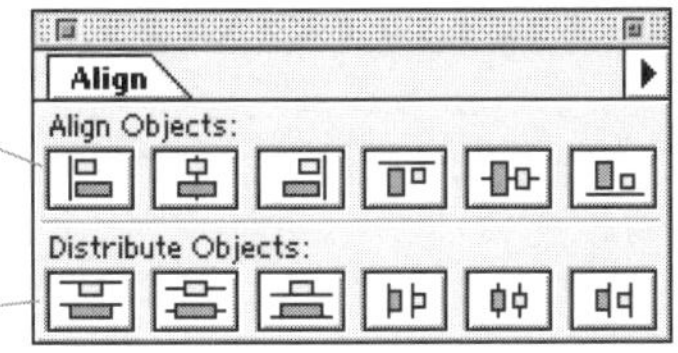

1 To align objects, use the Selection tool to select two or more objects. Make sure the Align palette is showing. (Window > Show Align.)

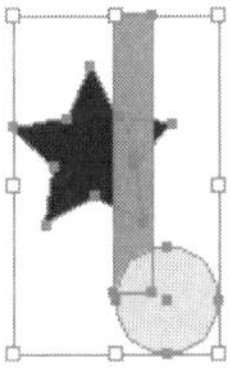

2 Click one of the horizontal alignment buttons to align the objects along their left edges, horizontal centres or right edges.

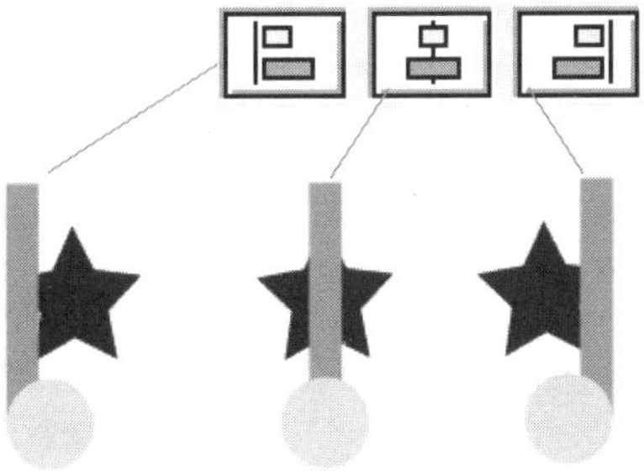

3 Click one of the vertical alignment buttons to align the objects along their top edges, vertical centres or bottom edges.

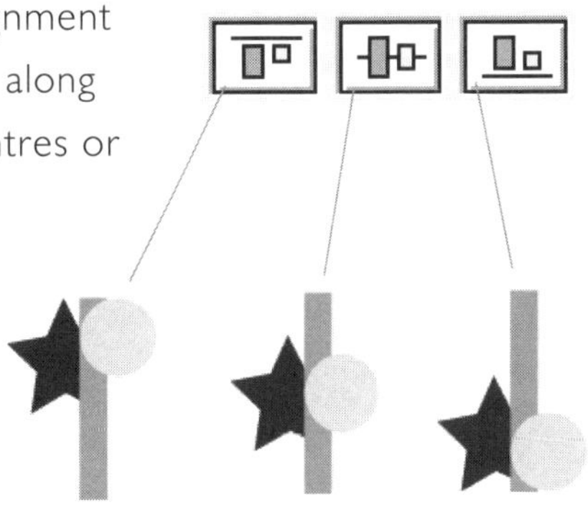

Distributing Objects

Distribute objects when you want to space objects evenly between two points. You use the bottom row of icons in the Align palette to distribute the space between specific parts of selected objects.

1. To distribute objects, use the Selection tool to select three or more objects that you want to distribute.

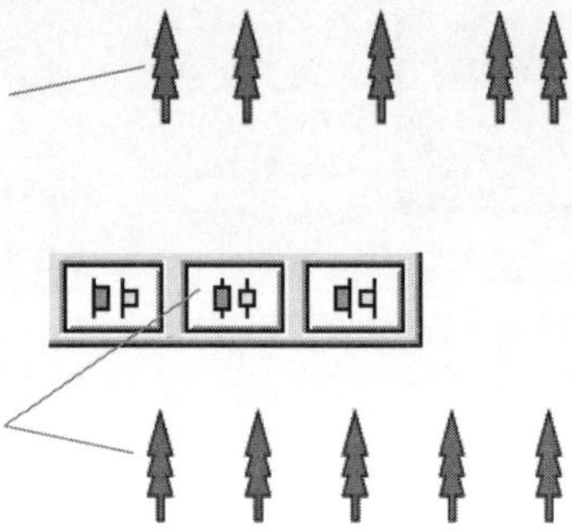

2. Click one of the Horizontal Distribute icons to create equal spacing between the left edges, horizontal centres or right edges of the objects.

You must select three or more objects before you can use the distribute options.

3. Click one of the Vertical Distribute buttons to create equal spacing between the top edges, vertical centres or bottom edges of the objects.

Distributing space equally between objects

1. Choose show options from the Align palette. This shows additional buttons at the bottom of the palette.

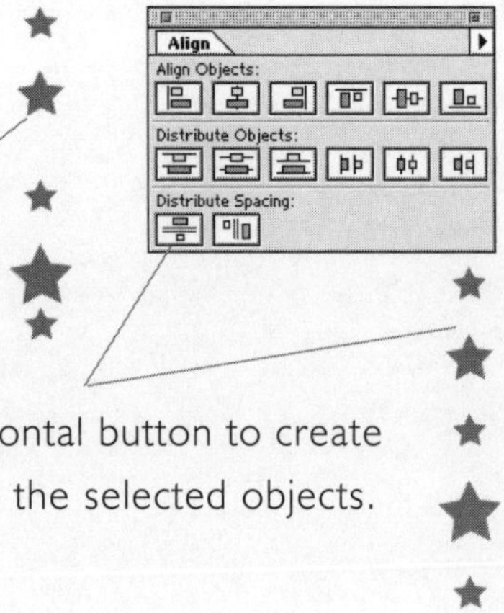

2. Use the Selection tool to select three or more objects.

3. Click either the Vertical or Horizontal button to create equal amounts of space between the selected objects.

Working with Groups

Group objects together when you want to work with them as a single unit. You can move, scale, transform and edit groups whilst keeping the relative size and positioning of objects intact.

If you group objects that are initially on separate layers, the objects are moved onto and grouped on the layer of the frontmost selected object.

1 To group selected objects, select two or more objects. Choose Object > Group. A bounding box with selection handles appears around the selected shapes. Any move, scale, rotate or other transformation will now apply to the whole group.

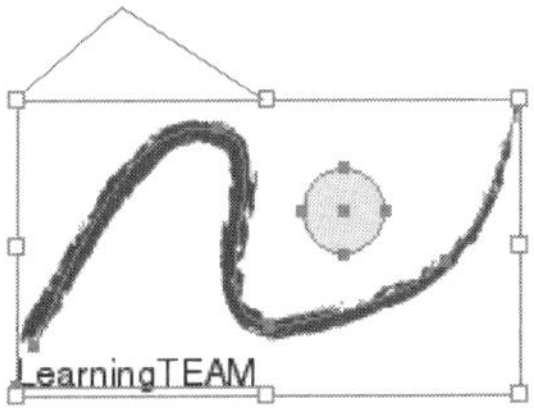

Hold down Shift, then drag a resize handle to resize the objects in the group in proportion.

2 Use the Selection tool to resize a group. Click on one of the objects in the group to select the group. Press and drag on a selection handle to resize all objects in the group.

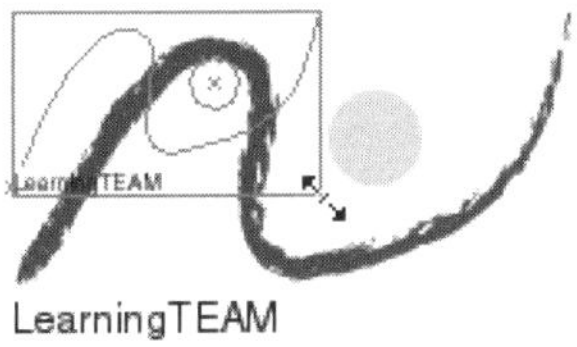

The keyboard shortcut for Ungroup is Command/Ctrl+ Shift+G (not Command/Ctrl+U).

3 To move a group, click on an object in the group to select it. Position your cursor on any object in the group, then press and drag to reposition the group. Hold down Shift, then drag an object in the group to constrain the move horizontally, vertically, or in multiples of 45 degrees. Start to drag the group, then hold down Alt to make a copy of the group.

4 To ungroup, select the group using the Selection tool. Choose Object > Ungroup. The objects are ungrouped, but initially all objects remain selected. To manipulate an individual object, click on some empty space to deselect all objects, then select the object you want to edit.

The Group-selection Tool

As illustrations become more and more complex you can group one group to another group and so on to create a nested hierarchy of groups. The Group-selection tool allows you to work on objects within a set of nested groups as individual objects, or on a group by group basis, without first having to ungroup the various groups.

1. To select objects with the Group-selection tool, select the Group-selection tool. Click on an object in a group. This will select one object only. If you wanted to at this stage, you could delete this individual object, or recolour it and so on.

In the screen shots used to illustrate the use of the Group-selection tool, the spokes of the sun form one group, the stars form another group, and the moon and the single displaced star form a third group. The spokes group was grouped to the star group and finally the moon and star group was grouped to the combined spoke–star group.

2. Click a second time on the same object to select all other objects in the same group. Again, it might be, for example, that you want to recolour all the objects in the group, or even delete the entire group.

3. Click a third time on the same object to select any other groups grouped with the first group. Continue to click on the same object, selecting outward through the grouping hierarchy.

Working with Colour/Appearance Attributes

Chapter Six

Colour can be one of the most powerful and essential ingredients of artwork you create in Adobe Illustrator. This chapter shows you how to use the Colour tools in the Toolbox, how to use the Color palette to create process and Spot colours and how to save, edit and manage colour swatches in the Swatches palette. It also covers selecting colours from colour matching systems such as the PANTONE® or FOCOLTONE® colour matching systems.

An appearance attribute changes the look or appearance of an object without permanently altering or changing the original object.

Covers

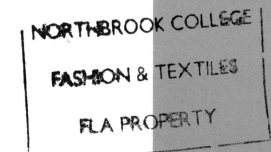

Applying Fill Colours

When you create an object or path in Illustrator, it fills with the currently selected fill colour and the path is stroked, or outlined, with the currently set stroke attributes. Even in the case of open paths, Illustrator fills in an imaginary line between the end points of the path. This can be disconcerting until you get used to it. Fills can be spot or Process colours, a gradient, or pattern.

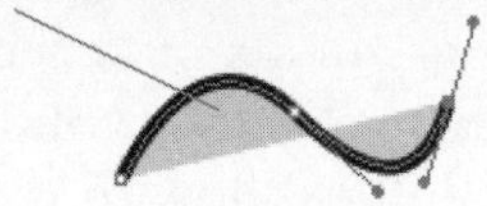

Use the Fill and Stroke boxes in the Toolbox to specify whether you want to apply a fill or stroke colour. Use the Default colours icon to revert to Black and White as the default fill/stroke colour.

When you click on either the Fill Box, or the Stroke Box, its icon comes to the front, indicating it is the 'active' icon. If you click on a swatch in the Swatches palette, or use the Color palette to define a new colour, the change is applied to the active icon.

1. To apply a fill colour to a selected shape, click on the Fill box to make it active.

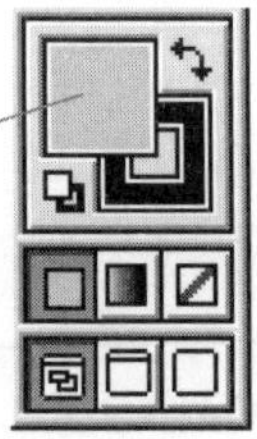

2. Click on one of the existing swatches in the Swatches palette. (Choose Window > Show Swatches if the Swatches palette is not showing.) The fill colour is applied to the selected shape and it becomes the default colour in the Fill box.

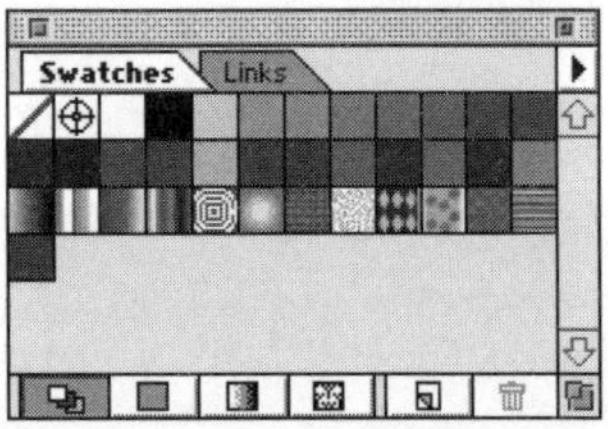

See pages 84-85 for further information on working with colour swatches in the Swatches palette.

3. Or use the Color palette to mix a new colour. (Choose Window > Show Colours if the Color palette is hidden). Make sure the Fill selector icon is selected then drag the colour sliders to create a colour, or click in the Colour Ramp on the palette base. The colour created is applied to the selected shape and it becomes the default colour in the Fill box.

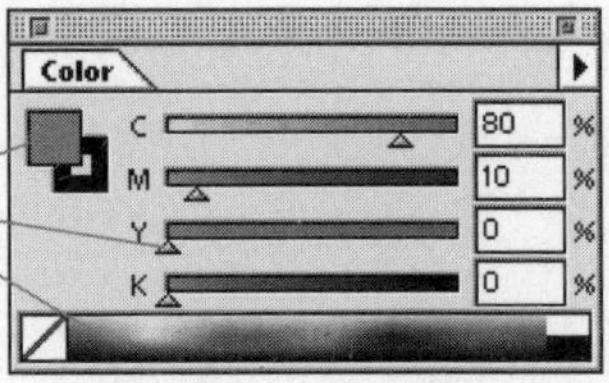

See page 82 for further information on creating colours in the Color palette.

If there is nothing selected when you change the fill colour, or stroke colour, these settings are applied to the next shape or path you draw.

Objects with a fill of none are transparent – you can see through them to objects placed behind.

The non Web-safe warning icon appears in the Color palette if the colour you create is not a Web-safe colour. Click the warning icon to change the colour to the nearest Web-safe colour.

The out of gamut warning icon appears if you create a colour that cannot be recreated using Process colours on a printing press. Click the warning icon to move the colour to the nearest printable colour.

4 Alternatively, you can position your cursor in the Colour box in the Color palette, or on one of the colour swatches in the Swatches palette, then 'drag and drop' the colour into a shape. For this technique, the shape does not have to be selected. The colour you drag and drop only becomes the default colour in the Fill Box if you drag and drop onto a selected object.

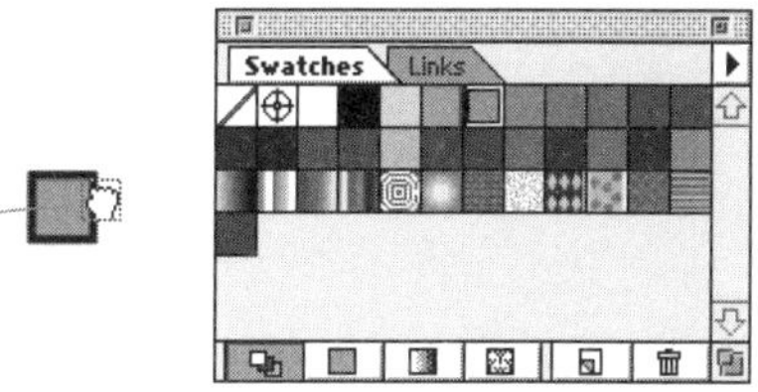

5 To apply a Fill of None to a selected shape, make sure the Fill box is selected, then click the None button. A red line through the Fill box indicates a fill of None. You can also click the None button in the Color palette or the Swatches palette.

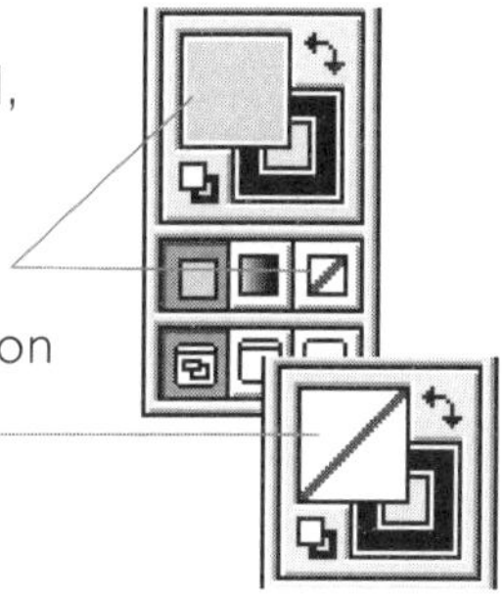

6 To apply a standard White Fill and Black Stroke to a selected object, click the Default colours icon below the Fill box, or press D on the keyboard.

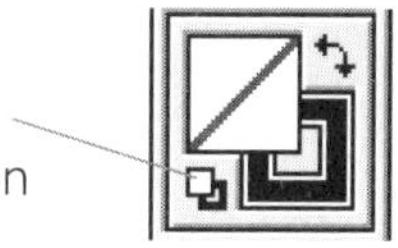

7 Click the Swap arrows (Shift+X) when you want to swap the Fill and Stroke colours.

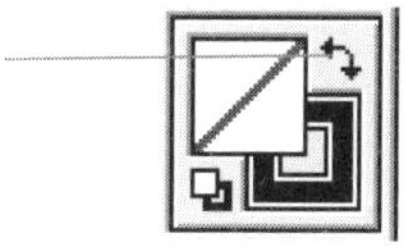

Applying Stroke Colour and Weight

A stroke is a colour applied to a path. You can think of a stroke as an outline on an object. A path does not have to have a stroke; many objects you create in Illustrator will have a stroke of none.

When you apply a stroke to a path, the stroke is centred on the path. For example, if you apply an 8pt stroke to a path, 4 points appear on the inside of the path, 4 points on the outside.

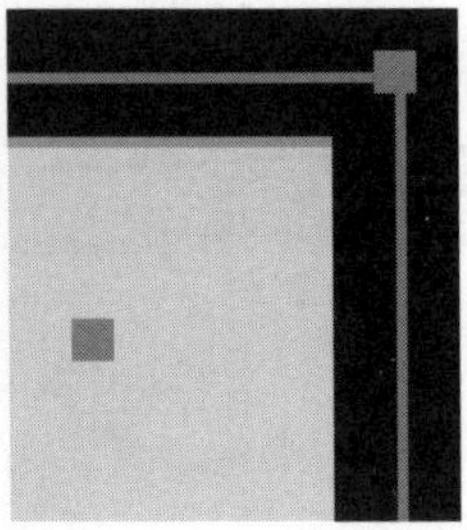

1 To apply a stroke colour to a path, make sure you have a path selected. Click on the Stroke Box to make it active.

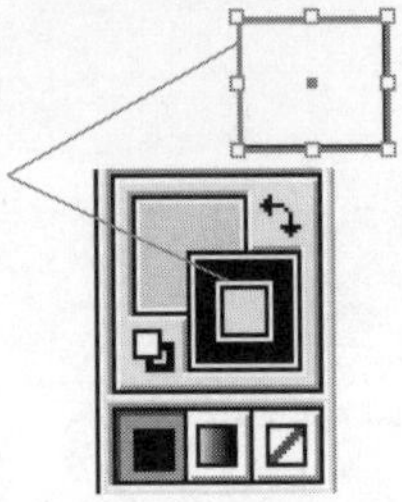

2 Click on one of the existing swatches in the Swatches palette. The colour is applied to the selected path and it becomes the default colour in the Stroke Box. The current Stroke weight is also applied.

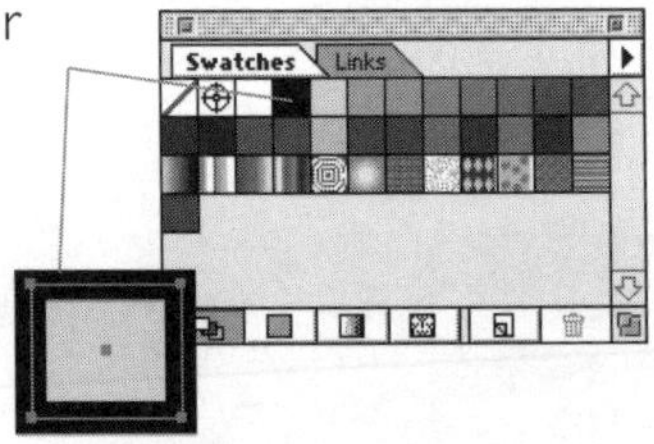

3 Or use the Color palette to mix a new colour. Click on the Stroke box to make sure that it is selected (it appears in front of the Fill box). Then drag the colour sliders to create a colour, or click in the Colour Ramp on the palette base. The new colour is applied as a stroke to the selected path and becomes the default colour in the main Stroke Box in the Tool box.

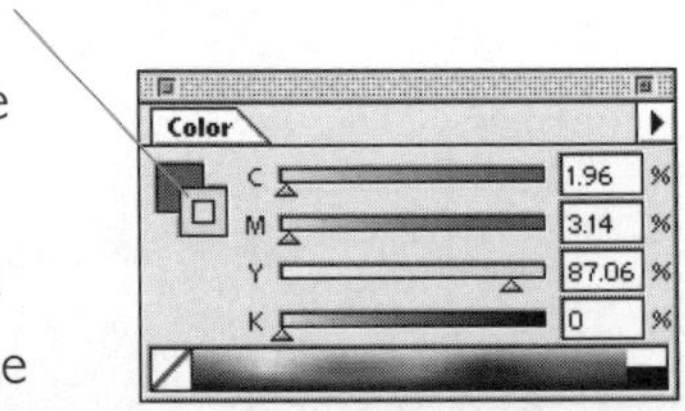

4 Alternatively, you can position your cursor in the Colour Box in the Color palette, or on one of the colour swatches in the Swatches palette, then drag the colour onto a path. Here, the path does not have to be selected. The colour you drag and drop only becomes the default colour in the main Stroke Box if you drag and drop onto a selected object.

5 To apply a stroke of None to a selected shape, make sure the Stroke Box is selected, then click the None button. A red line through the Stroke Box indicates a stroke of None. You can also click the None button in the Color palette or the Swatches palette.

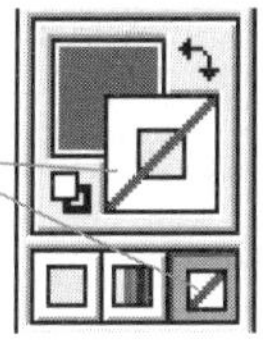

Applying a stroke weight to a selected path

1 Select an open or closed path.

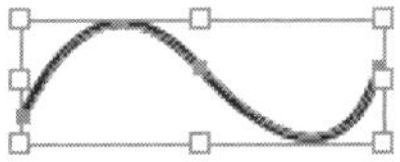

If no object is selected when you change the Stroke weight value, the new value will be applied to the next object you create.

2 Choose Window > Show Stroke if the Stroke palette is not already showing. By default, the Stroke palette is docked at the bottom of the Color palette.

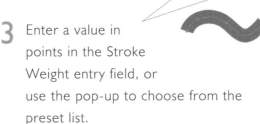

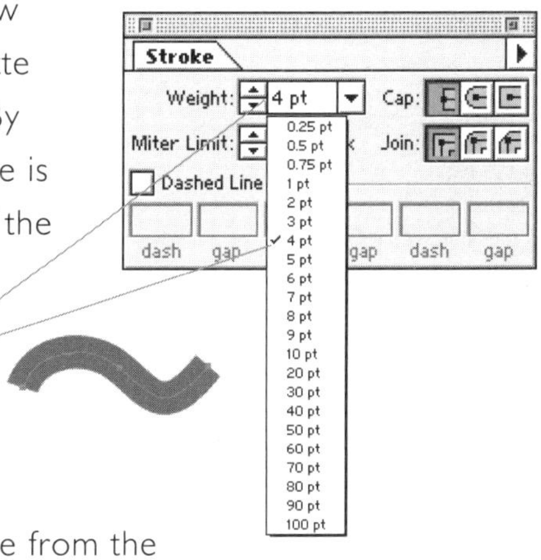

3 Enter a value in points in the Stroke Weight entry field, or use the pop-up to choose from the preset list.

The Color Palette

A Spot colour is printed with a premixed ink on a printing press. At 100% (i.e. no tint), a Spot colour is printed as a solid colour and has no dot pattern. Spot colours create their own separate plate when you print separations.

Use the Color palette to create Spot, Process and Web-safe colours which you can then save in the Swatches palette to use whenever necessary. Colours you save in the Swatches palette are saved with the document. Choose Window > Show Colours if it is not showing or click the Colour button below the Toolbox Fill and Stroke boxes.

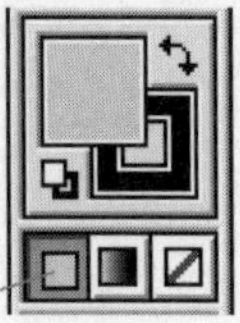

1 To create a Process or a Spot colour, use the Color palette pop-up menu to choose CMYK. Click either the Fill or Stroke box icon to make the colour you create apply to the Fill or Stroke of a selected object.

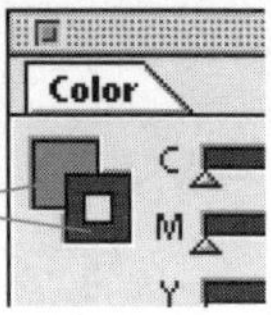

Process colours are printed using the four process inks – cyan, magenta, yellow and black (CMYK).

2 Either drag the sliders to mix the required colour, or enter values in the CMYK entry fields. You can also click anywhere in the Colour Ramp at the bottom of the palette. The colour is displayed in the Fill or Stroke box in the palette. If no object is selected, the colour you create appears in the Fill/Stroke Box in the Toolbox and the colour is applied to the next object you create.

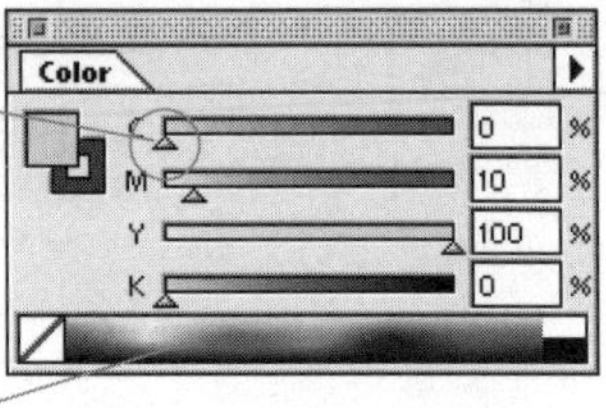

All Spot colours, including Spot colours from colour matching libraries, are converted to Process colours when separated, unless you deselect the Convert to Process option in the Separations Setup dialogue box.

3 To save the colour, show the Swatches palette. Choose New Swatch from the Swatches palette pop-up menu. Enter a name for the colour in the New Swatch dialogue box. Use the Colour Type pop-up to specify Spot or Process colour. The Colour Mode should indicate CMYK, provided you specified this in the New Document dialogue box. OK the dialogue box. The colour is added to the Swatches palette.

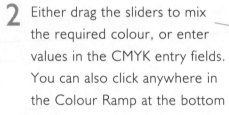

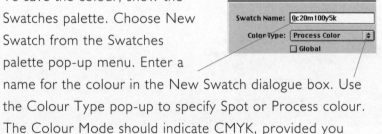

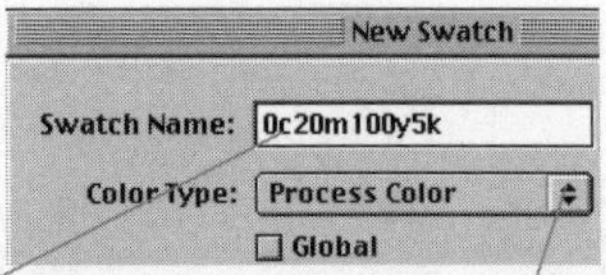

Managing and Editing Swatches

You use the Swatches palette to store colours you want to use more than once in an illustration. Think of the Swatches palette as a colour library for use in a particular illustration. Customised Swatches palettes are saved with the file.

To control the appearance and content of the Swatches palette you can use a number of commands in the Swatches pop-up menu together with the buttons at the bottom of the palette.

Each time you relaunch Adobe Illustrator, the Swatches palette reverts to its default settings.

You can also use the Swatches palette to convert colours from Spot to Process and vice versa, to delete colours you no longer need, and to duplicate colours.

1 To view swatch categories, make sure the Swatches palette is showing.

2 Click one of the Swatch category buttons at the bottom of the palette. The Swatch palette display updates to show the swatch category you selected.

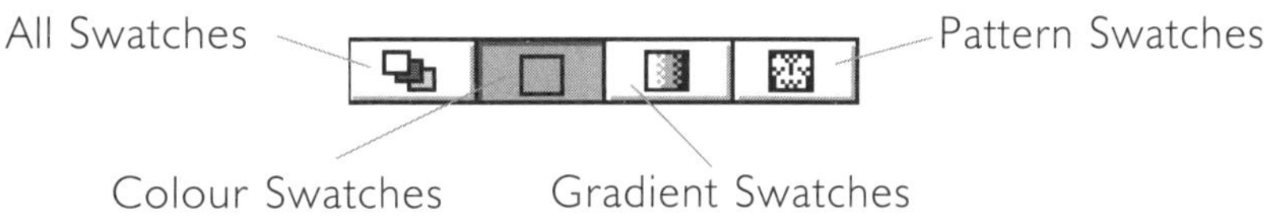

3 To view swatches as a list, choose Name View from the pop-up menu in the Swatches palette. The list view also shows icons next to each colour which indicate the colour mode of the colour as well as whether the colour is spot or process.

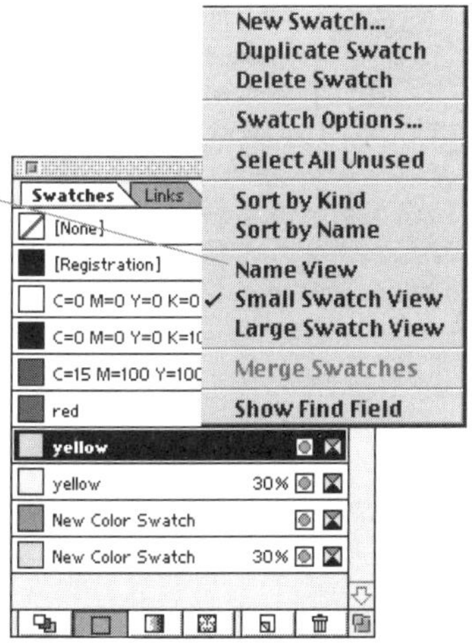

To select more than one non-consecutive swatch, select a swatch, then hold down Command/Ctrl and click on the additional swatches to add them to the selection.

The Process colour icon (CMYK quarters) indicates that the colour is in CMYK mode. A grey circle indicates that a colour is a Spot colour. Three bars (red, green, blue) indicate that a colour is an RGB colour.

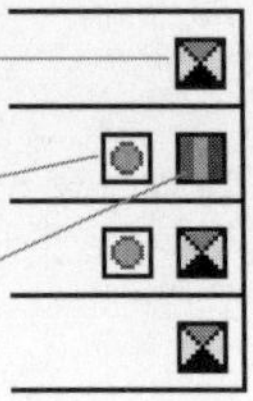

Deleting a swatch from the Swatches palette

1. Make sure that no object is selected. Click on a swatch to select it. A highlight box appears around the swatch.

2. Choose Delete Swatch from the pop-up in the Swatches palette. Or drag the swatch onto the Wastebasket icon at the bottom of the palette.

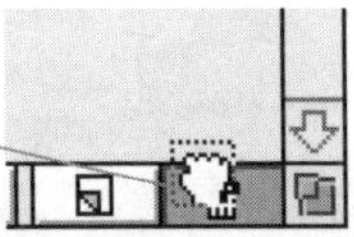

To select a range of consecutive swatches, click on the first swatch in the range, move your cursor to another swatch, hold down Shift and click on the swatch to identify it as the last swatch in the range. All swatches in between are selected.

Creating a new colour

1. Choose New Swatch from the Swatches pop-up menu.

2. Enter a name for the new colour.

3. Choose either Spot or Process using the Colour Type pop-up (see page 88 for more on global colours).

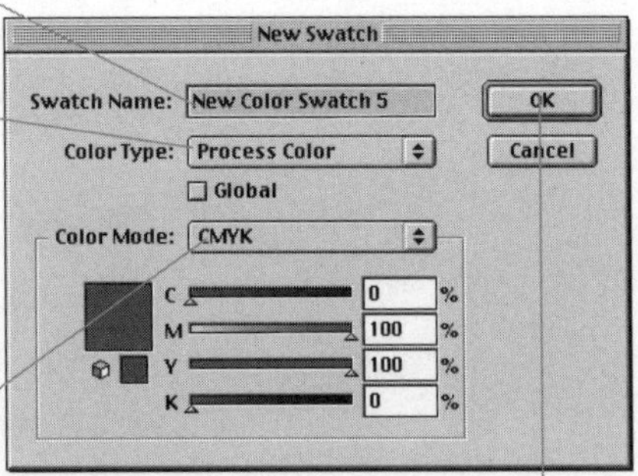

When you create a new document, if you choose CMYK as your colour mode in the New Document dialogue box, you cannot create an RGB colour in that document, and vice versa.

4. Choose a colour mode from the Colour Mode pop-up. Enter values in the entry boxes, or use the sliders to create the colour you want.

5. Click OK.

Editing an existing colour

1. Make sure no objects are selected. Click on a colour swatch to select it.

2. Choose Swatch Options from the pop-up menu.

3. Edit settings in the Swatches options dialogue box, then OK the dialogue box. Any objects to which the colour has already been applied are updated according to whether they are global or non-global.

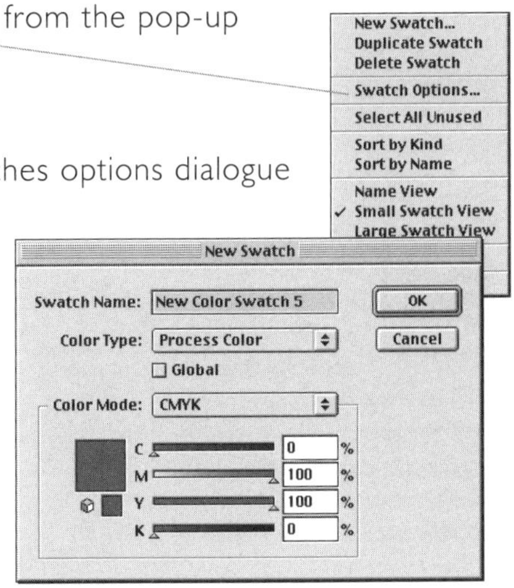

Global Process colours are indicated by a small white triangle in the bottom right corner of the swatch when the palette is in Small/Large Swatch View:

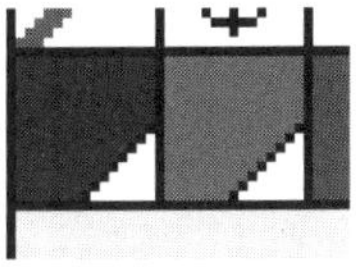

Converting a Process colour to Spot and vice versa

1. Click on the swatch to select it, then choose Swatch options from the Swatches pop-up menu.

2. Or double-click on a swatch.

3. Use the Colour Type pop-up in the Swatch Options dialogue box to change the colour from one type to another.

Spot colour swatches are identified by the small white triangle with a dot in it in the bottom right corner of the swatch when the palette is in Small/Large Swatch View:

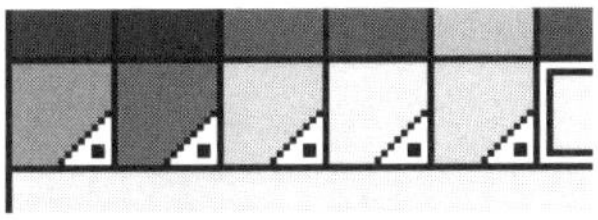

Colour Matching Systems

Use the Swatch Libraries sub-menu when you want to choose a colour from a colour matching system such as PANTONE® colour matching system, FOCOLTONE® colour system or Trumatch™ colour swatching system. You can also select a colour library designed specifically for illustrations intended for the World Wide Web.

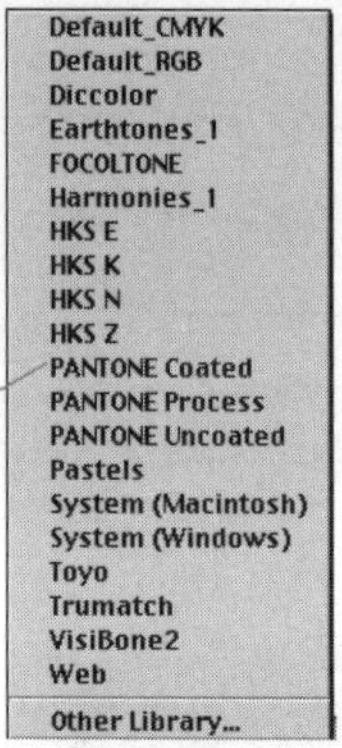

The Web colour library consists of 216 RGB colours most commonly used by Web browsers to display 8-bit images. Use this Color palette to ensure consistent results on both Windows and Macintosh platforms.

1. To load the PANTONE colour matching library, choose Window > Swatch Libraries and choose the library name from the list.

2. The library opens as a separate palette in the Illustrator window.

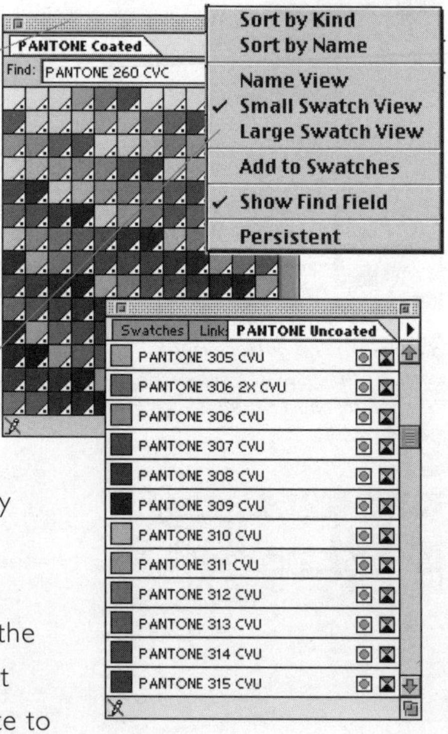

3. Choose either Name View, Small Swatch View or Large Swatch View from the pop-up menu to control the appearance of the Library palette.

4. Choose Persistent from the pop-up menu if you want the Colour Library palette to open automatically whenever you open the Illustrator file.

Hold down Alt and click on a swatch in the colour matching library to add it to the Swatches palette.

Selecting a colour from the library

1 Scroll to the colour you want, then click on it to select it.

2 Or make sure the Find entry box is either empty, or that the existing entry is highlighted. Enter the matching system number of the colour you want to select.

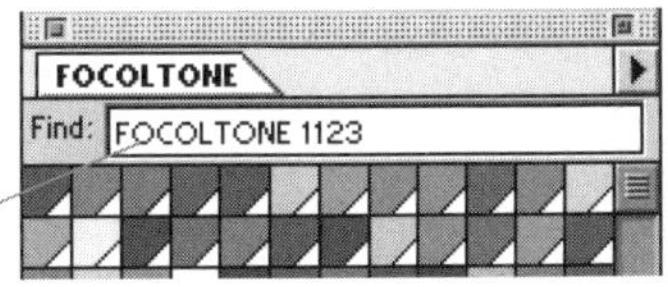

3 If you have hidden the Find entry box, You can hold down Command/Ctrl+Alt, then click in the Colour Library palette. A black selection border appears around the colours in the palette. Type the number, e.g. 314, of the PANTONE colour you want to select. You need to enter the numbers in reasonably quick succession.

Adding a colour from the library to the Swatches palette

1 Drag a swatch from the library into the Swatches palette.

2 Or click on a colour to select it, and choose Add to Swatches from the pop-up menu in the Library palette. You can now close the Colour Library palette unless you want to choose further colours. Any colours you add to the Swatches palette are saved with the file.

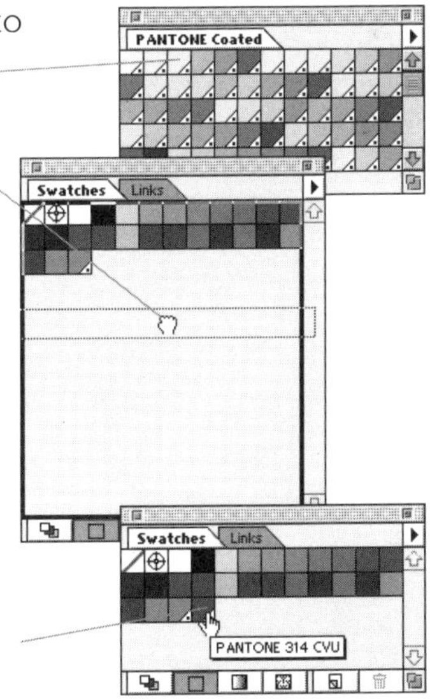

Global Process Colours

If you create a global Process colour and apply it to several objects in your artwork, then edit the colour, all objects to which the global colour has been applied are automatically updated to reflect the change made to the colour swatch.

By contrast, if you create a non-global Process colour (non-global is the default for Process colours), apply the colour to several objects in your artwork, then edit the colour, objects to which the colour has been applied are not updated to reflect the change to the colour.

Global Process colours are colours that automatically update throughout a document when the colour swatch is edited – every object to which the colour has been applied will update when the swatch is modified.

Non-global colours do not automatically update throughout a document when the colour swatch is edited.

A Process colour is non-global by default. Spot colours are global by default – you do not have the option of making them non-global.

1. To create a global Process colour, choose New Swatch from the pop-up menu in the Swatches palette.
2. Enter a name for the swatch.
3. Make sure the Colour Type pop-up is set to Process Colour.
4. Select the Global option to make the colour a global colour.

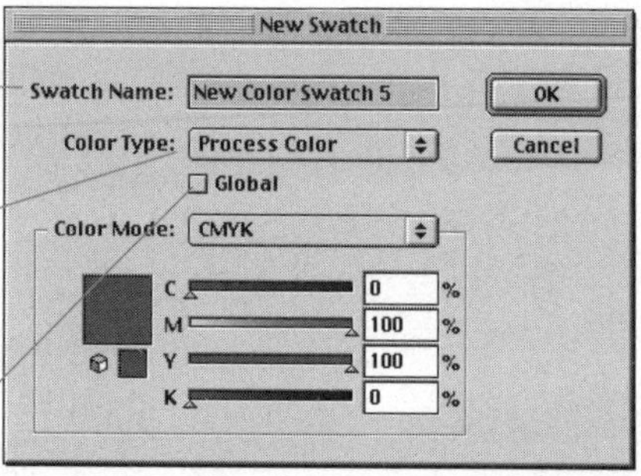

5. Adjust the CMYK sliders as necessary, or enter % values to create the colour you want. OK the dialogue box. The swatch is added to the Swatches palette. The global Process colour is indicated by a white triangle (no dot) in the bottom right corner of the swatch.

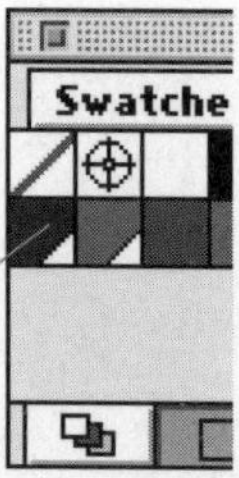

In the Color palette, the representation of a global colour is similar to that for a Spot colour.

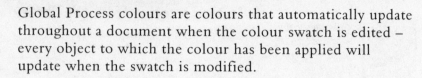

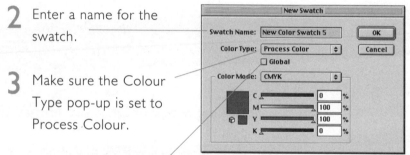

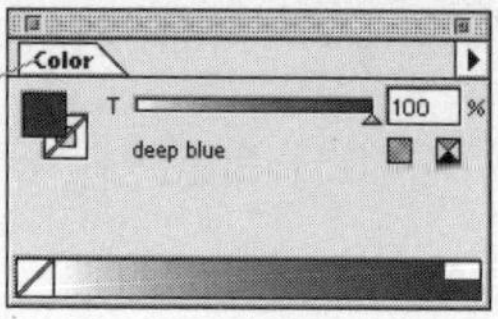

Creating Tints

Use the Color palette to create tints of spot colours, including PANTONE spot colours, and global Process colours.

1 To create a tint of a spot or global Process colour, make sure the Swatches palette is showing. Click on an existing spot or global Process colour to select it.

2 Make sure the Color palette is showing. The swatch colour you clicked on in the Swatches palette appears in the Fill or Stroke selector icon.

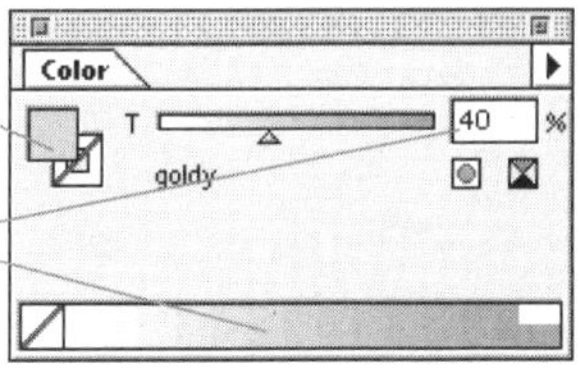

3 Drag the tint slider to the left to create a tint of the base colour, or enter a tint percentage in the entry field. You can also click in the colour ramp at the bottom of the palette to choose a tint visually. Depending on which is active, the Fill or Stroke selector updates according to the value you set. The Fill/Stroke of any selected object updates.

Tints of the same base colour remain related. Edits to the base colour will affect associated tint swatches and objects in the artwork to which the tints have been applied.

4 To store the tint in the Swatches palette so that you can use it repeatedly, drag the Fill/Stroke selector swatch into the Swatches palette. Or click the New button in the Swatches palette.

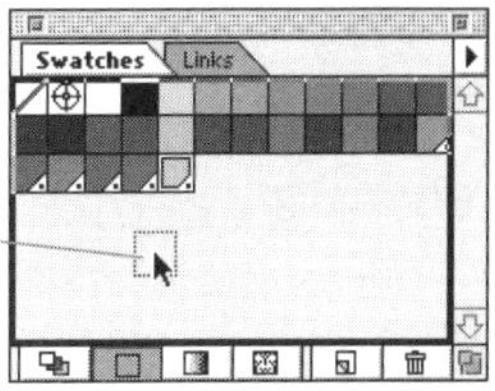

5 Choose Name View from the pop-up in the Swatches palette to identify tints easily from their percentage value. Tints are saved with the same name as the base colour, with the tint % also indicated, e.g. 'Goldy 40%'.

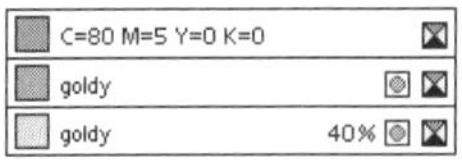

Appearance Attributes

An appearance attribute changes the way an object looks and prints, without permanently changing or transforming the original object. You apply an appearance attribute to an object, group or layer using the Attributes palette (Window > Show Attributes).

Think of an appearance attribute as a lens that, when placed over an object, changes the way the object looks. When the lens is removed, the original object remains in its original state.

Fills and Strokes are examples of appearance attributes – both change the appearance of the object without changing its original shape. Other appearance attributes include transparency settings and effects applied via the Effects menu. (See page 187)

Using appearance attributes streamlines editing tasks for objects that share the same appearance (e.g. a set of Web site navigation buttons). The Appearance palette provides a visible and editable record of the properties of an object.

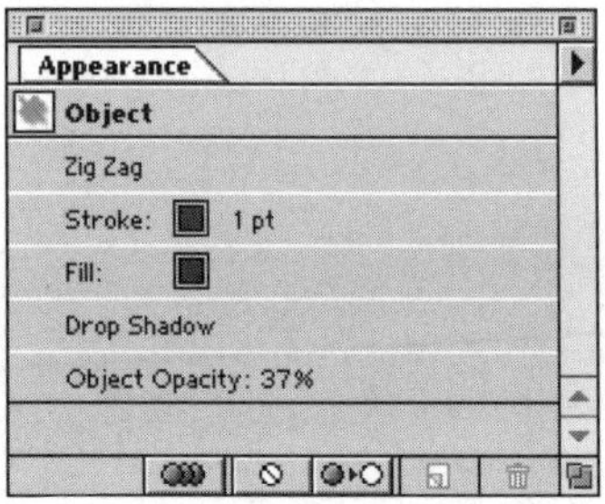

1 Notice how, as you apply fill and stroke, transparency or effects, these are recorded in the Appearance palette.

Use appearance attributes for the flexibility they offer. Attributes applied to a layer, group or object can be modified or removed at any time without changing the original object.

2 To edit an attribute's setting you can double-click it in the Appearance palette. This opens the corresponding dialogue box where you can make changes.

3 Fill and Stroke attributes can be modified independently. For example, click on the Fill attribute, then apply an effect such as ZigZag. The Effect is added to the Fill attribute as a sub attribute, without affecting the Stroke or Transparency attributes.

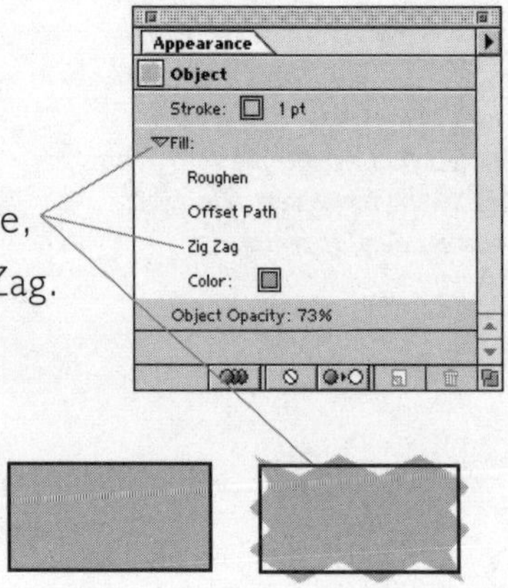

Use the Expand triangle in the Appearance palette to access appearance attributes that you have applied specifically to the fill or stroke of an object.

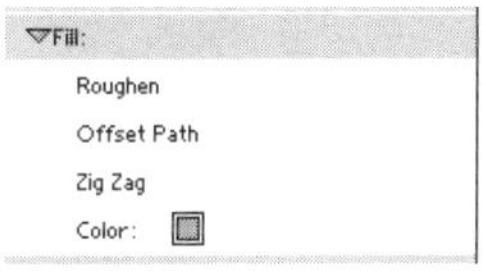

4 To apply an existing set of appearance attributes to an object using the Appearance palette, select an object with the attributes you want to apply. Drag the appearance icon to the left of the Object entry onto a different object.

5 To remove an appearance attribute from an a selected object, in the Appearance palette, click on the appearance attribute you want to remove. Click the Wastebasket icon at the bottom of the palette, or drag the appearance attribute onto the Wastebasket icon.

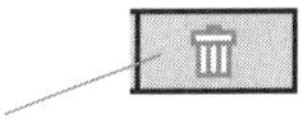

6 To remove all appearance attributes including Fill and Stroke from a selected object, click the Clear Appearance button, or choose Clear Appearance form the pop-up menu.

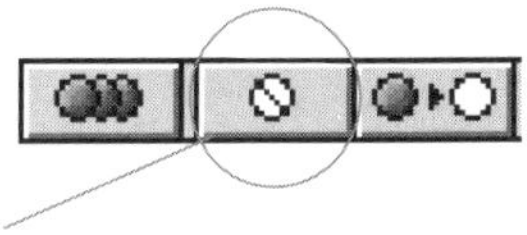

7 To remove all appearance attributes except basic Fill and Stroke for a selected object, click the Reduce to Basic Appearance button or choose the command in the pop-up.

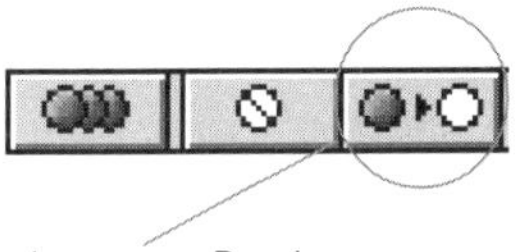

8 You can specify that newly created objects appear with basic fill and stroke attributes only, or that they appear with all current appearance attributes applied. Click the New Art Button to toggle between the two options, or use the command in the palettes pop-up menu.

Has Basic Appearance

Maintains Appearance

Transparency

To apply a transparency effect/setting to a layer, you must first target the layer then drag the transparency slider.

You can apply transparency to any object (including text), group or layer. Underlying artwork becomes more and more visible as you decrease the opacity setting. Choose Window > Transparency to show the palette if necessary.

An opacity setting of 100% means that the object, group or layer is completely solid. An opacity setting of 0% gives a completely see-through result.

When you apply transparency settings to a group, you do not always get the result you expect. If necessary, ungroup the objects, then apply transparency to change transparency on an object by object basis.

When you save or export a file with transparency settings, the transparent objects are flattened using the current settings in the Transparency panel of the Document Setup dialogue box. Use the Quality/ Speed slider to control the quality and printing speed of the transparent areas.

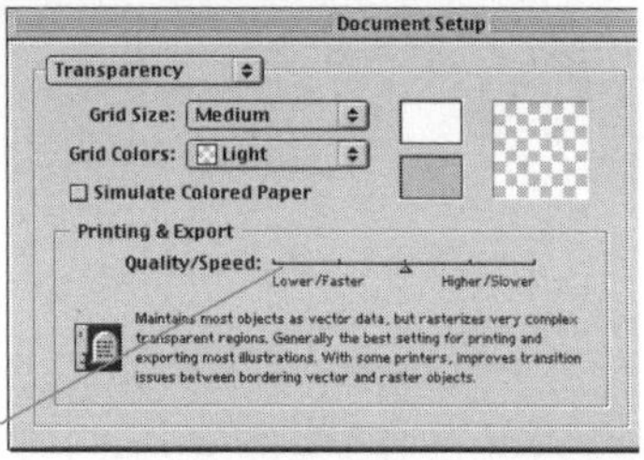

To achieve transparency effects, Illustrator has to convert, either fully or partially, some of your vector artwork into a bitmap or raster format. The degree to which transparent areas of artwork are rasterised is controlled by the slider/settings in the Transparency panel of the Document Setup dialogue.

1. To apply basic transparency to an object, first select the object. A thumbnail of the object appears in the Transparency palette.

2. In the Transparency palette, enter a value in the Opacity field, or drag the Transparency slider.

3. Transparency settings also appear in the Appearance palette as an appearance attribute.

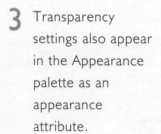

Keep a version of the file in Illustrator format if you might conceivably need to make further adjustments to opacity settings.

Cutting and Joining Paths

Chapter Seven

This chapter looks at a variety of techniques for cutting and joining paths. The commands in the Pathfinder palette take much of the hard work out of cutting and joining paths manually.

Covers

The Scissors Tool and Slice Command

When you click on a closed path with the Scissors tool you create an open path. When you click on an open path you create two separate paths.

The Scissors Tool

Use the Scissors tool to split open or closed paths.

1 To split a path, select an object. Select the Scissors tool. Position your cursor on an anchor point, or anywhere on a curve or straight line segment, then click. The path is split at the point where you click. Select the Direct-selection tool, then click on either part if you want to make further changes to the shape of the path.

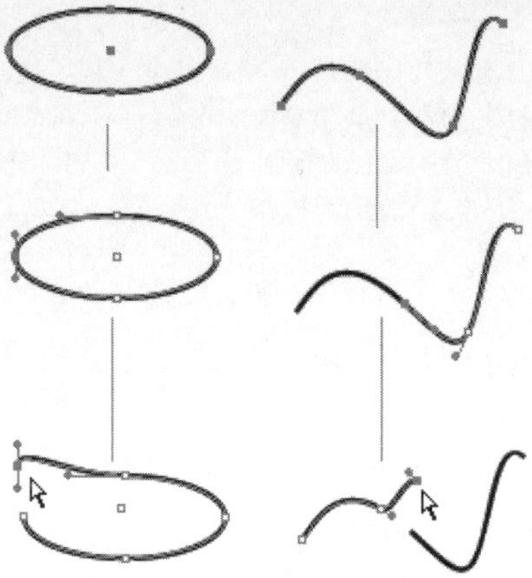

The Slice Command

The Slice command works on two or more overlapping paths. The topmost path slices through any underlying paths it touches. The effect is similar to that of a pastry cutter.

1 To slice objects, use the Selection tool to select the 'slicing' or topmost object. Do not select the objects you want to slice.

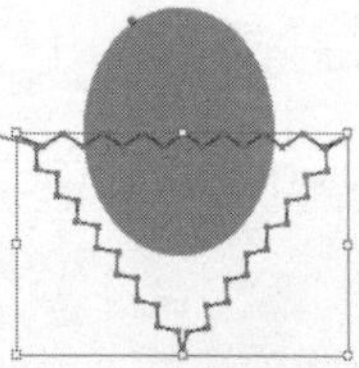

2 Choose Object > Path > Slice. The path of the topmost shape slices or cuts through the underlying paths. The newly sliced shapes are all initially selected. Click away to deselect, then reselect any individual shapes to which you want to make changes.

The topmost, slicing object is discarded after applying the Slice command.

Average

You can use the Direct-selection or the Direct-lasso tool to create a marquee around the points you want to select, or you can use Shift and click to add anchor points to a selection:

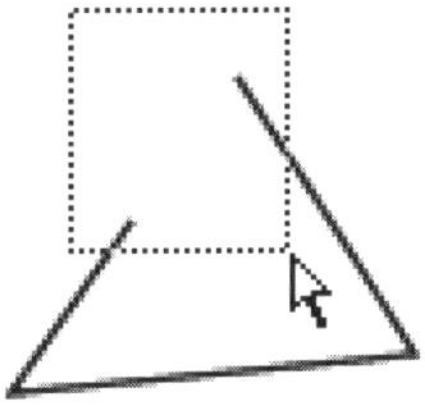

The Average command aligns two or more anchor points vertically and/or horizontally.

1. To average anchor points, use the Direct-selection tool to select two or more points.

2. Choose Object > Path > Average.

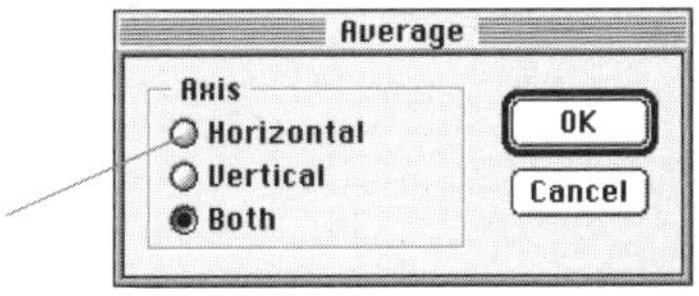

3. Select Horizontal to align points along the horizontal axis:

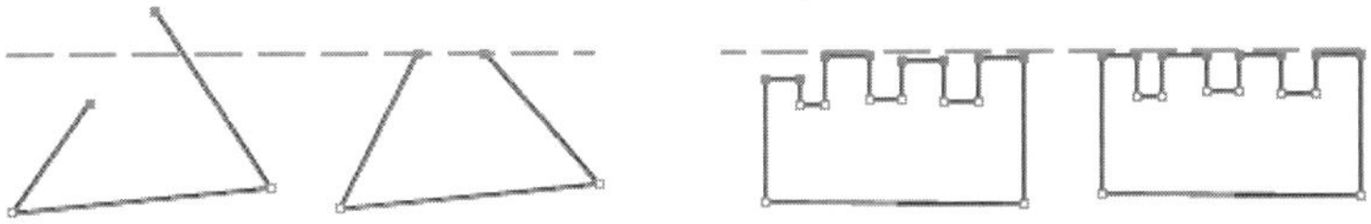

4. Select Vertical to align points along the Vertical axis:

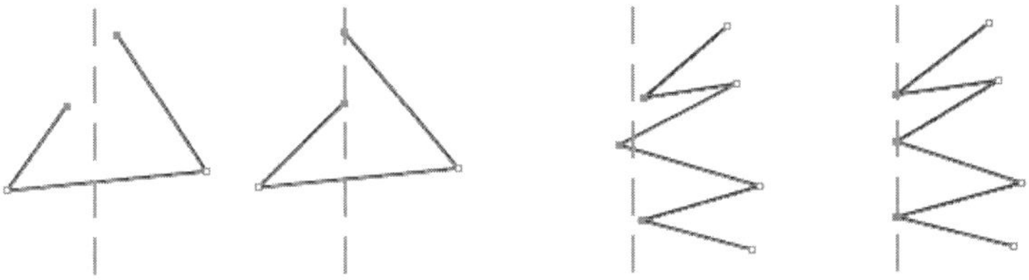

'Both' is useful when you want to join two points to form a single point. After you OK the Average dialogue box, you then need to use the Join command. (See page 96).

5. Select Both to align points along both horizontal and vertical axes:

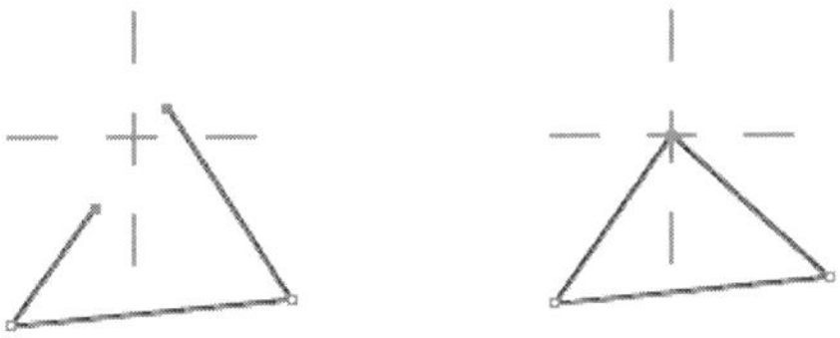

6. Click OK.

Join

The Join command joins the end points of two separate paths, or the two end points of an open path with a straight line segment. If you have first used the Average command, then selected Both, so that the two points are directly one on top of another, Join simply merges the two points into one.

1 To join two separate paths, use the Direct-selection tool to select the two end points of two paths you want to join. Choose Object > Path > Join. Illustrator draws a straight line segment between the two end points.

2 To create a closed path, use the Direct-selection tool to select the two end points of the open path. Choose Object > Path > Join. Illustrator draws a straight line segment between the two end points to create a closed path.

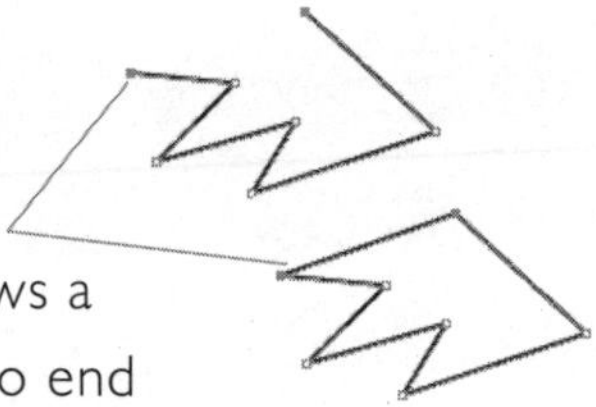

3 To average both then join, use the Direct-selection tool to select the two end points you want to average before you join. Choose Object > Path > Average. Select the Both option then OK the dialogue. At this stage the two end points are placed directly one on top of another.

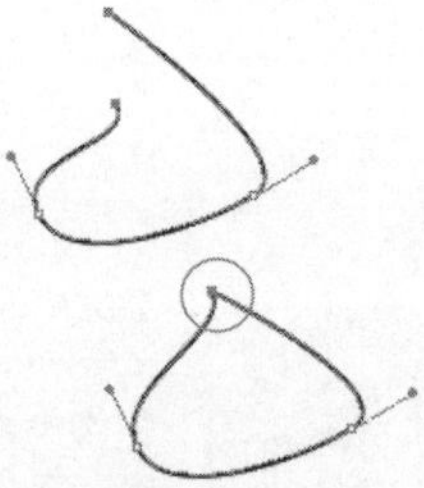

4 Choose Object > Path > Join. Select either Smooth or Corner, according to the type of point you want to create. Click OK. The two points are merged into a single anchor point.

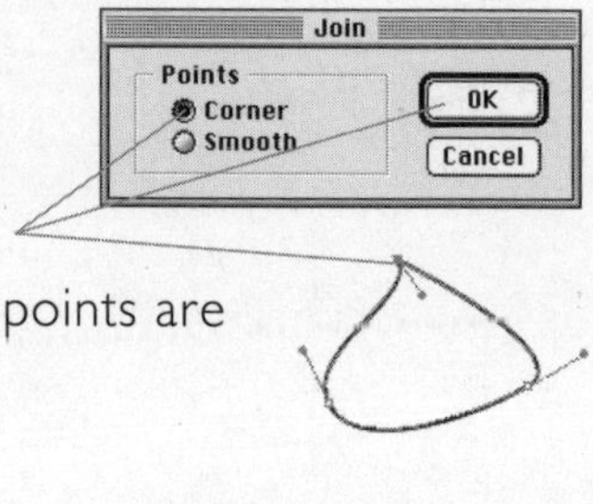

The Knife Tool

The Knife tool is perfect when you want to cut through an object with a freeform line and end up with closed paths. The Knife tool is located with the Scissors tool group.

1. To cut a closed path with the Knife tool, select the Knife tool. The object you cut through does not have to be selected.

2. Position your cursor outside the object, then press and drag across the object. Make sure your cursor crosses the path to finish the cut. The result is two closed paths. The cut follows the movement of your cursor.

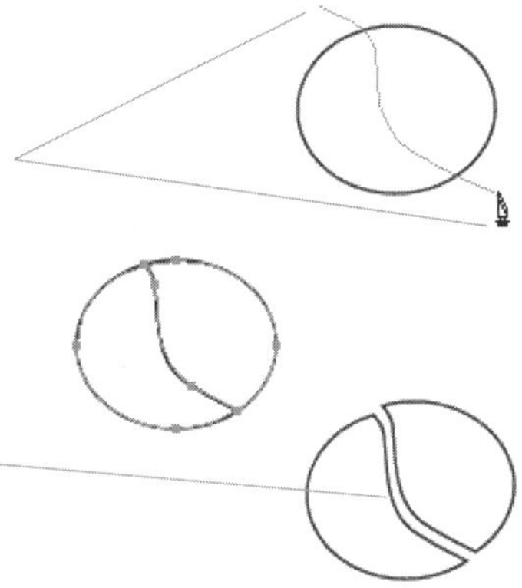

3. To cut with a straight line, select the Knife tool. The object you cut through does not have to be selected.

4. Position your cursor outside the object, hold down Alt, then press and drag through the object. Make sure your cursor crosses the path to finish the cut. The result is two closed paths. The cut follows the movement of your cursor.

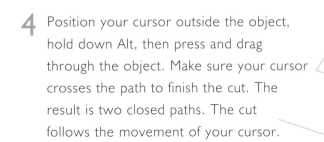

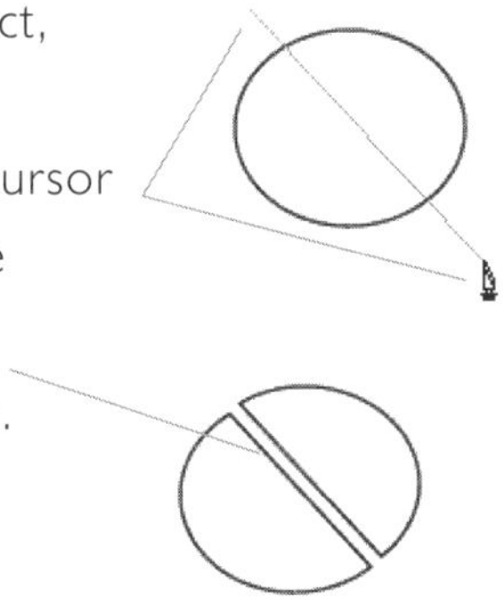

HOT TIP

The Knife tool will now cut through grouped objects.

Pathfinder Combine Commands

Choose Window > Pathfinder to show the Pathfinder palette.

In early versions of Adobe Illustrator, in order to create complex shapes, you often had to use many individual objects, then cut and join paths to finally achieve the more complex path you wanted.

The Pathfinder commands short circuit what used to be a tedious, time consuming procedure. They automatically create new paths, based on where separate overlapping paths intersect.

The Pathfinder commands work most successfully on closed paths with a fill. Using Pathfinder commands on open, stroked paths sometimes gives unpredictable results.

The Combine Commands

The Combine group of commands typically create a single, new, combined or compound path based on the overlapping areas of the original paths. The individual commands determine precisely how the resultant objects are formed and which areas or paths are discarded.

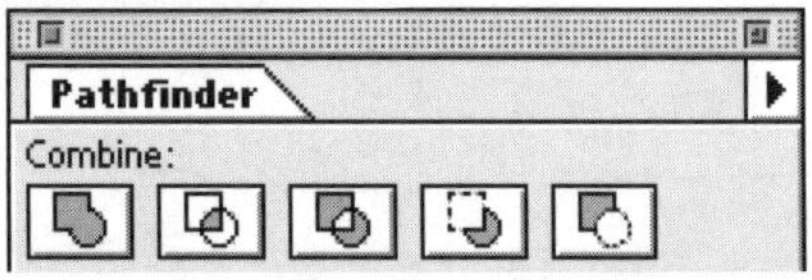

In the majority of instances, the new path(s) created by using the Pathfinder commands are assigned the fill and stroke attributes of the frontmost path.

Many of the Pathfinder commands can now be applied as an effect. *(See page 187 for information on the Effects menu.)*

The Combine Pathfinders and Divide and Trim are covered in this chapter.

Unite

Unite combines two or more selected objects into one merged object. Paths that were inside the outer perimeter of the original shapes are discarded. The stroke and fill attributes of the frontmost object are assigned to the new object.

Use unite when you want to create a complex outline from a series of simpler objects.

The Pathfinder commands do not work on Gradient Mesh objects.

1. To unite shapes, select two or more overlapping shapes.

2 Click the Unite button on the Pathfinder palette. The shapes become one merged object. The fill and stroke attributes of the frontmost shape are applied. Objects inside the selected objects are deleted.

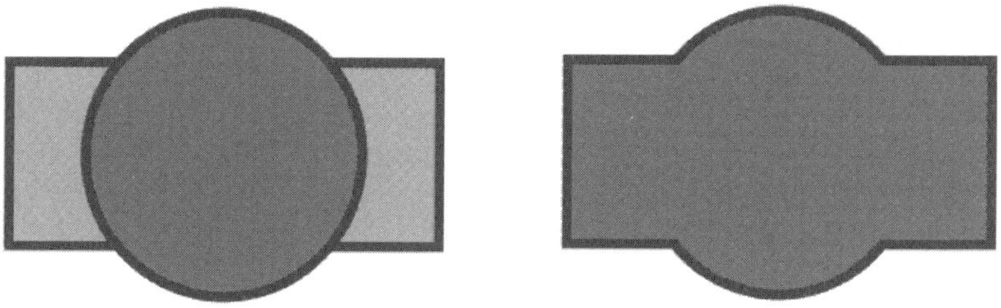

You can often create interesting effects by applying Intersect to a copy of a shape. For example, select the circle, then choose Edit > Copy to copy it. Next, choose Edit > Paste in Front. Select the front copy of the circle and the other shape, then click the Intersect button.

Pathfinder – Intersect

Intersect creates a new shape where the original paths overlap. Areas that do not overlap are deleted. Do not select more than two objects – this command works only on two objects at a time.

1 To create an intersect, select two objects.

2 Click the Intersect button in the Pathfinder palette.

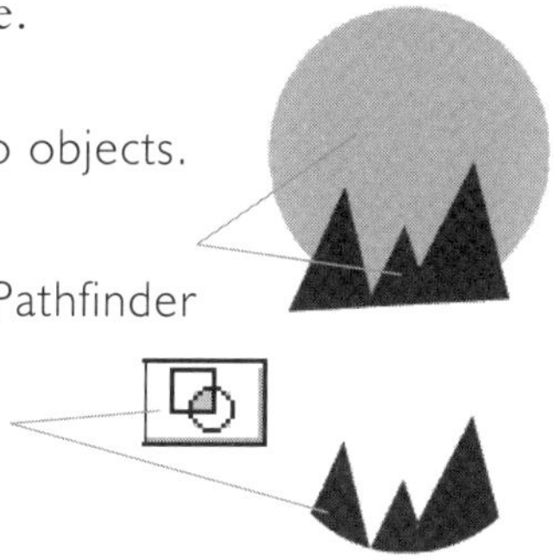

Pathfinder – Exclude

Exclude makes areas where paths overlap transparent. The result is a compound path. (For further information on compound paths see page 103.)

1 To use Exclude, select the overlapping objects. In this example the letters 'd' and 'o' have been converted to paths.

You can often create interesting effects by applying Exclude to a copy of a shape. For example, select the circle, then choose Edit > Copy to copy the circle. Next, choose Edit > Paste in Front. Select the front copy of the circle and both the characters, then click the Exclude button.

2 Click the Exclude button in the Pathfinder palette.

The fill and stroke attributes of the frontmost shapes are applied to the new, compound path. The white areas in this example are transparent.

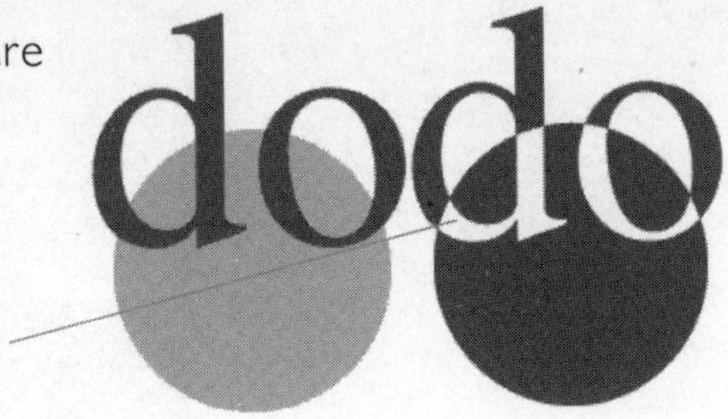

Pathfinder – Minus Front

Objects in front of the backmost selected object cut away areas of the backmost object where they overlap. Objects originally in front of the backmost object are deleted. The backmost object retains its original fill and stroke attributes.

Use Minus Front when you want the front object(s) to cut away areas of the backmost shape.

1 To use Minus Front, select two or more objects.

2 Click the Minus Front button.

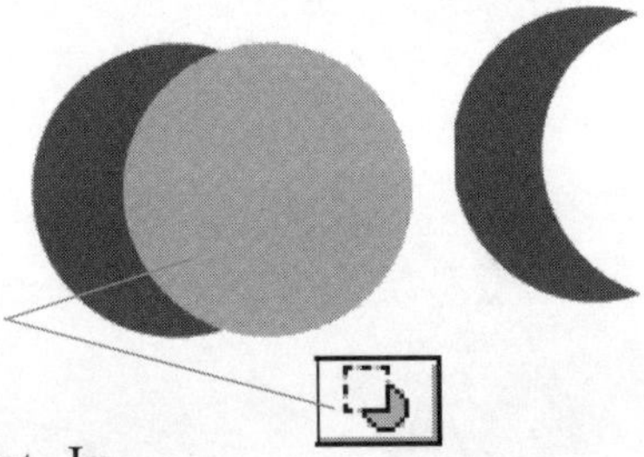

Minus Back

This is the reverse of Minus Front. In this example there are two backmost shapes – a rectangle and a circle.

Objects behind the frontmost selected object cut away areas of the frontmost object where they overlap. Objects originally behind the frontmost object are deleted. The frontmost object retains its original fill and stroke attributes.

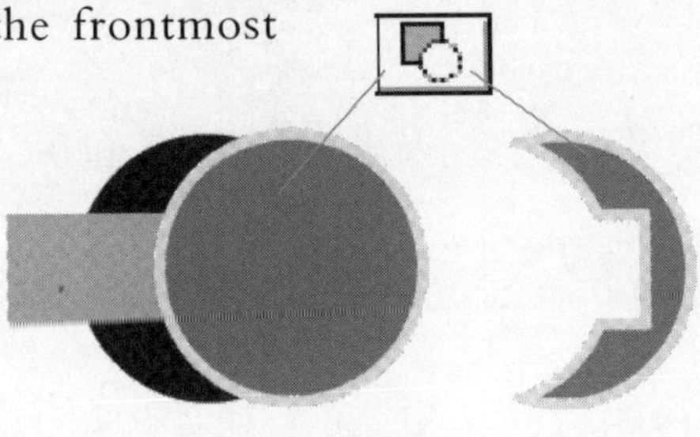

Pathfinder – Divide

In contrast to the Combine Pathfinder commands, the Divide Pathfinder commands create new, separate objects or paths based on where the original overlapping paths intersect.

You must select two or more overlapping objects in order to use the Divide commands.

After applying a Pathfinder command to two or more overlapping shapes, the resultant objects or paths are initially grouped. Ungroup the resultant objects if you want to further manipulate them.

Pathfinder – Divide

Divide command divides selected overlapping shapes into a series of new objects based on where the original paths intersect. The new shapes created are termed faces – areas that are not divided or crossed by a line segment.

1 To divide objects, select two or more overlapping objects. Click the Divide button.

2 Choose Object > Ungroup to ungroup the resultant shapes if you want to further manipulate individual objects.

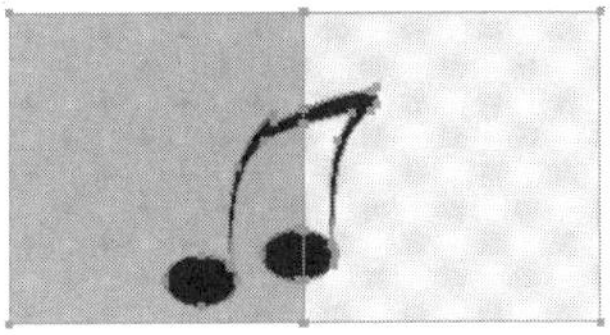

3 Click on a shape with the Direct-selection tool, then apply a fill colour if you want to apply colour without ungrouping the shapes.

4 To control whether or not unfilled objects are deleted or kept when you apply the Divide command, choose Pathfinder Options from the pop-up menu in the Pathfinder palette.

Pathfinder – Trim

Trim does not divide the frontmost object – this preserves its original shape and fill, but not any stroke. The frontmost object removes parts of objects behind it that it obscures. It removes strokes from the backmost shapes. It does not merge objects with the same colour fill.

1 To trim objects, select two or more overlapping objects.

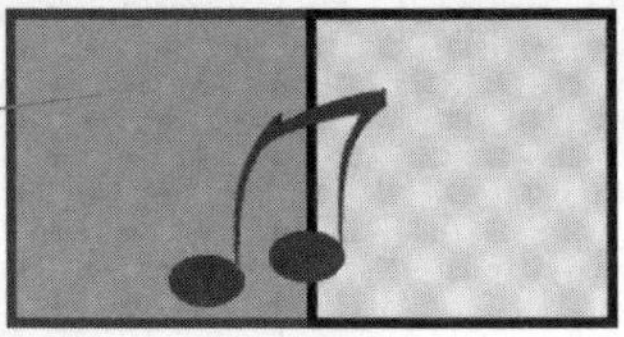

2 Click the Trim button.

3 Choose Object > Ungroup to ungroup the resultant shapes if you want to further manipulate individual objects.

4 Click on a shape with the Direct-selection tool, then apply a fill colour if you want to apply colour without ungrouping the shapes.

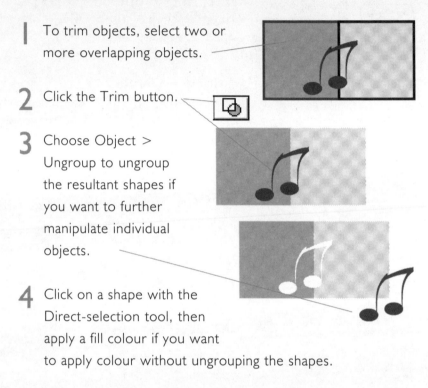

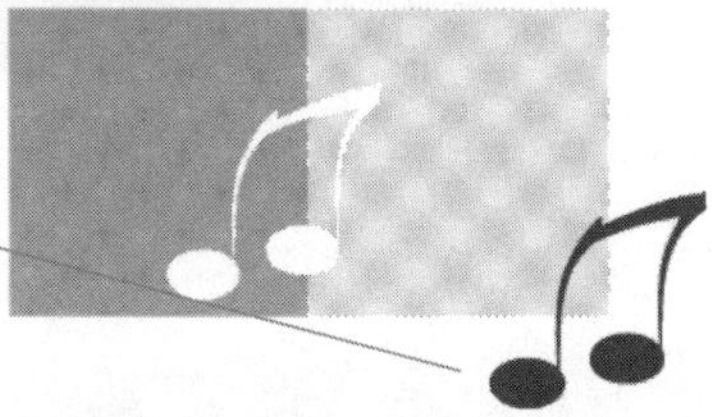

Compound Paths

Compound paths formed from complex shapes, or several compound paths in the same Illustrator file, can cause printing problems. Simplify paths, or reduce the number of compounds to solve the problem.

You can use a compound path to create areas of transparency in objects. Compound paths handle like grouped objects, but they are not the same as a group. A compound path is one object formed from more than one path.

1 To create a compound path, use the Selection tool to select two or more overlapping paths.

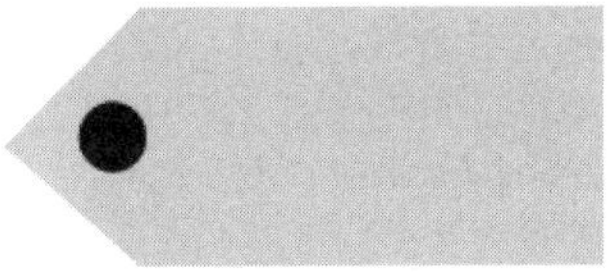

2 Choose Object > Compound Path > Make. The outer path forms the perimeter of the compound path, the inner object forms the inner boundary of the path. The area between the outer and inner path is filled with the fill and stroke attributes of the backmost object. The area inside the inner path is transparent.

3 Use the Direct-selection tool to select and edit a specific part of the compound path – either the inner or outer path.

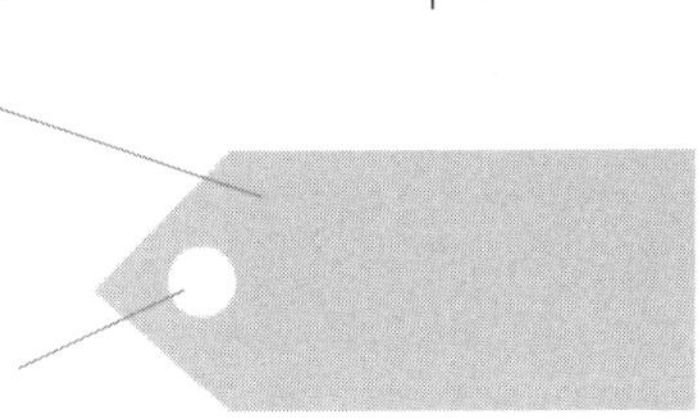

4 To release a compound path, select the compound using the Selection tool. Choose Object > Compound Paths > Release. The compound separates into the original objects. The frontmost object does not regain its original stroke and fill attributes.

Clipping Masks

A Clipping Mask is a path that controls the visibility of other objects. Objects, or portions of objects, that fall within the boundary of the masking path are visible. Objects or portions of objects that fall outside the path are invisible and do not print.

The object you use to create the mask can be an individual path, or a compound path. Type can also be used to create a mask.

1 To create a Clipping Mask, create the shape you want to act as the mask on top of the objects you want to mask. In this example, the circle is the masking shape, the face, spiral and rectangle underneath are the objects to be masked.

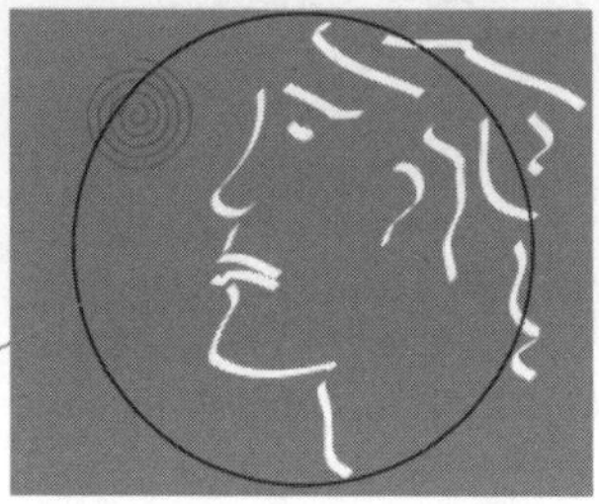

2 Select the masking object and the objects you want to mask. Choose Object > Clipping Mask > Make (Command/Ctrl+7). The fill and stroke attributes of the masking shape are discarded.

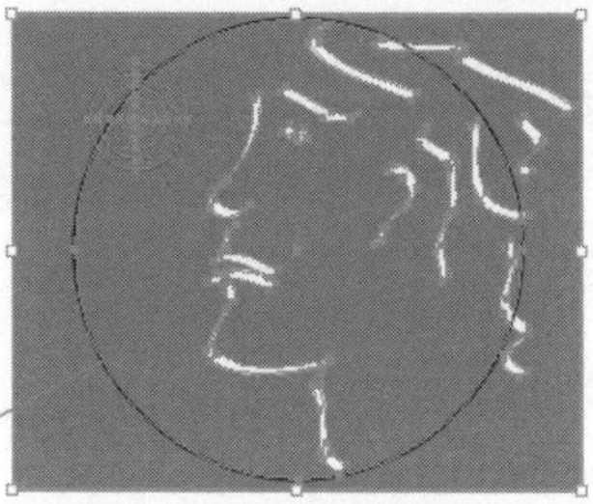

3 To release a mask, select the mask object. Choose Objects > Clipping Mask > Release (Command/Crtl+Alt+7). The masking shape remains unfilled with a stroke of none.

Blending Paths

The Blend tool creates a transition from one path and its fill colour to another path and its fill, by creating a series of intermediate shapes and colours.

You can blend between two open paths, between two closed paths, between two gradients or two blends.

1 To create a blend between two objects, use the Selection tool to select both objects you want to blend.

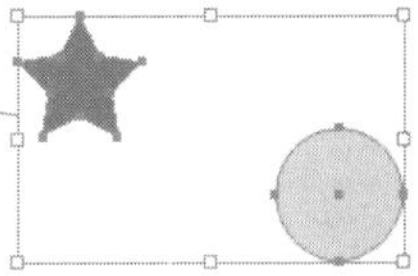

2 Select the Blend tool. Click one of the anchor points on one of the paths. Position your cursor on an anchor point on the second object, then click to create the blend. Alternatively, with two objects selected, you can choose Object > Blend > Make.

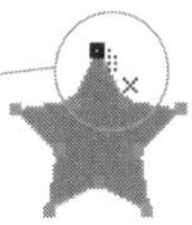

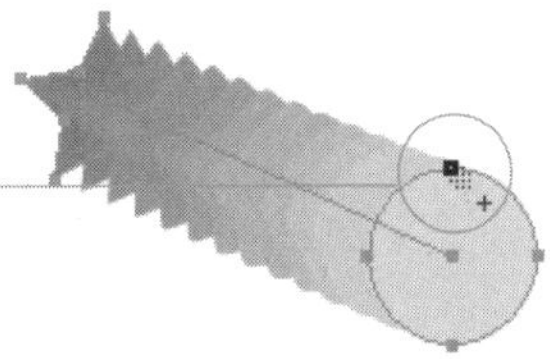

3 Select one of the Selection tools to make further changes to the blend.

4 To release a blend, select the blend with any of the selection tools. Choose Object > Blend > Release. When you release a blend, the path or spline along which the objects blended remains as a separate object. (This is most obvious if you work in Outline mode.) Make sure you delete the path if you have no further use for it.

Controlling Blend Steps

1. To control the number of steps in a blend, select the blend. Either, Choose Object > Blends > Blend Options, or double-click the Blend tool.

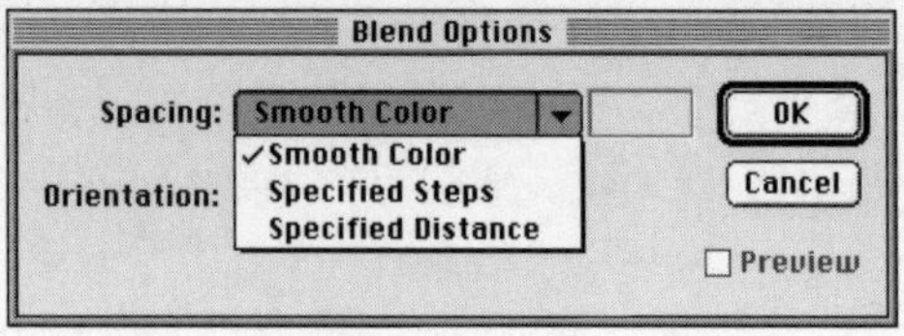

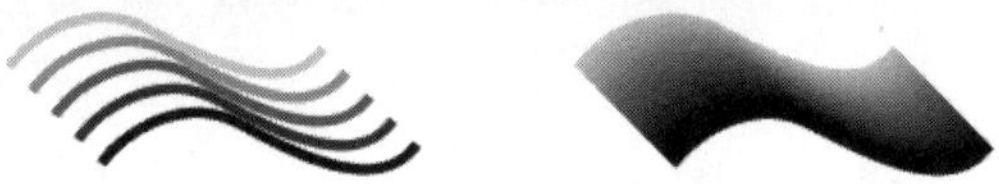

3 steps

36 steps

2. Choose Specified Steps from the Spacing pop-up, then enter a value to specify the exact number of steps you want in the blend. If you prefer, you can enter a value for Specified Distance. This value specifies the distance between steps in the blend.

3. Alternatively, choose Smooth Color from the Spacing pop-up to create a blend which has an optimum number of steps calculated to produce a smooth colour transition in the blend.

Creating and Editing Type

When you add type to a document, you create a text object, which can consist of a letter, a word, or multiple paragraphs. You can move, copy, delete, transform, group and paint a text object as you can for any graphic object.

Covers

Chapter Eight

Point Type

The default Type tool can be used to create two kinds of type – Point type and Rectangle type.

1 To create Point Type, select the Type tool. The pointer changes to an I-beam cursor within a dotted box. Position the cross-hair of the I-beam where you want to begin typing.

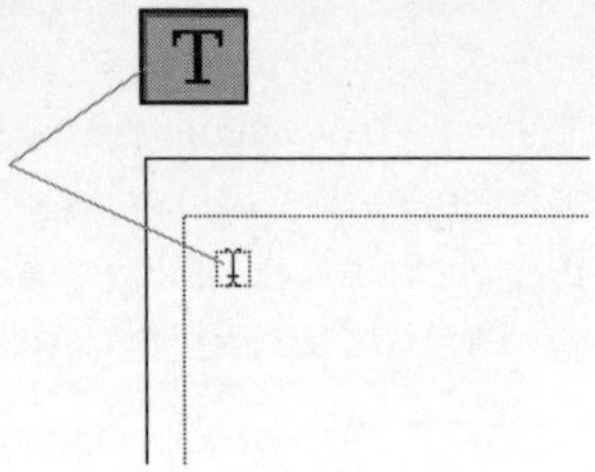

Point-type will not 'wrap' automatically. To begin a new paragraph, press the Return/Enter key.

2 Click to place a flashing insertion point. Begin typing.

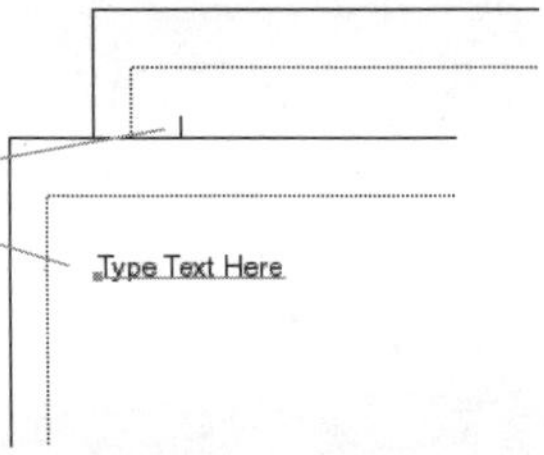

3 When you click on Point type with the Selection tool, a standard bounding box with selection handles appear. Drag handles to change the type size of the text, and also the Horizontal/Vertical scaling.

Hold down Shift, then drag a selection handle to scale type without introducing horizontal or vertical scaling.

4 When you click on Point type with the Direct-selection tool, it is identified by a solid rectangle (the 'point') and a line along the base of the text. Drag the point or the line to reposition the text.

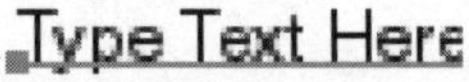

Rectangle Type

Use the default Type tool to create Rectangle type when you want to work with one or more paragraphs of type. When you enter type into a text rectangle the type will automatically wrap to fit within the area defined by the rectangle.

Type wraps to fit within the rectangle. Press Return/Enter to begin a new paragraph.

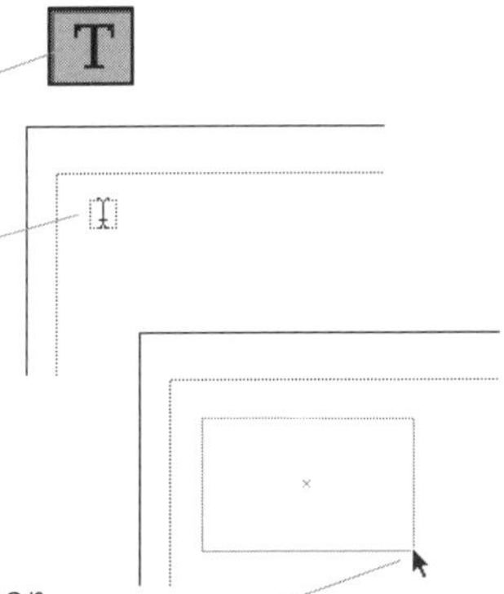
T

1 To create rectangle type, select the Type tool.

2 Position the cursor at one corner of the rectangle or column you want to create.

If you enter more text than will fit within the rectangle, a '+' in a box appears towards the bottom right corner of the rectangle.

3 Press and drag to the opposite corner to define the size of the rectangle. When you release the mouse, the pointer cursor reverts to the I-beam. An insertion point appears at the start point for the text.

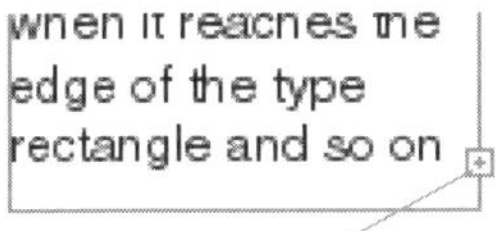
when it reaches the
edge of the type
rectangle and so on

Excess text

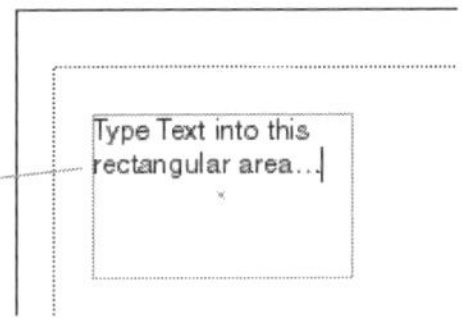
Type Text into this
rectangular area...

4 Enter type.

Resizing text rectangles with the Selection tool

1 Select the Selection tool. Click on the type rectangle to select it. A standard bounding box with selection handles appears, indicating the current size of the text rectangle.

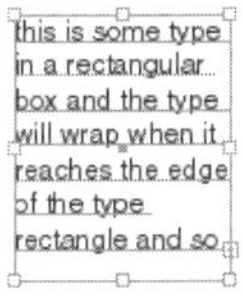
this is some type
in a rectangular
box and the type
will wrap when it
reaches the edge
of the type
rectangle and so

Dragging selection handles of Rectangle type does not change the size of the type inside it. It changes the dimension of the text rectangle.

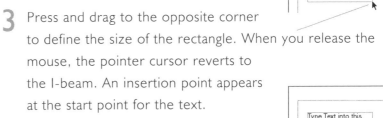

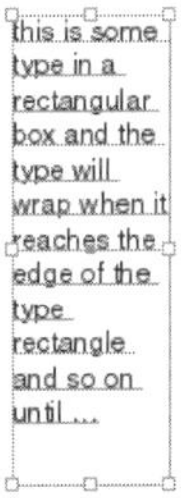
this is some
type in a
rectangular
box and the
type will
wrap when it
reaches the
edge of the
type
rectangle
and so on
until ...

2 Drag a handle to change the dimensions of the text rectangle. Text inside the text rectangle will wrap according to the new dimensions.

To resize a text rectangle with the Direct-selection tool:

1. Select the Direct-selection tool.

2. Click outside the text rectangle to deselect it.

3. Click on an edge of the text rectangle. Make sure you do not select any of the text baselines.

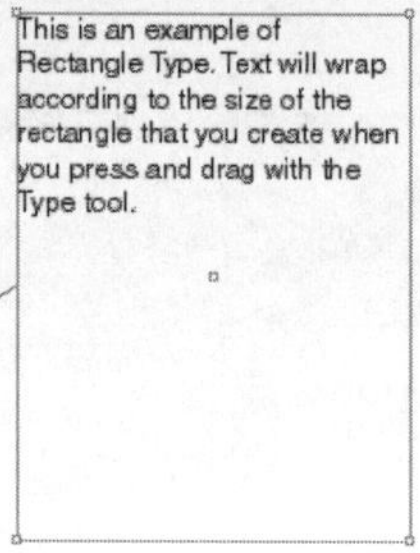

This is an example of
Rectangle Type. Text will wrap
according to the size of the
rectangle that you create when
you press and drag with the
Type tool.

4. Drag one of the line segments to adjust the size. Start to drag a line segment, then hold down Shift as you drag, to constrain the shape to a rectangle.

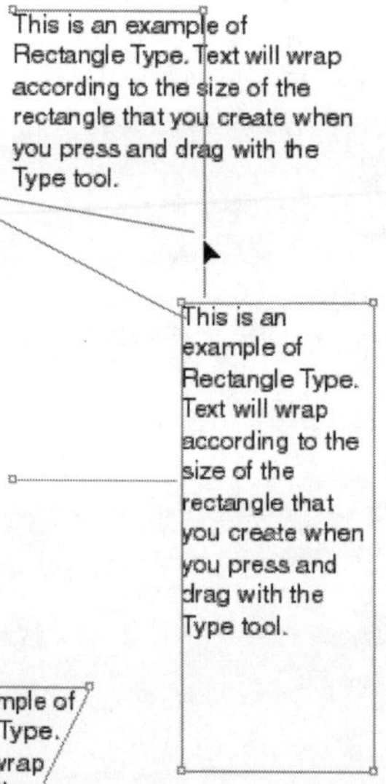

This is an example of
Rectangle Type. Text will wrap
according to the size of the
rectangle that you create when
you press and drag with the
Type tool.
This is an
example of
Rectangle Type.
Text will wrap
according to the
size of the
rectangle that
you create when
you press and
drag with the
Type tool.

5. Drag a corner anchor point to change the shape of the rectangle.

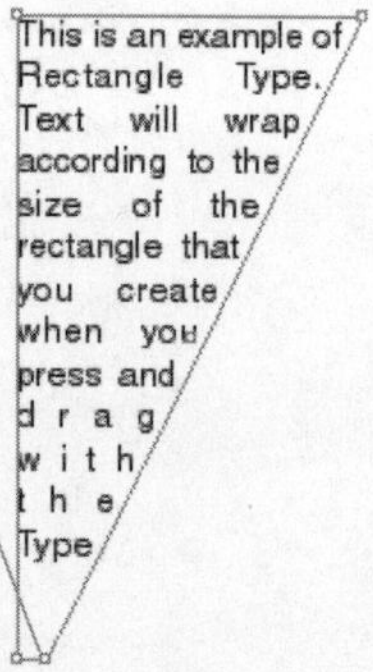

Area Type

When you select the Area-type or Path-type tools, you must click on a path to begin entering type.

Use the Area-type tool to enter type inside a path. The type is constrained by the path and wraps within it. Type can be created in any path except compound and masking paths.

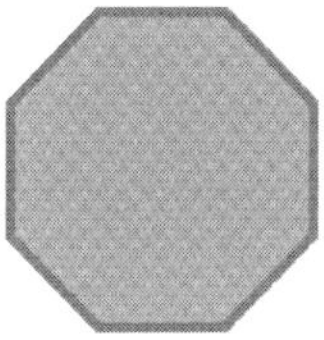

1. To create type within an area or path, select the Area-type tool.

2. Position the cursor on an existing path.

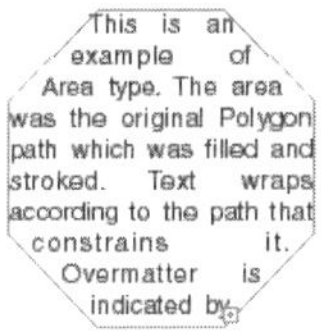

This is an example of Area type. The area was the original Polygon path which was filled and stroked. Text wraps according to the path that constrains it. Overmatter is indicated by

A small '+' near the bottom of the text area indicates overmatter – more text than will fit inside the path.

3. Click to place the insertion point, then enter text. The text wraps according to the constraints of the path.

Painting Area-type Paths

When you turn a path into a text path as above, the path becomes unstroked and unfilled, even if it was originally stroked and filled. You can paint the path after you enter type by selecting the path with the Direct-selection tool.

1. To fill or stroke an Area-type Path, select the Direct-selection tool. Click outside the Area-type path to deselect it.

2. Click on the edge of the of the path to select only the path. If baselines appear below the lines of text you need to deselect the path and try again.

3. Click on the Fill Box or the Stroke Box in the Tool palette, then apply a fill or stroke as detailed in Chapter Six, 'Working with Colour/Appearance Attributes'.

Colouring Area Type

Just as you may want to stroke or fill an Area Type path, you will often need to colour the type inside the path. There are two techniques you can use.

1. To colour Area Type, select the Type tool you used to create the type in the path.

2. Click into the type to place the text insertion point. Either drag across type to select specific ranges; double or triple-click to select a word or paragraph respectively; or choose Edit > Select All to select all the type.

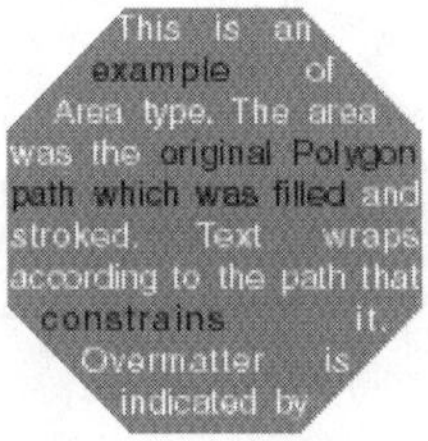

3. Click the Fill Box to make it active, then apply colour as explained in Chapter Six, 'Working with Colour/Appearance Attributes'.

4. As an alternative, select the Area Type with the Selection tool. The path should highlight and a baseline will appear along the base of all lines of type. Apply a Fill colour.

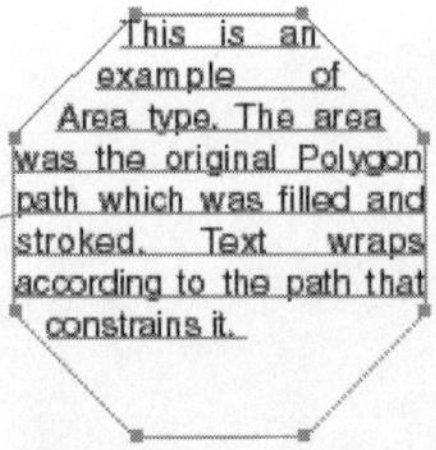

Type on a Path

You can only have one text object on a path.

You can enter type that follows an open or a closed path that you have already drawn.

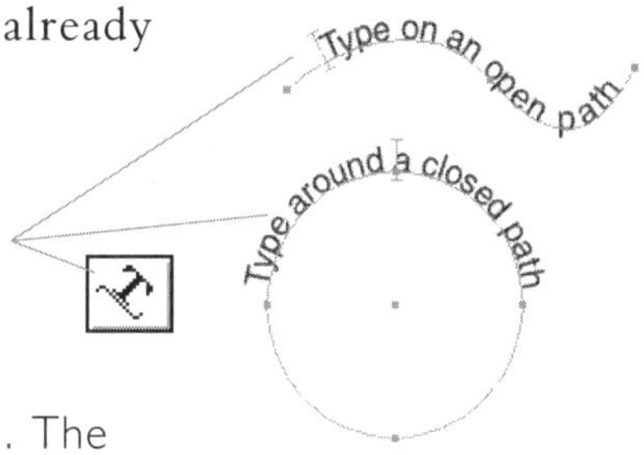

1 To enter type along a path, select the Path-type tool.

When you create Path-type, the path is reset to unstroked and unfilled. You can reapply stroke and fill attributes, if desired, by selecting the path with the Direct-selection tool.

2 Place the cursor on the path. The cursor changes to the Path-type cursor.

3 Click the mouse to place an insertion point on the path. Enter type. The type flows along the path.

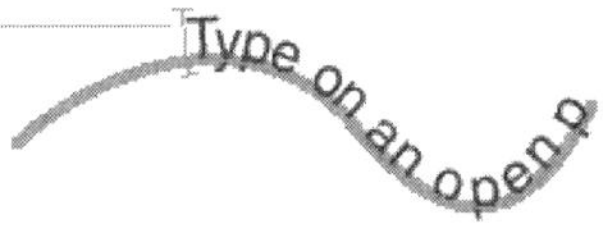

4 To move type on a path, select the text object using the Selection tool. Drag the I-beam at the beginning of the type along the path.

5 To flip type across a path, select the text object using the Selection tool. Drag the I-beam across the path. Or, double-click the I-beam.

To move type across a path without flipping the type, you must use Baseline Shift from the Character palette.

6 To colour the type, either highlight a specific range of text using the Type tool, or select the type using the Selection tool. Apply a fill colour.

7 To change the stroke colour/weight, deselect the Type path, select the Direct-selection tool and click on the path. Make sure only the path is selected. Apply a stroke colour/weight.

Vertical Type Tools

The Vertical Type tools create vertical text. Use the same techniques for working with the Vertical Type tools as you do for the standard Type tools.

1. To create Vertical Point type, select the Vertical Type tool. Position your cursor on the page. The cursor changes to the Vertical Type cursor. Click to set the text insertion point. Enter text. Vertical Point type does not wrap. Press Return/Enter to start a new vertical line.

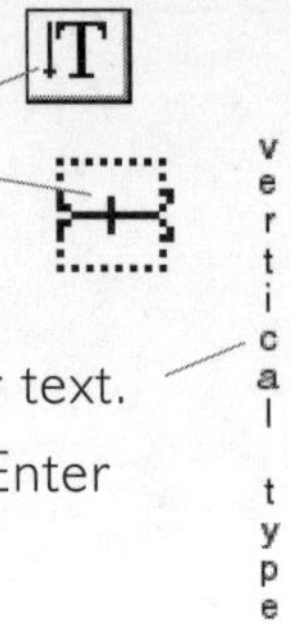

2. To create Vertical Rectangle Type, select the Vertical Type tool. Place your cursor on the page, then drag to define the size of the text rectangle. Enter type. The text aligns to the right of the text rectangle by default and will wrap to the left when it reaches the bottom of the rectangle.

3. To create vertical area type, select the Vertical Area Type tool. Position your cursor on a path. (The path does not have to be selected.) The cursor changes to the Vertical Area Type cursor. Click on path, then enter text. Any fill or stroke attributes are automatically removed.

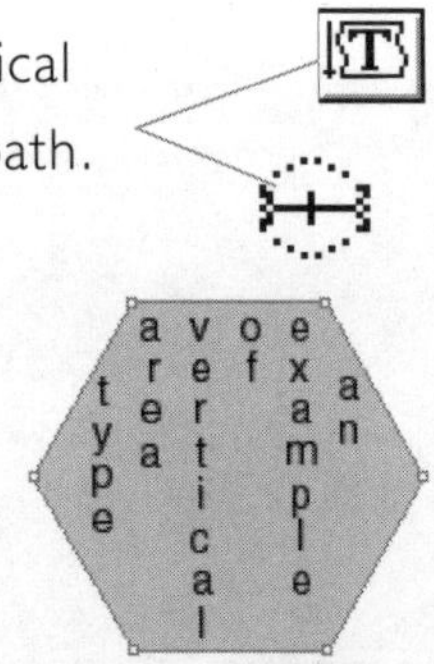

See pages 111-112 for information on re-colouring the type or the path.

4. To create vertical path type, select the Vertical Path Type tool. Position your cursor on a path. The cursor changes to the Vertical Path Type cursor. Click on the path, then enter text. The path is automatically unstroked.

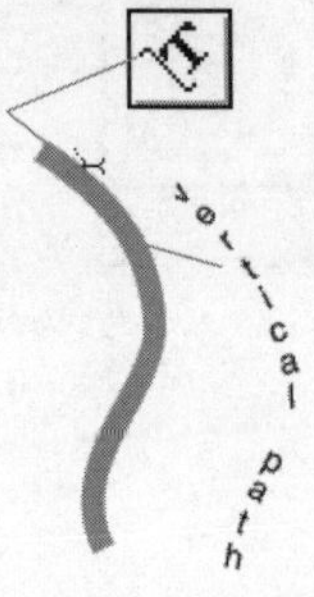

Importing Text

You can import text prepared in other applications in a variety of common text formats which include: text only (ASCII), MS RTF, MS Word 6.0 or later.

1 To import a text file, choose File > Place. When you place the text file it will create a default sized rectangular text area.

2 The Open dialogue box appears. Use standard Macintosh/ Windows dialogue boxes to navigate to the relevant text file.

3 Click on the text file to select it.

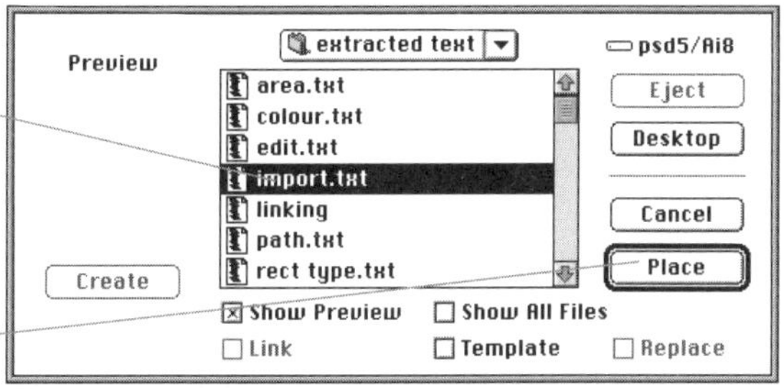

4 Click the Place button. The text will now flow into your artwork, creating a default size rectangular text area. Adjust the dimensions of the rectangle as necessary.

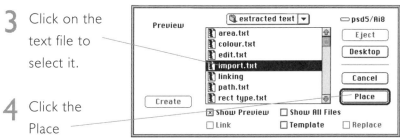

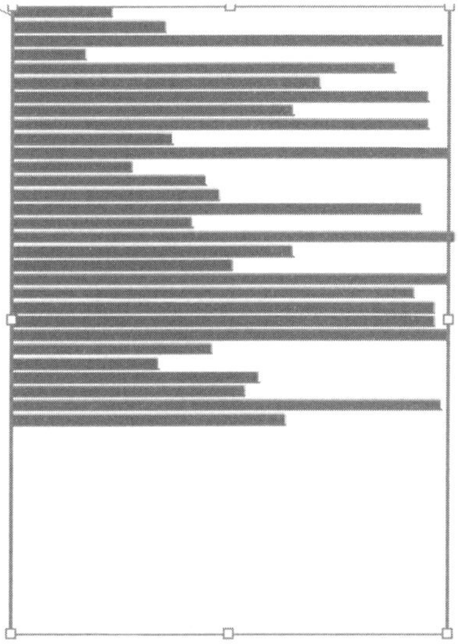

Wrapping Text Around Objects

If your illustration contains text and objects that overlap, there will be times when you require the text to wrap or run around the objects, rather than on top or underneath.

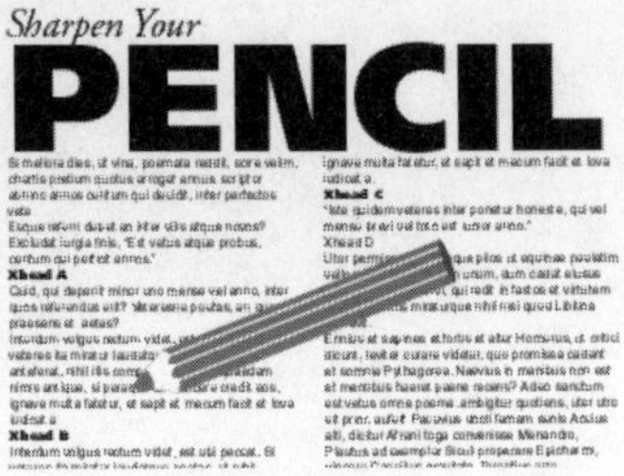

1 To wrap type around an object, make sure the object is in front of the text objects.

2 Select the text objects and the graphic object you want text to wrap around, using the Selection tool.

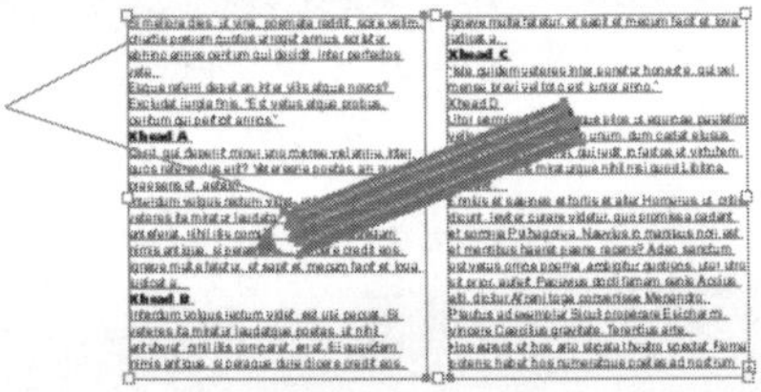

3 Choose Type > Wrap > Make.

4 To create a desirable effect it is often necessary to create an additional object using the rectangle tool, or any other drawing tool, to act as boundary outside the original graphic object. The additional object should have a fill and stroke of none and can be used as a graphic boundary to control how closely the text wraps around the object.

Releasing text wrap

1 Select the text and graphic objects. Choose Type > Wrap > Release.

Formatting Type

Type can often form an integral part of the artwork you create. Illustrator provides a complete set of sophisticated typographic controls that give you the precision you need to create interesting, attractive and readable type.

Covers

Highlighting Type

You can format an entire text object by selecting it with the Selection tool and then making changes to character and paragraph settings. Or, you can make changes to specific ranges of text by highlighting the text you want to format and then changing the character and paragraph settings. Use the following techniques to highlight text:

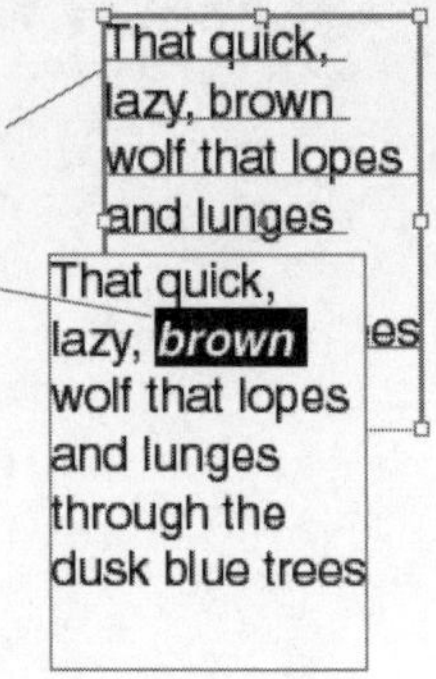

To deselect text, using the Type tool, just click anywhere within the text.

1. To highlight text, select the Type tool. Click into a text rectangle and make sure that the text insertion point is flashing somewhere in the text. The cursor changes to the I-beam cursor.

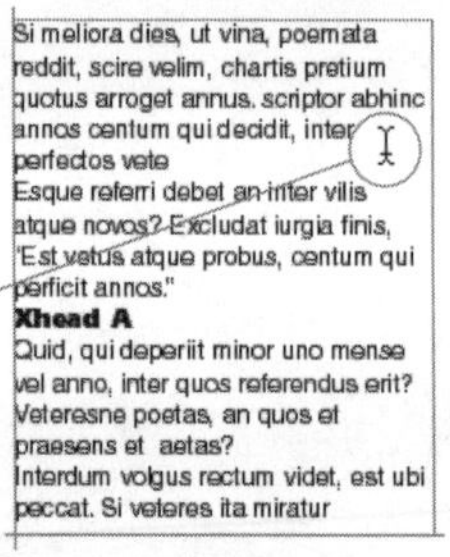

Si meliora dies, ut vina, poemata reddit, scire velim, chartis pretium quotus arroget annus. scriptor abhinc annos centum qui decidit, inter perfectos vete
Esque referri debet an inter vilis atque novos? Excludat iurgia finis, "Est vetus atque probus, centum qui perficit annos."
Xhead A
Quid, qui deperiit minor uno mense vel anno, inter quos referendus erit? Veteresne poetas, an quos et praesens et aetas?
Interdum volgus rectum videt, est ubi peccat. Si veteres ita miratur

2. Position the I-beam cursor at the start of the text you want to highlight. Press and drag across the text. As you do so, the text will reverse out or highlight to indicate exactly which characters are selected. Drag your cursor horizontally, vertically or diagonally depending on the range of text you want to select. Using this technique you must select all the text you want to highlight with one movement of the mouse. You can't release, then drag to add to the original selection. Practice this technique a number of times to get used to it. Use the technique to select any amount of visible text.

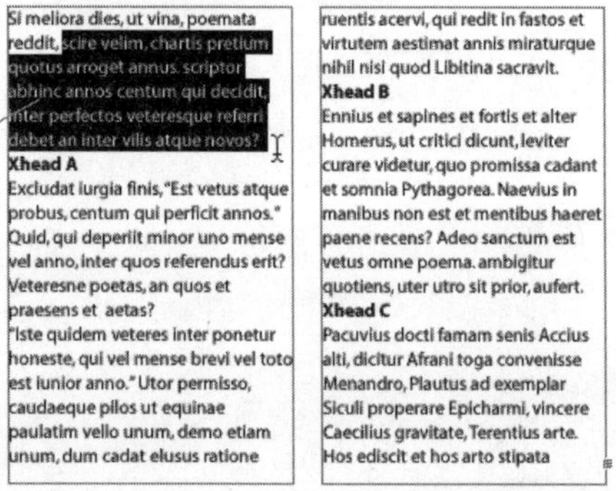

Si meliora dies, ut vina, poemata reddit, scire velim, chartis pretium quotus arroget annus. scriptor abhinc annos centum qui decidit, inter perfectos veteresque referri debet an inter vilis atque novos?
Xhead A
Excludat iurgia finis, "Est vetus atque probus, centum qui perficit annos." Quid, qui deperiit minor uno mense vel anno, inter quos referendus erit? Veteresne poetas, an quos et praesens et aetas?
"Iste quidem veteres inter ponetur honeste, qui vel mense brevi vel toto est iunior anno." Utor permisso, caudaeque pilos ut equinae paulatim vello unum, demo etiam unum, dum cadat elusus ratione
ruentis acervi, qui redit in fastos et virtutem aestimat annis miraturque nihil nisi quod Libitina sacravit.
Xhead B
Ennius et sapines et fortis et alter Homerus, ut critici dicunt, leviter curare videtur, quo promissa cadant et somnia Pythagorea. Naevius in manibus non est et mentibus haeret paene recens? Adeo sanctum est vetus omne poema. ambigitur quotiens, uter utro sit prior, aufert.
Xhead C
Pacuvius docti famam senis Accius alti, dicitur Afrani toga convenisse Menandro, Plautus ad exemplar Siculi properare Epicharmi, vincere Caecilius gravitate, Terentius arte. Hos ediscit et hos arto stipata

3 Position your cursor on a word, then double-click the mouse button to highlight one word.

4 Position your cursor within a paragraph, then triple-click to highlight an entire paragraph.

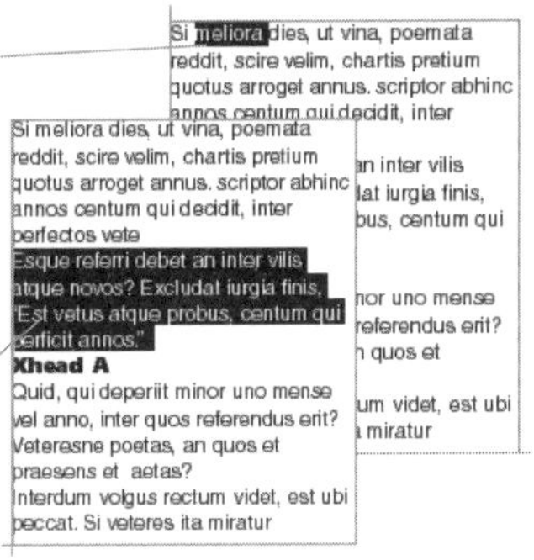

When you have a range of text highlighted, if you press any key on the keyboard you are effectively overtyping the selected text – whatever you type on the keyboard replaces the selected text. If this happens unintentionally, choose Edit > Undo immediately.

5 Position your cursor at the start of the text you want to highlight. Click the mouse button to place the text insertion point and to mark the start of a range of text you want to highlight. Move the cursor to the end of the text you want to highlight. It is important that you do not press and drag with the mouse at this stage, simply find the last bit of text you want to highlight. Hold down Shift, then click the mouse button to indicate the end of the text you want to highlight. All the text between the initial click and the Shift+click is highlighted.

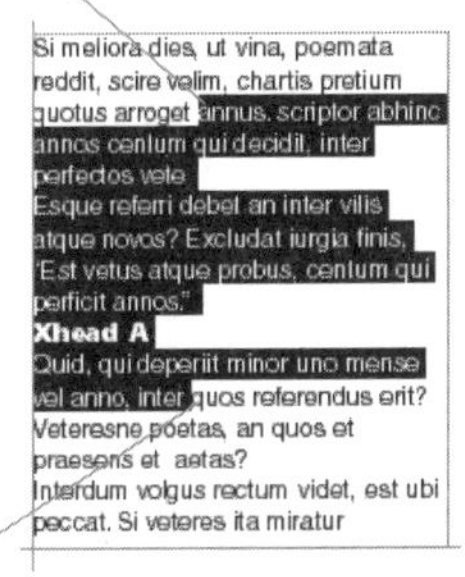

You can use the same techniques for highlighting Area type, Vertical Area type, Path Type and Vertical Path type.

6 Choose Edit > Select All (Command/Ctrl+A) to select an entire text file. This includes any overmatter, even though you cannot see it.

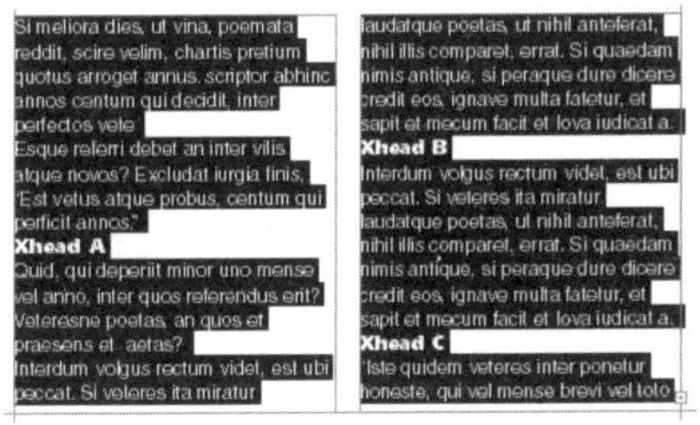

Font, Style, Size

Font and Style

A Font is a complete set of characters (upper case, lower case, numerals, symbols and punctuation marks) in a particular typeface, size and style. The term typeface refers to the actual design or cut of the characters. For example, Gill Sans is a typeface. There are many variations of Gill Sans within the Gill Sans typeface family.

1. To change the font for a particular range of text, make sure you select the text using the Type tool. Select a text rectangle with the Selection tool if you want to change the font for the entire text rectangle. If nothing is selected when you choose a new font you will set a text default – the next time you enter text it will be formatted according to the font you choose.

2. Either choose Type > Font and select a typeface and style from the Font sub-menus.

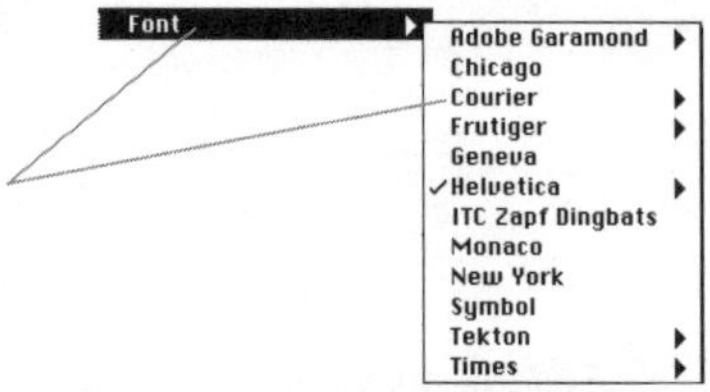

You can format text using options in the Type menu, using the Character palette and using keyboard shortcuts. To show the Character palette choose Type > Character (Command/Ctrl+T).

3. Or use the Font pop-up in the Character palette. Choose a type face, such as Frutiger, and a style, such as Light.

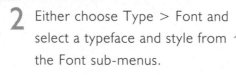

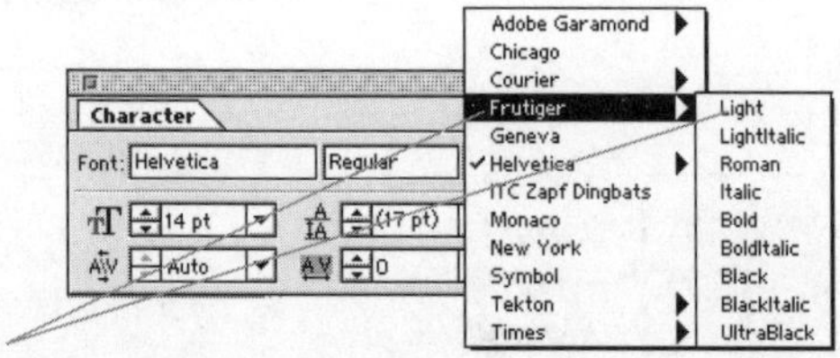

You can also specify increments to 0.01 point accuracy.

Size

You can specify type size from 0.1–1296 points.

1. To specify a type size, choose Type > Size and select a size from the Size sub-menu. If you choose Other from the sub-menu the Character palette will open if it is not already showing.

2 Use the Size pop-up in the Character palette and choose from the preset list of sizes.

3 Or highlight the existing value in the entry field, enter a new value, then press Return/Enter to apply the change.

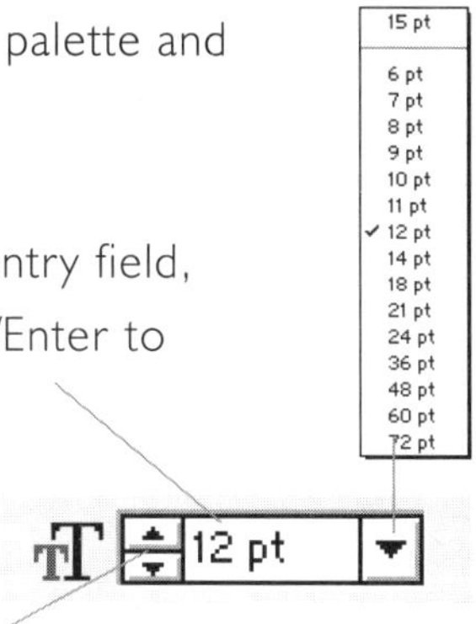

4 Or, click the up/down arrows to increase/decrease the size in single point increments. Hold down Command/Ctrl+Shift then click the Up/Down arrows to change type size in double the default increments (set in Type Preferences – see below).

5 For text highlighted with the Type tool, hold down Command/Ctrl+Shift, then use the '<' or '>' keys to decrease/increase the size in increments. The standard default for this keyboard shortcut is 2 points. If necessary, choose File > Preferences > Type and Auto Tracing, then change the value in the Size/Leading entry field.

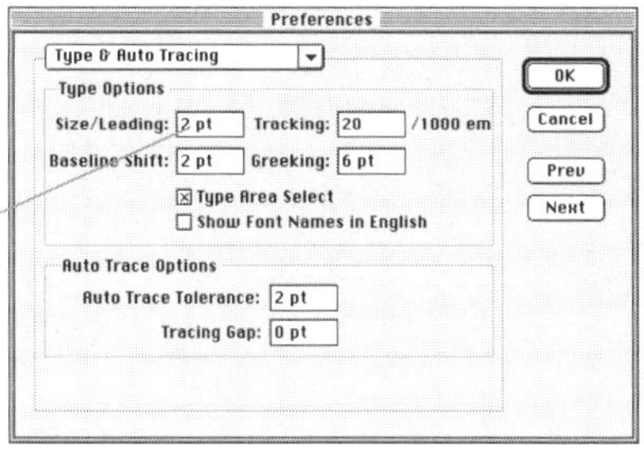

6 For highlighted text , hold down Command/Ctrl+alt/Alt+Shift, then use the '<' or '>' keys to decrease/increase the size in increments of 5 times the default Type Size/Leading preference setting. For example, with the Type Size/Leading setting at 1 point, this keyboard shortcut will decrease/increase the size in 5 point increments.

Leading

Leading is an important consideration for setting readable and attractive type.

Leading is the distance from one baseline of text to the next. A baseline is an imaginary line that runs along the base of text characters

That quick, lazy,
brown wolf that
stretches, sniffs
and squeezes
through the dusk

Absolute Leading

Absolute leading is a fixed value. If you change the point size of your type, the leading does not change, it remains fixed. For example, if you are working with 14 point type with a leading value of 20 (14/20), then change the type size to 18, the leading value remains at 20 points.

Leading is set relative to the point size you are working with. Typically the leading value, measured in points, will be greater than the point size with which you are working. In headlines at larger point sizes, leading may need to be the same value as the size of the headline, or could even be slightly less than the headline size (negative leading).

1. To set leading for an entire text rectangle, select the text with the Selection tool. To set leading for a complete paragraph(s), use the Type tool to select the paragraph(s). To set leading for a line of type, use the Type tool and select at least one character – leading is set according to the highest leading value applied to any character in the line.

2. Highlight the Leading field in the Character palette and enter a value.

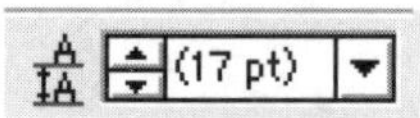

   Press Return/Enter to apply the value to the selected text.

3. You can also use the leading pop-up to choose from the preset list. Or use the arrows to increase/decrease leading in single point increments.

Hold down Command/Ctrl+Shift then click the leading arrows to increase/decrease the leading in double the default leading increments.

Auto Leading

Auto Leading sets leading to an additional 20% of the point size with which you are working. If you increase or decrease the point size, the leading value changes automatically.

1. Choose Auto from the Leading pop-up. Auto Leading appears as a value in brackets.

Kerning

The kerning/ tracking unit used in Adobe Illustrator is 1/1000th EM.

Use kerning – often referred to as 'pair kerning'– to reduce the space between two adjacent characters. Digital fonts have in-built, automatic pair kerning values. Auto Kerning is the default when you create type in Adobe Illustrator. At larger point sizes, certain combinations of character may need manual kerning; body text sizes do not normally require any manual kerning.

Automatic pair kerning amounts are indicated in the Character palette by a value enclosed in brackets. Manual pair kerning amounts are not enclosed in brackets.

1 To manually kern characters, select the Type tool. Place the text insertion point between the character pair you want to kern. Make sure the Character palette is showing. Highlight the Kerning entry field, enter a value, then press Return/ Enter to apply the new value.

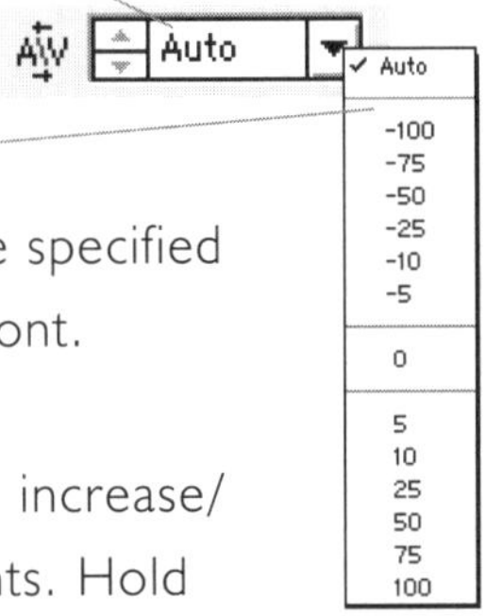

3 You can also use the Kerning pop-up to choose from the preset list. Choose Auto to apply the kerning value specified by the font designer and built into the font.

Negative values bring characters closer together, positive values move characters further apart.

4 Or use the Kerning increment arrow to increase/ decrease the kerning in single increments. Hold down Shift and click the increment arrows to increase/decrease the kerning value in increments of 10.

5 Hold down Alt then use the left/right arrows to vary kerning values. The keyboard shortcut uses the value set in the Type and Auto Tracing Preferences dialogue box. The default value is 20/1000th Em.

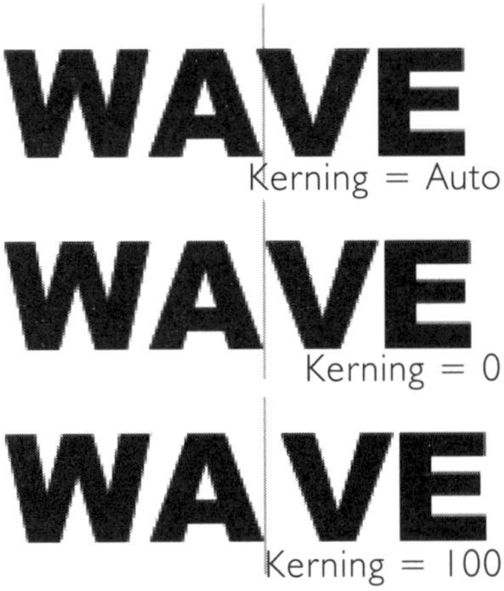

To reset kerning to 0, use the keyboard shortcut Command/Ctrl+Shift+Q.

Tracking

Tracking is used to increase or decrease the space between a range of highlighted characters – sometimes referred to as 'range kerning'.

Set the Tracking preference to 5/1000th to kern by the equivalent amount used by the QuarkXPress tracking shortcut.

The default tracking unit used in Adobe Illustrator is 1/1000th Em. When you track text using the keyboard shortcut Illustrator tracks in 20/1000th Em increments. Choose Edit > Preferences > Type & Auto Tracing and change the Kern/track amount to specify the tracking increment used by the keyboard shortcut.

1. To track a range of text, select the Type tool, then highlight the range of text you want to track. Make sure the Character palette is showing.

2. Highlight the Tracking entry field, enter a value then press Return to apply the new value. Positive values increase the space between characters, negative values decrease it. Or you can use the Kerning pop-up to choose from the preset list.

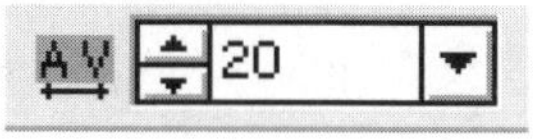

To reset tracking to zero, use the keyboard shortcut Command/Ctrl+Shift+Q on a range of highlighted text.

3. Or use the Tracking increment arrow to vary the tracking in single increments. Tracking increases in 1/1000th Em. Hold down Shift and click the increment arrows to increase/decrease tracking values in double the default increment.

4. Hold down Alt then use the left/right arrows to vary tracking values. This uses the value set in the Type and Auto Tracing Preferences dialogue.

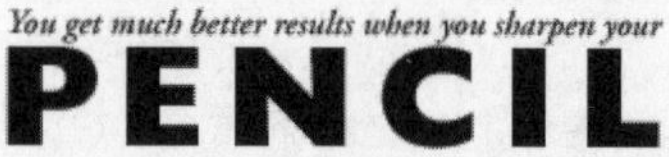

Horizontal and Vertical Scale

Exaggerated Horizontal or Vertical Scale settings will visibly distort the characters, creating pronounced differences between the relative weights of vertical and horizontal strokes in the letterforms:

L L

Use Horizontal or Vertical Scale to expand or condense selected characters, making them fatter or thinner. Horizontal and Vertical scale can be useful for headlines/special effects. The default value for this is 100%.

1 To scale type horizontally or vertically, select the range of type you want to scale using the Type tool.

2 Make sure you have the Character palette showing (Command/Ctrl+T). Use the pop-up menu to choose Show Options. The palette expands to show Horizontal and Vertical Scale and Baseline Shift fields.

3 Highlight the Vertical or Horizontal entry field, then

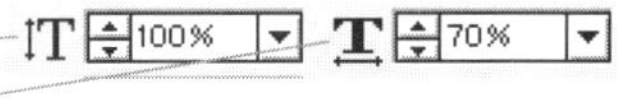

enter a new value and press Return/Enter to apply the change. Or, use the pop-up to choose from the preset options. You can also use the increment arrows to increase/decrease the settings in 1% increments.

CONSTANTINOPLE T = 100%, IT = 100%
CONSTANTINOPLE T = 70%
CONSTANTINOPLE IT = 70%
CONSTANTINOPLE T = 120%

Use the keyboard shortcut Command/Ctrl+Shift+X to reset Horizontal Scale to 100% for a highlighted range of text.

4 Also, you can manually scale point type horizontally or vertically. Select the Selection tool, click on some point type then press and drag centre top or bottom, centre left or right handles to scale vertically or horizontally.

Baseline Shift

A 'baseline' is an imaginary line that runs along the base of text characters. The Baseline Shift control enables you to move highlighted characters above or below their original baseline to create a variety of effects.

Typically, you need to baseline shift text when you place type on a path which has a visible stroke.

1. To baseline shift, use the Type tool to highlight the characters you want to baseline shift.

2. Make sure you have the Character palette showing (Command/Ctrl+T). Use the pop-up menu to choose Show Options. The palette expands to show Horizontal and Vertical Scale and Baseline Shift fields.

3. Highlight the Baseline Shift entry field, then enter a new value and press Return/Enter to apply the change. Positive values shift characters upward, negative values shift characters downward. Or, use the pop-up to choose from the preset options. You can also use the increment arrows to increase/decrease the baseline shift in 1 point increments.

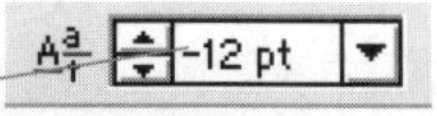

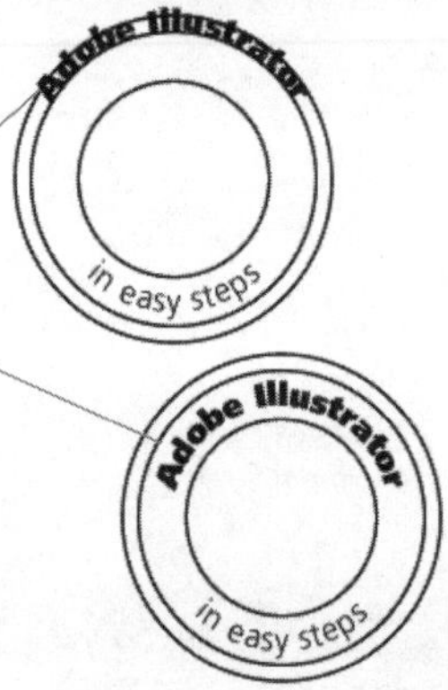

4. Or, hold down Alt+Shift, then use the up/down arrow keys to increase/decrease baseline shift in increments of 2 points. The increment is set in the Type Options preferences. Choose Edit > Preferences > Type & Auto Tracing, then enter a value in the Baseline Shift entry field to change the increment.

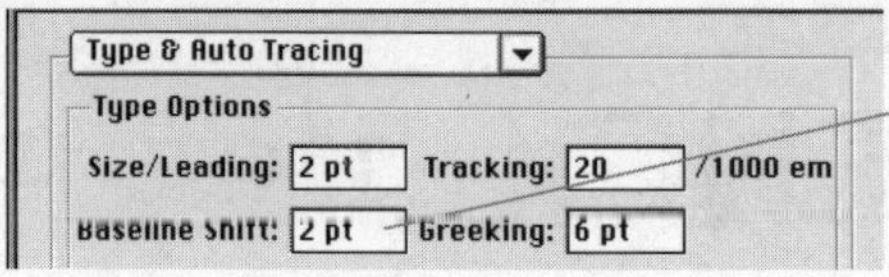

Paragraph Indents

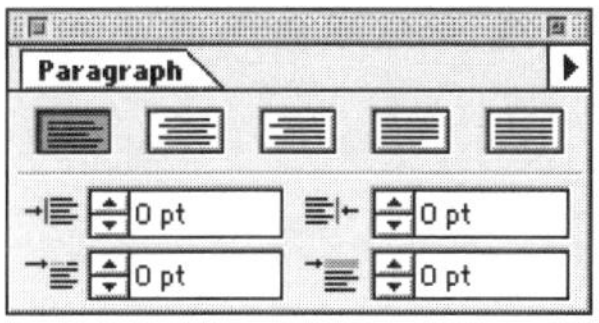

Use the Paragraph palette to set indents. Left and Right indents can be set to push type inward from the left/right edge of the text rectangle. This can be useful when the text rectangle has a fill colour, preventing the text from running right up to the edge of the rectangle. Indents are also useful for creating bullet points. First Line indents can be used to visually indicate the start of a new paragraph.

1. To set left and/or right indents, select the Type tool and highlight the paragraph(s) you want to indent. Make sure the Paragraph palette is showing (Command/Ctrl+M).

To set an indent using millimetres, enter a value followed by 'mm'. When you press Return/Enter, Illustrator converts this millimetre measurement into its points equivalent.

2. Enter a value in the Left/Right indent entry fields, then press Return/Enter to apply the change. Or click the increment arrows to increase/decrease the indent setting in 1 point increments.

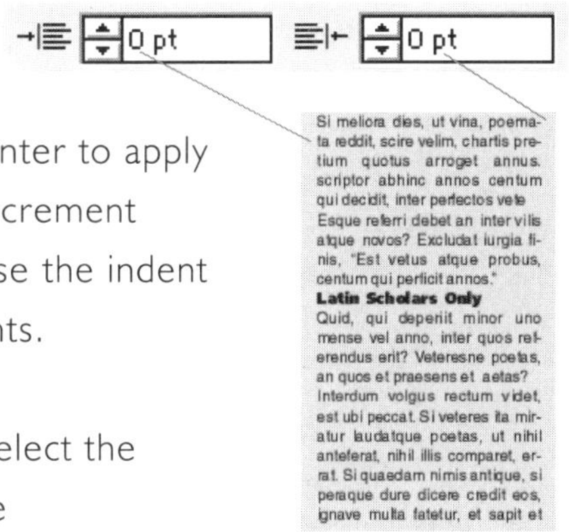

3. To set a first line indent, select the Type tool and highlight the paragraph(s) you want to indent.

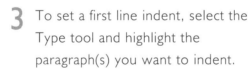

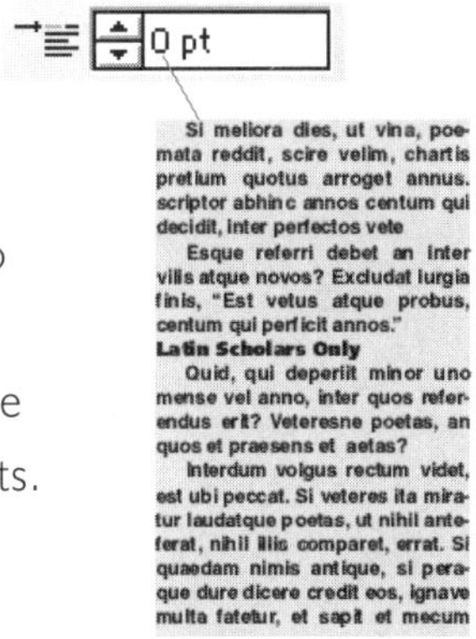

4. Enter a value in the First Line indent entry field, then press Return/Enter to apply the change. Or, click the increment arrows to increase/decrease the indent setting in 1 point increments.

Alignment

Alignment is a paragraph level control. If your text insertion point is flashing in a paragraph of text and you choose a different alignment option, the entire paragraph changes according to the alignment option you choose. Highlight a range of paragraphs if you want to change the alignment of more than one paragraph at a time. There are five alignment options to choose from – Left, Right, Centre, Justify Full Lines, Justify All Lines.

1 To change the alignment of a paragraph(s), select the Type tool, then click into a paragraph to place the text insertion point, or highlight a range of paragraphs.

2 Make sure the Paragraph palette is showing (Command/Ctrl+M).

3 Click one of the alignment buttons.

4 Alternatively, use one of the alignment keyboard shortcuts: Command/Ctrl+Shift+L (Align Left), +R (Align Right), +C (Align Centre), +J (Justify Full Lines).

BEWARE

Justify All Lines produces unsightly gaps in the last line of justified paragraphs, but can sometimes be used on headlines.

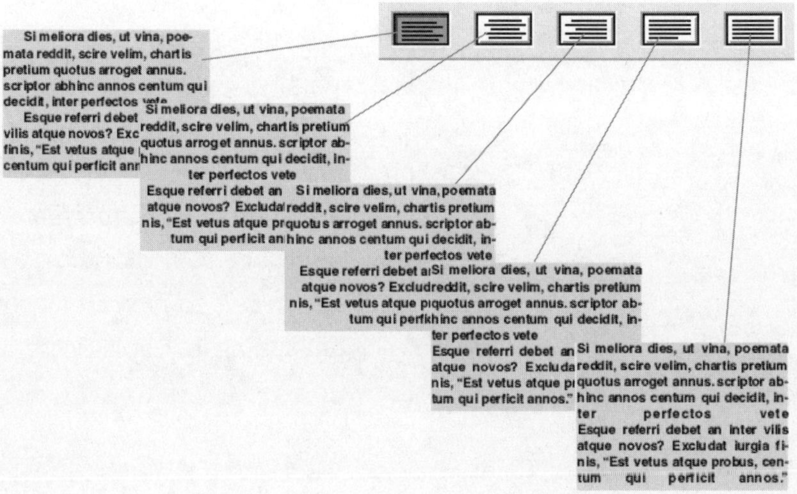
Si meliora dies, ut vina, poemata reddit, scire velim, chartis pretium quotus arroget annus. scriptor ab- hinc annos centum qui decidit, in- ter perfectos vete
Esque referri debet an inter vilis atque novos? Excludat iurgia fi- nis, "Est vetus atque probus, cen- tum qui perficit annos."

Hyphenation

Automatic hyphenation is a paragraph level control. Switch on hyphenation if you want Illustrator to hyphenate words automatically where appropriate at the ends of lines. Hyphenation is off as a default.

1 To switch on hyphenation, select the Type tool, then click into a paragraph to place the text insertion point, or highlight a range of paragraphs.

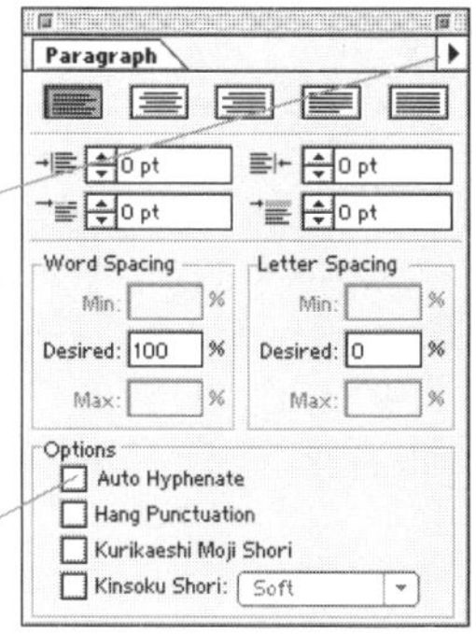

2 Make sure the Paragraph palette is showing (Command/Ctrl+M). Use the pop-up menu to choose Show Options. The Paragraph palette expands to show further options.

3 Click the Auto Hyphenate option. The text is hyphenated according to the settings in the Hyphenation Options dialogue box.

Changing Hyphenation Options

1 Choose Hyphenation from the pop-up menu in the Paragraph palette.

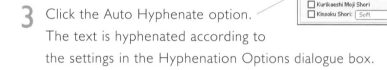

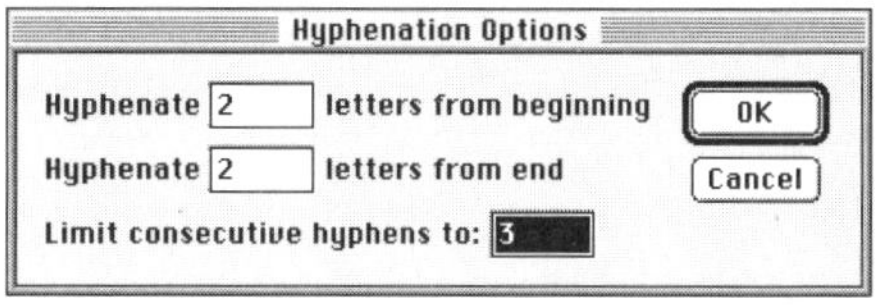

2 Enter a value, typically either 2 or 3, in the 'Hyphenate ... letters from beginning/end' entry fields. This setting specifies the minimum number of letters there must be preceding a hyphen at the end of a line, and how many letters of a word there must be after a hyphen at the beginning of a new line, for hyphenation to be allowed.

3 Enter a value in the consecutive hyphens field to limit the number of consecutive hyphens. A value of 2 or 3 will prevent the possibility of a 'step ladder' effect being created in the eventuality of Illustrator being able to create hyphens at the end of several consecutive lines.

Creating a discretionary hyphen

Illustrator always breaks a word, when appropriate, at a discretionary hyphen, whether the Auto Hyphenate option is on or off.

1. Select the Type tool. Click to place the text insertion point where you want to hyphenate a word.

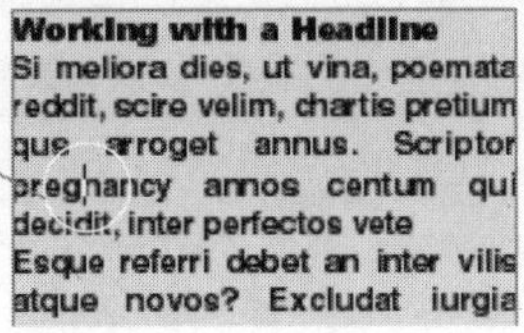

Working with a Headline
Si meliora dies, ut vina, poemata reddit, scire velim, chartis pretium qus arroget annus. Scriptor pregnancy annos centum qui decidit, inter perfectos vete
Esque referri debet an inter vilis atque novos? Excludat iurgia

2. Use Command/Ctrl+Shift+'-' (hyphen) to insert a discretionary hyphen. If text is edited and reflows so that the hyphenated word appears in the middle of a line of type, the discretionary hyphen will not appear.

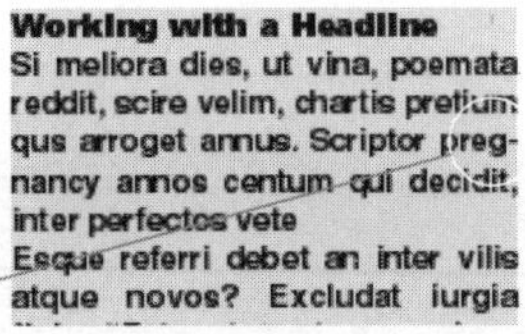

Working with a Headline
Si meliora dies, ut vina, poemata reddit, scire velim, chartis pretium qus arroget annus. Scriptor preg-nancy annos centum qui decidit, inter perfectos vete
Esque referri debet an inter vilis atque novos? Excludat iurgia

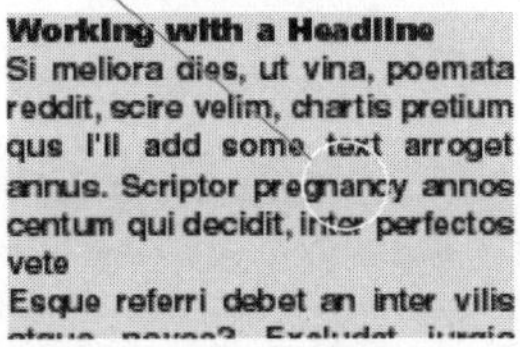

Working with a Headline
Si meliora dies, ut vina, poemata reddit, scire velim, chartis pretium qus I'll add some text arroget annus. Scriptor pregnancy annos centum qui decidit, inter perfectos vete
Esque referri debet an inter vilis

Transforming Objects

There are four transformation tools – the Rotate, Reflect, Scale, and Shear tools. You can use the tools to transform objects manually, or you can use a dialogue box to transform objects numerically. You can also use the Transform palette to transform objects with numerical precision. The Free Transform tool also enables you to transform objects. You can transform any object you have created in Adobe Illustrator.

Covers

Chapter Ten

Rotating Objects

All the Transformation tools take effect around a point of origin. The Point of Origin Marker appears at the centre of a selected object as soon as you select one of the basic Transformation tools.

Rotating manually

An important point to understand when you rotate an object is that there must be a point around which it rotates. This is called the point of origin.

The further away from the point of origin that you position the arrowhead cursor, the greater the control you will have over the transformation.

1. To rotate an object manually, select the object(s) you want to rotate.

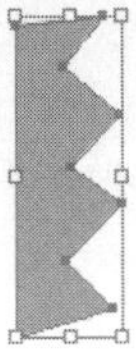

2. Click on the Rotate tool to select it. The point of origin marker automatically appears at the centre point of the object.

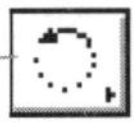

3. Place your cursor some distance away from the point of origin marker (the cursor changes to an arrowhead), then drag in a circular direction to rotate the object around its centre point.

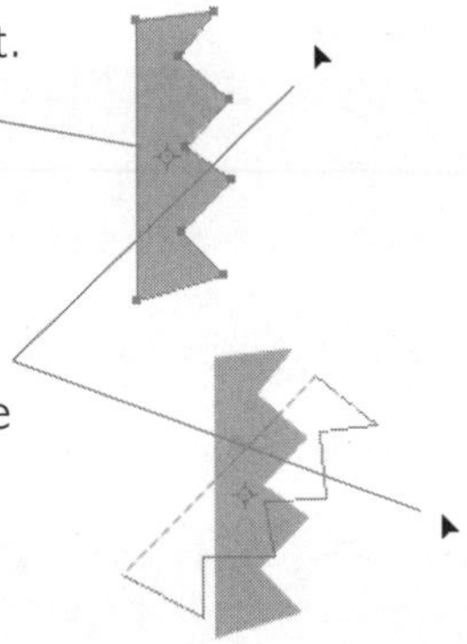

To constrain the rotation to 45 degree increments, start to rotate the object, then hold down the Shift key. Release the mouse button before you release the Shift key, otherwise the constraint effect will be lost.

4. Alternatively, click anywhere on the object or elsewhere on the page to specify a new point of origin around which you want to rotate the object. The point of origin marker moves to where you clicked. You can also drag the point of origin marker to a new position.

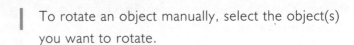

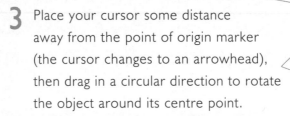

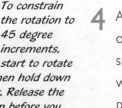

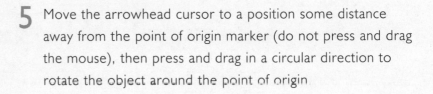

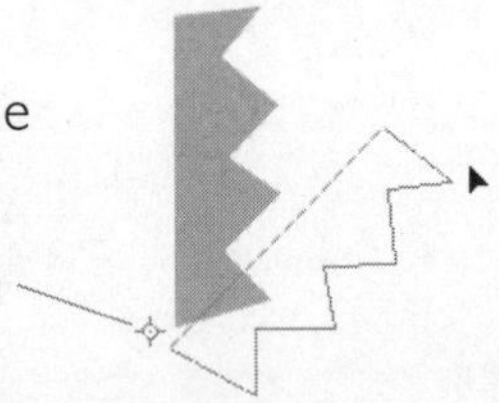

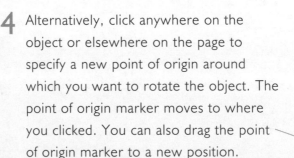

5. Move the arrowhead cursor to a position some distance away from the point of origin marker (do not press and drag the mouse), then press and drag in a circular direction to rotate the object around the point of origin.

To manually rotate a copy of the object, start to rotate the object, then hold down Alt.

The Rotate dialogue box

The Rotate dialogue box is useful when you need to rotate an object by a precise amount.

1. To rotate using the Rotate dialogue box, select the object(s) you want to rotate.

2. Double-click the Rotate tool. Notice the point of origin marker which appears at the centre of the object. This marks the point around which the transformation takes place.

If your object is filled with a pattern, select the Pattern option to rotate the pattern as well as the object.

3. Enter a value from -360 to 360. Negative numbers rotate an object in a clockwise direction; positive numbers rotate in an anticlockwise direction.

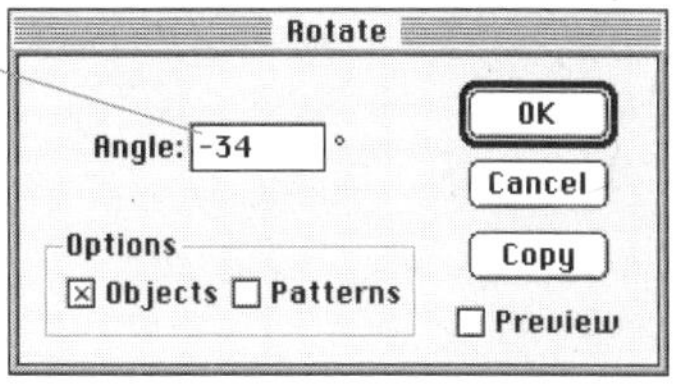

4. Click the Preview option if you want to see a preview of the rotation before you OK the dialogue box. Click OK to rotate the object around its centre point.

In the Rotate dialogue box, if your object is filled with a pattern and you want to rotate the pattern and not the object, deselect the Object option and select the pattern option. The pattern will rotate by the specified amount.

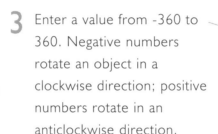

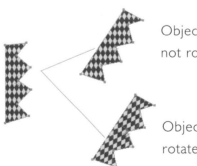

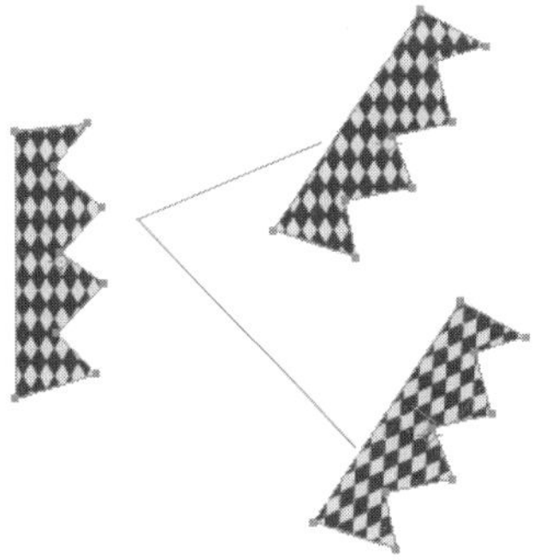

Object rotated, pattern not rotated.

Object and pattern rotated.

Scaling Objects

You can scale objects manually using the Scale tool, or using the Scale dialogue box. As with all transformations, scaling takes place around the point of origin marker.

Hold down Shift, then press and drag to scale in proportion.

1 To scale an object manually, select the object(s) you want to scale. Select the Scale tool.  The point of origin marker appears automatically at the centre point of the object. Position your cursor some distance away from the point of origin marker.

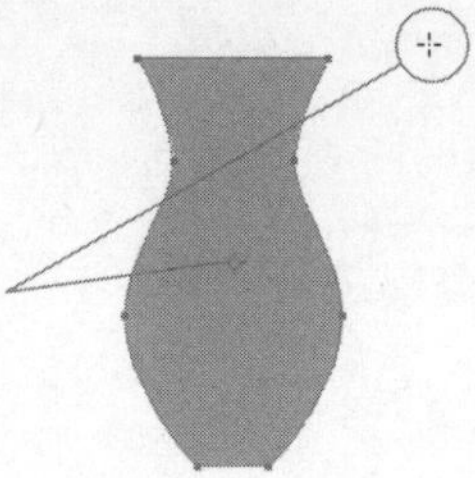

The further away from the point of origin that you position the cursor before you start to scale, the greater the control you will have over the transformation.

2 Press and drag to scale the object. Press and drag horizontally to scale horizontally; press and drag vertically to scale vertically. If you drag past the point of origin you will 'flip' the object horizontally and/or vertically.

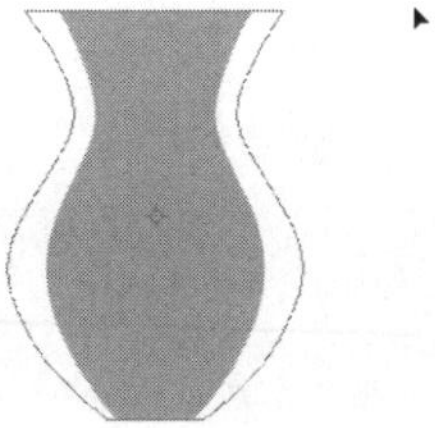

To make a copy of the object as you scale, start to scale the object, then hold down Alt.

3 Alternatively, click on the object or elsewhere on the page to specify a new point of origin around which you want to scale the object. The point of origin marker moves to where you clicked. You can also drag the point of origin marker to a new position.

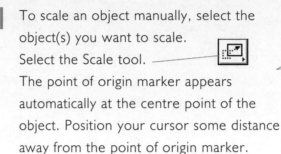

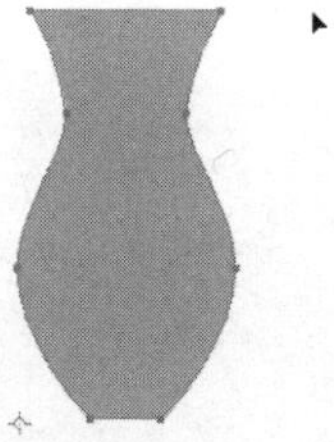

4 Move the arrowhead cursor to a position some distance away from the point of origin marker (do not press and drag), then press and drag to scale the object.

The Scale dialogue box

The Scale dialogue box is useful when you need to scale an object by a precise amount.

If your object is filled with a pattern, select the Pattern option to scale the pattern as well as the object.

1 To scale using the Scale dialogue box, select the object(s) you want to scale.

2 Either, double-click the Scale tool, or choose Object > Transform > Scale. Notice the point of origin marker which appears at the centre of the object, setting the point around which the transformation takes place.

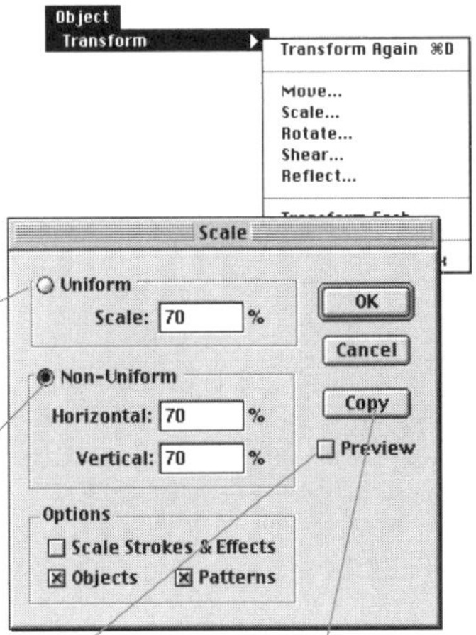

If your object is filled with a pattern and you want to scale the pattern and not the object, deselect the Object option and select the Pattern option. The pattern will scale by the specified amount.

3 Click the Uniform button to maintain the proportions of the object as you scale. Click the Non-Uniform button to scale the object non-proportionally. Enter the scale values you require.

4 Click the Preview option if you want to see a preview of the scale before you OK the dialogue box to scale the object around its centre point.

5 Click the Copy button to create a scaled copy of the original object.

Scaling Line Weights

When you scale an object, any stroke weight is not scaled by default. For example, if you scale a circle with a 6pt stroke to 50% of its original size, the smaller circle still has a 6 point stroke.

1. To scale an object and its stroke weight, select the object(s). Either double-click the Scale tool, or choose Object > Transform > Scale.

2. Select the Scale Stroke and Effects option. Now if you scale a circle with a 6 point stroke to 50%, the stroke weight will be scaled to 3 points.

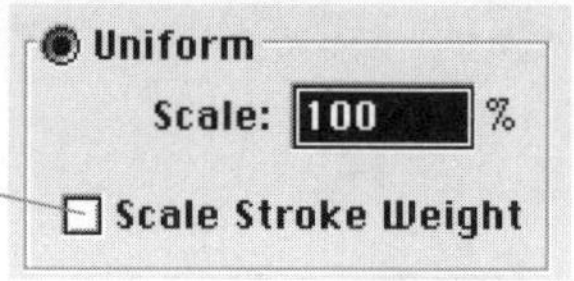

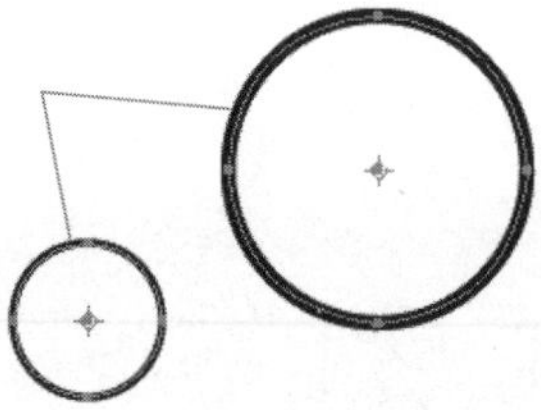

3. To scale line weights as you scale an object manually with the Scale tool, choose Edit > Preferences > General. Select the Scale Stroke Weight & Effects option.

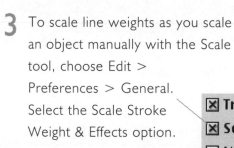

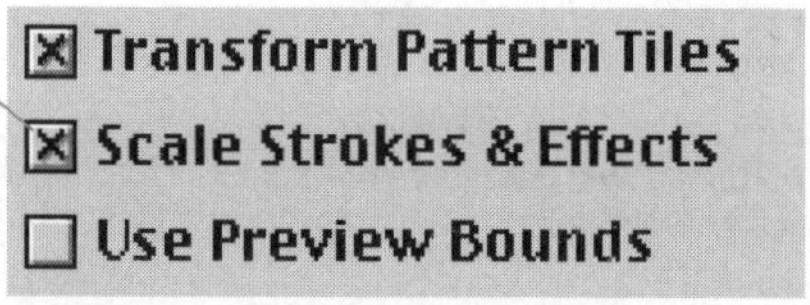

Reflecting Objects

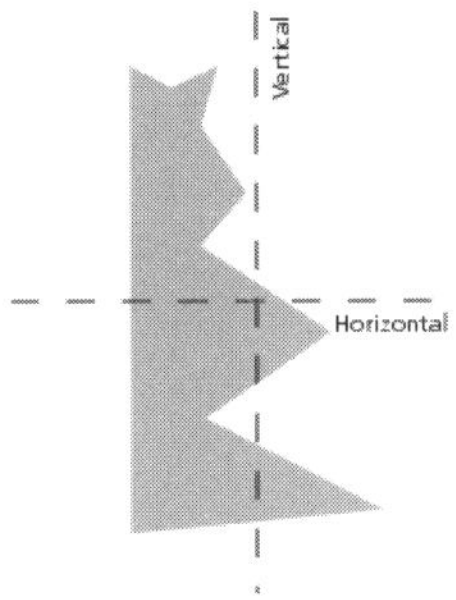

Reflecting shapes is useful when you need to create a mirrored version of your object and for creating perfectly symmetrical shapes. You can reflect objects manually using the Reflect tool, or using the Reflect dialogue box.

1 To reflect an object manually, select the object(s) you want to reflect. Select the Reflect tool: The point of origin marker appears automatically at the centre point of the object.

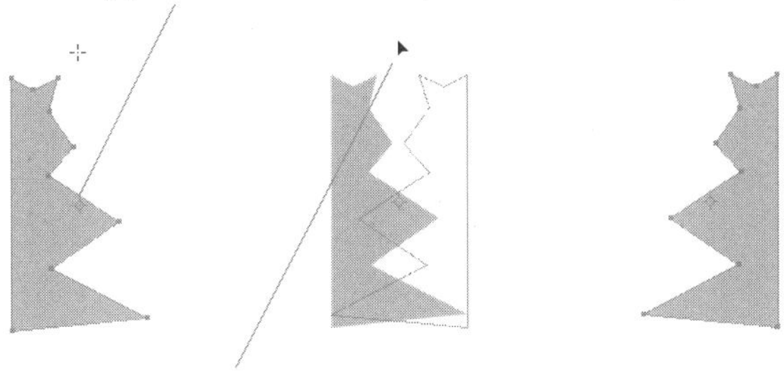

Hold down Shift, then press and drag to constrain the reflection to multiples of 45 degrees.

2 Position your cursor some distance above the point of origin marker, then press and drag upward to reflect the object across its vertical axis.

3 Position your cursor some distance to the right or left of the point of origin marker, then press and drag horizontally to reflect the object across its horizontal axis.

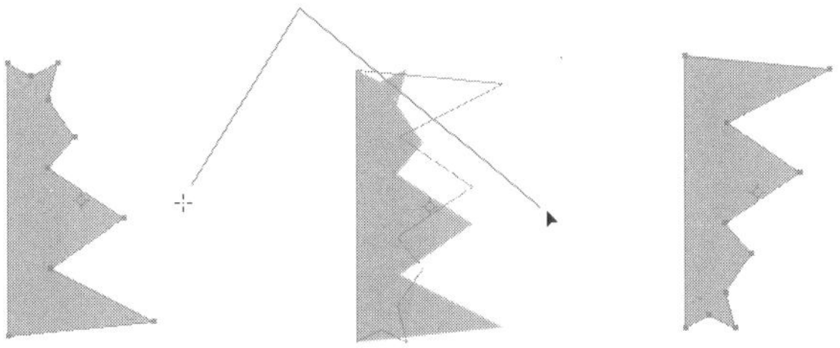

To make a copy of the object as you reflect, start to reflect the object, then hold down Alt.

4 Alternatively, click on the object or elsewhere on the page to specify a new point of origin around which you want to reflect the object. The point of origin marker moves to where you clicked. You can also drag the point of origin marker to a new position.

5 Move the arrowhead cursor to a position some distance away from the point of origin marker (do not press and drag), then press and drag to reflect the object.

The Reflect dialogue box

The Reflect dialogue box is especially useful for reflecting an object precisely across either the horizontal or vertical axis.

1 To reflect using the Reflect dialogue box, select the object(s) you want to reflect. Either double-click the Reflect tool, or choose Object > Transform > Reflect. The point of origin marker appears at the centre of the object.

If your object is filled with a pattern, select the Pattern option to reflect the pattern as well as the object.

2 Click the Horizontal button to create a horizontal reflection, click the Vertical button to create a vertical reflection.

Reflect

Axis
○ Horizontal
● Vertical
○ Angle: 90 °

OK
Cancel
Copy

Options
☒ Objects ☒ Patterns
□ Preview

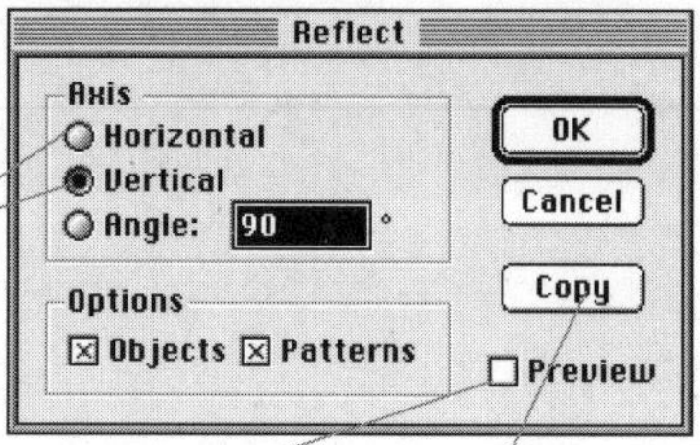

3 Click the Preview option if you want to see a preview of the reflection before you OK the dialogue box.

To reflect the pattern and not the object, deselect the Object option and select the Pattern option.

4 Click the Copy button to create a reflected copy of the original object.

Shearing Objects

Shearing an object slants the object along its horizontal or vertical axis. Shear is useful for creating shadow-like effects.

You get good control over the Shear operation if you move your cursor away from the point of origin at an angle of 45 degrees, before you start to press and drag to perform the shear.

1. To Shear an object manually, select the object(s) you want to shear. Select the Shear tool: The point of origin marker appears automatically at the centre point of the object.

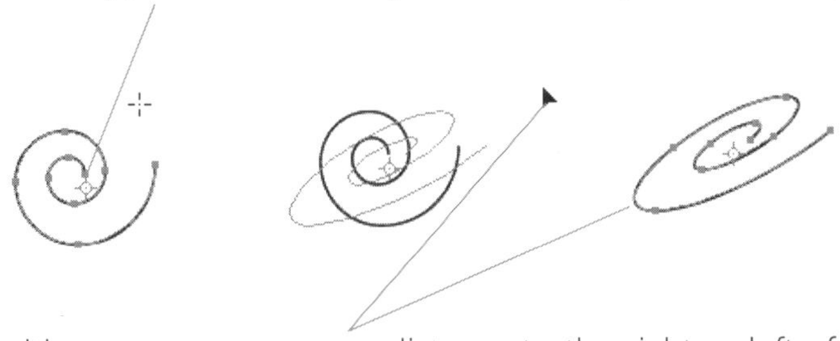

2. Position your cursor some distance to the right or left of the point of origin marker, then press and drag horizontally to shear the object across its horizontal axis.

Hold down Shift, then press and drag to constrain the shear to multiples of 45 degrees.

3. Position your cursor some distance above the point of origin marker, then press and drag upward to shear the object across its vertical axis.

4. Alternatively, click on the object or elsewhere on the page to specify a new point of origin around which you want to shear the object. The point of origin marker moves to where you clicked. You can also drag the point of origin marker to a new position.

To make a copy of the object as you shear, start to shear the object, then hold down Alt.

5. Move the arrowhead cursor to a position some distance away from the point of origin marker (do not press and drag), then press and drag to shear the object.

The Shear dialogue box

The Shear dialogue box is especially useful for shearing an object precisely along either the horizontal or vertical axis.

If your object is filled with a pattern, select the Pattern option to scale the pattern as well as the object.

To shear a pattern and not the object, deselect the Object option and select the Pattern option.

1. To shear using the Shear dialogue box, select the object(s) you want to shear. Either double-click the Shear tool, or choose Object > Transform > Shear. The point of origin marker appears at the centre of the object.

2. Enter a value for the Shear angle, then click the Horizontal button to create a horizontal shear, click the Vertical button to create a vertical shear.

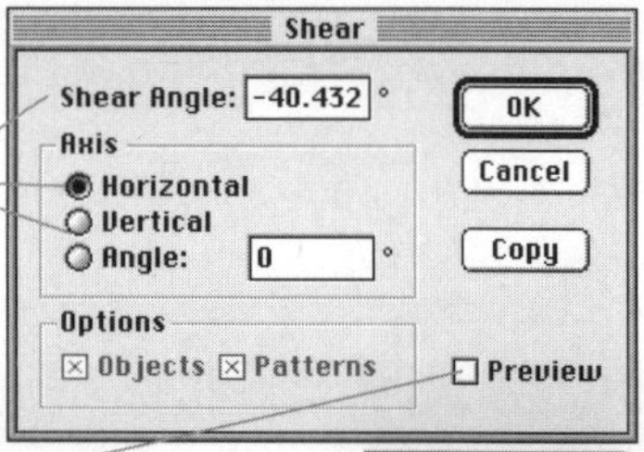

3. Click the Preview option if you want to see a preview of the shear before you OK the dialogue box.

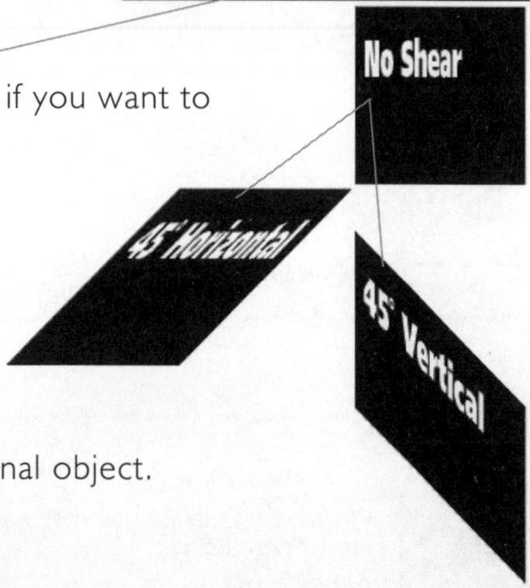

4. Click the Copy button to create a sheared copy of the original object.

The Free Transform Tool

The Free Transform tool provides a convenient and powerful method for transforming and distorting objects.

Rotating objects

1 To rotate an object, use the Selection tool to select the object. Select the Free Transform tool.

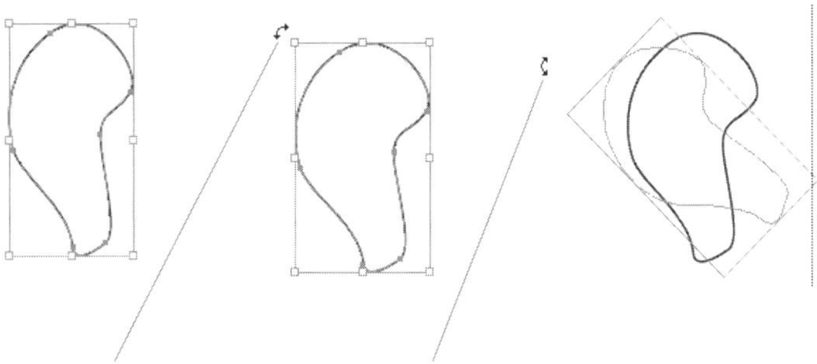

2 Position your cursor just outside the bounding box of the object(s). The cursor changes to a bidirectional, curved arrow. Press and drag in a circular direction.

Hold down Shift, then drag a corner handle to maintain the proportions of the object as you scale.

Reflecting an object

1 Use the Selection tool to select the object. Select the Free Transform tool.

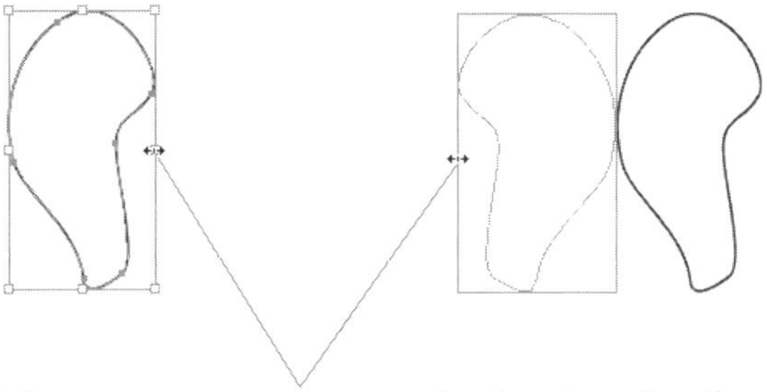

Hold down Alt and drag a resize/selection handle to scale from the centre of the object.

2 Position your cursor on a selection handle, then drag the handle completely across the opposite handle or edge.

Hold down Shift as well to constrain the tool to multiples of 45 degrees.

Scaling an object

1. Use the Selection tool to select the object. Select the Free Transform tool. Drag a selection handle on the bounding box.

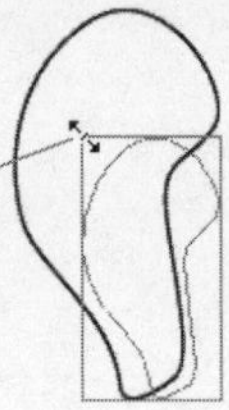

Shearing an object

1. Use the Selection tool to select the object. Select the Free Transform tool.

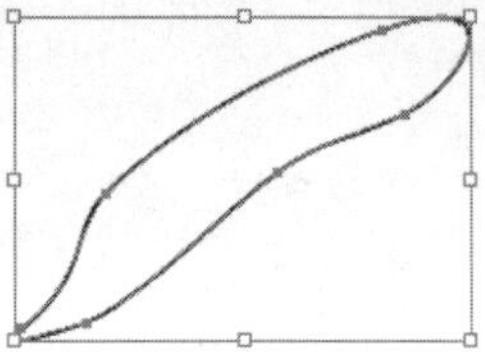

2. Position your cursor on a side handle (centre top or bottom, centre left or right, but not a corner handle). Start to drag the handle, then hold down Command/Ctrl+Alt as you drag.

Distorting an object

1. Use the Selection tool to select the object. Select the Free Transform tool.

2. Position your cursor on a corner handle, start to drag, then hold down Command/Ctrl.

3. To create a perspective effect, position your cursor on a corner handle, start to drag, then hold down Command/Ctrl+Alt+Shift.

The Transform Palette

You can use the Transform palette to position, scale, rotate and shear objects. Options in the Transform palette's pop-up menu allow you to reflect objects, scale stroke weights and specify whether or not pattern fills are transformed.

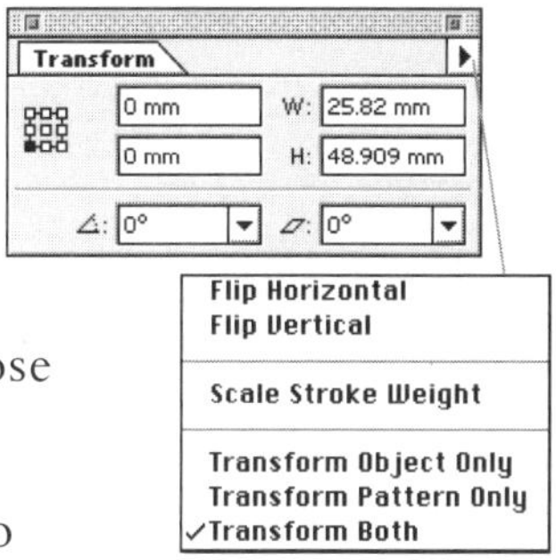

To show the Transform palette, choose Window > Show Transform.

The Transform palette enables you to choose a reference point on a selected object which becomes the point of origin for the changes you make.

1 To choose a reference point, click one of the reference point handles in the Transform palette. These reference point handles refer to the corresponding selection handles on the bounding box of the selected object. A centre reference point is also available. The selected reference point goes solid.

Repositioning an object

1 Enter values in the X and/or Y entry fields. The X value positions the reference point from the left edge of the page; the Y value positions the object from the bottom of the page (assuming that the zero point has not been changed).

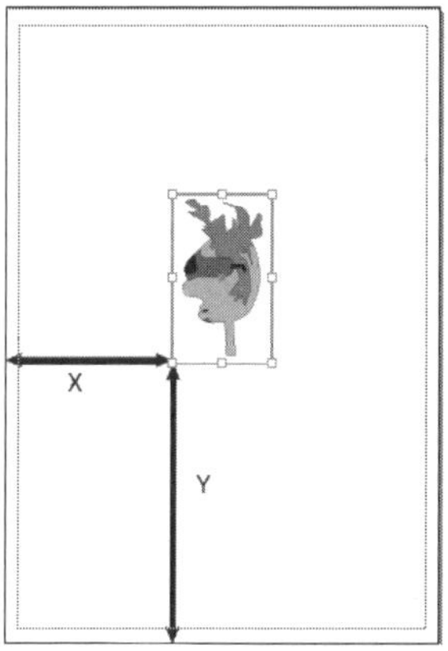

2 Press Return/Enter to apply the change.

Scaling an object

1. Enter the exact dimensions for width and height in the W and H fields to scale the object to that size.

Select an object(s) before you make any changes to the fields in the Transform palette, otherwise nothing will happen.

2. Press Return/Enter to apply the change.

Rotating an object

1. Enter a value in the Rotate entry field, or use the pop-up to choose from the preset list. You can enter positive or negative number from 0 to 360 degrees.

2. Press Return/Enter to apply the change.

Press the Enter/Return key to apply any new value you enter in the Transform palette.

Shearing an object

1. Enter a value in the Shear entry field, or use the pop-up to choose from the preset list.

2. Press Return/Enter to apply the change.

Bezier Paths and the Pen Tool

Bezier curves are the fundamental building blocks of all objects you create in Adobe Illustrator. An understanding of Bezier curves is essential for working efficiently in Illustrator and if you want to unlock the full creative possibilities of the application. The ideas and techniques associated with working with Bezier curves can take a little while to master, but it is well worth spending the time to do so.

Covers

Chapter Eleven

Bezier Paths

Paths form the skeleton of all the shapes you create in Adobe Illustrator. You can edit anchor points, curve and line segments and you can also adjust direction points which control the shape and length of curve segments.

You can apply a fill and/or stroke to an open or closed path. (See Chapter Six, Working with Colour.)

Points and Line Segments

A path consists of two or more anchor points joined by curve or straight line segments.

Open Paths

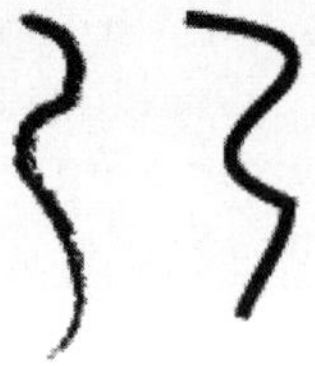

Create open paths using the Pen, Pencil and Brush tools and the Spiral tool. The start and end points of an open path do not join up.

Closed Paths

Create closed paths using tools such as the Oval, Rectangle, Star, and Polygon tools. These tools automatically create a closed path. You can also create closed paths using the Brush and Pencil tools (see Chapter Four) and the Pen tool (see page 147).

You must use the Direct-selection tool to edit the anchor points which form a path.

Anchor points

Illustrator sets anchor points automatically when you create most paths. Using the Pen tool you can control exactly where anchor points are created and which type of anchor point you create. Anchor points help define the exact shape of the path. You can edit anchor points to change the shape of the path.

Direction points and lines

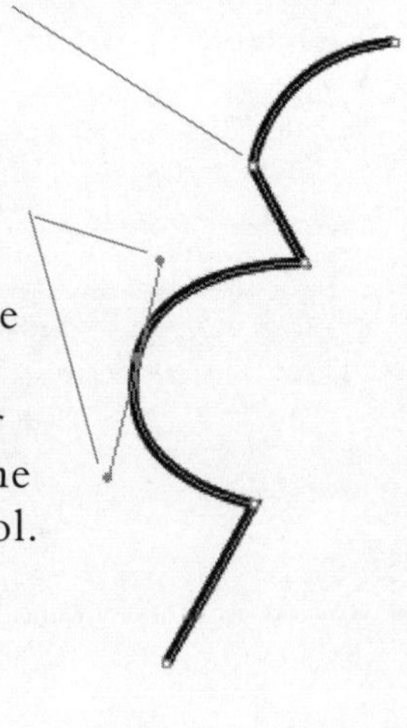

Anchor points connecting curve segments have associated direction points, joined to the anchor point by a direction line. Direction points control two aspects of the curve – its length and direction. The direction points associated with an anchor point become visible when you click on the anchor point with the Direct-selection tool.

The Pen Tool

When you start to draw an open path, if there is a Fill colour set in the Toolbox, Illustrator fills the path along an imaginary line running from one end point to the other. If you find this disconcerting, set the Fill box to none before you start to use the Pen tool.

Hold down Shift, then click to constrain segments to vertical, horizontal or multiples of 45 degrees.

You can use both the above techniques to create paths consisting of curve and straight line segments.

Use the Pen tool to create open or closed paths. Using the Pen tool gives you complete control over where anchor points are positioned and the type of anchor point that is created. You can use the Pen tool to create straight line segments, curve segments, or a mixture of both.

1 To create a straight line segment, select the Pen tool. Position your cursor on the page, then click. This sets the first anchor point. Move the cursor to a new position (do not press and drag), and then click. This sets the next anchor point and a line segment is drawn between the anchor points. Continue the procedure to create as many straight line segments as you need.

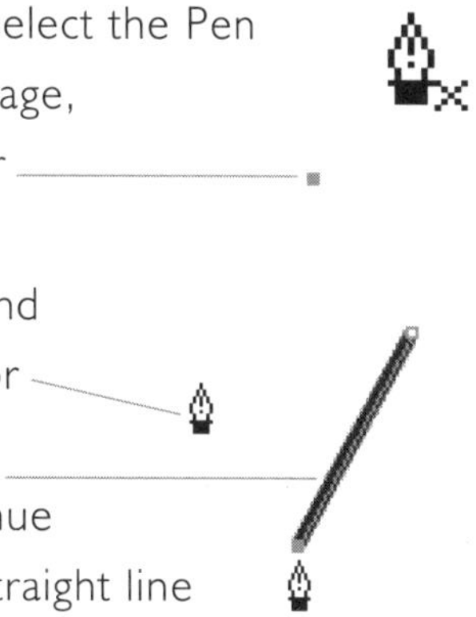

2 To finish drawing the path, either position your cursor back at the start point (a small loop appears with the cursor), then click to create a closed path. Or, click on the Pen tool (or any other tool) in the Toolbox to create an open path. You can also choose Edit > Deselect All to create an open path.

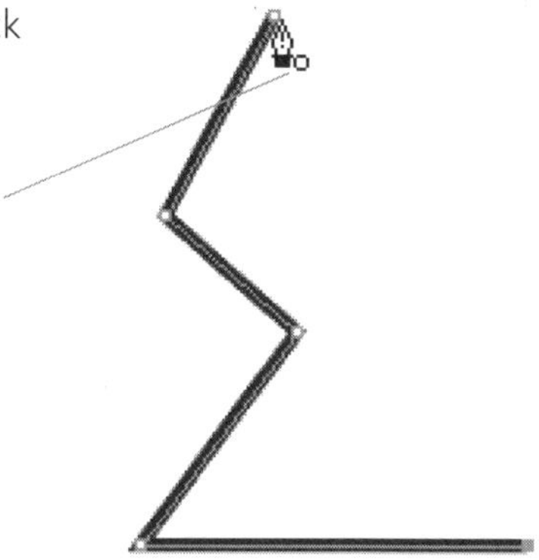

To make adjustments to a path as you draw it, hold down Command/Ctrl to temporarily access the Direct-selection tool. Make adjustments, then release the Command/Ctrl key to continue drawing the path with the Pen tool.

3 To create Curve segments, select the Pen tool. Position your cursor on the page, then press and drag. This action sets the first anchor point and defines its associated direction points.

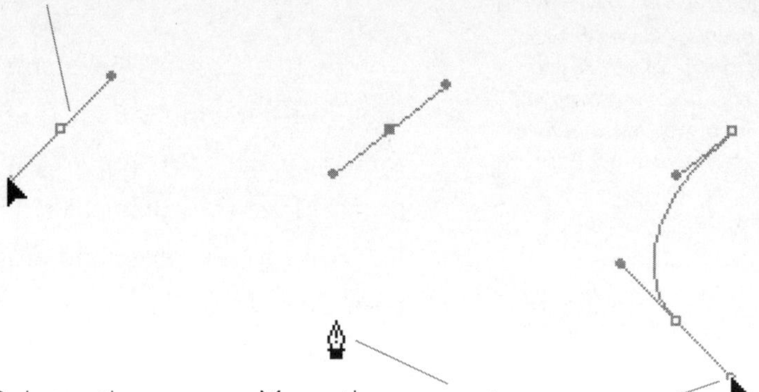

Release the mouse. Move the cursor to a new position. Press and drag to set another anchor point and to define the associated direction points. Continue the procedure to create as many curve segments as you require.

To add straight line or curve segments to an existing path, select an end point using the Direct-selection tool, then select the Pen tool. Click on the end point, or press and drag on the end point, move your cursor to a new position, then continue to press and drag or click to add to the path.

4 To finish drawing the path, either position your cursor back at the start point (a small loop appears with the cursor), then click to create a closed path. Or, click on the Pen tool (or any other tool) in the Toolbox to create an open path. You can also choose Edit > Deselect All to create an open path.

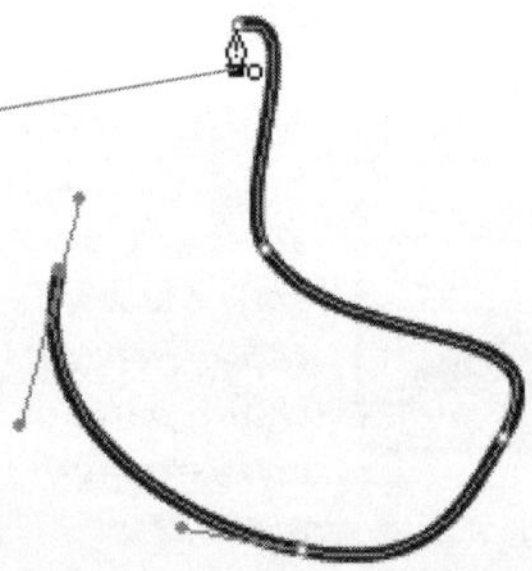

Adding/Deleting Anchor Points

You can add and delete anchor points using the Add-anchor point and Delete-anchor point tools respectively.

1 To add an anchor point to a path, select the Add-anchor point tool: Position your cursor on the path (the path does not have to be selected), then click to add a point. Points added on a curve segment automatically appear with direction points. Points added to straight line segments do not have direction points.

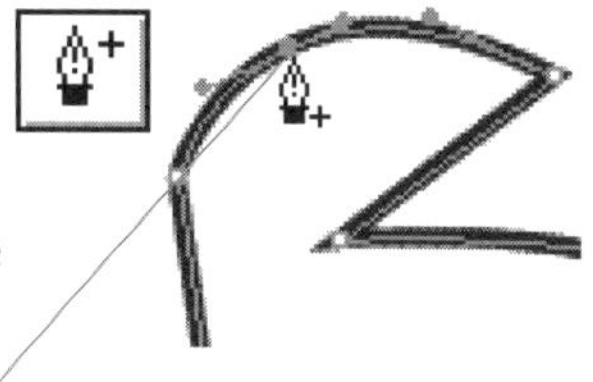

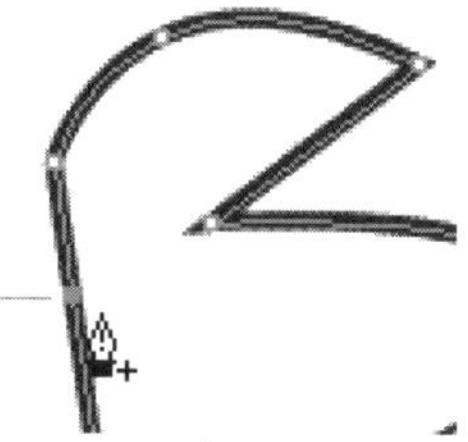

You can add and delete points to basic shapes such as ovals, rectangles, stars, etc.

2 To delete anchor points, make sure the path is selected. Select the Delete-anchor point tool: Position your cursor on an existing anchor point, then click to delete the point. The path is redrawn without the point.

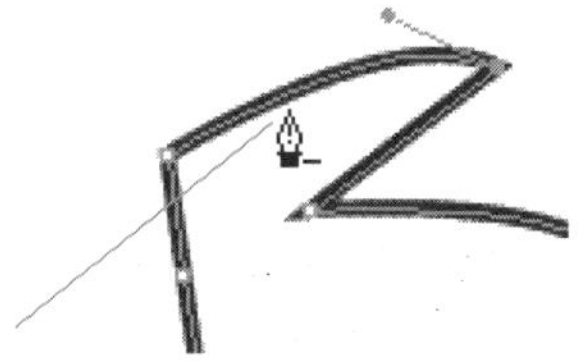

The more points there are in an illustration, the more complex it becomes and the longer it takes to print. It is always a good idea to work with as few points as necessary to achieve the shapes you require. This helps to ensure trouble-free output.

Using the Pen tool to add and delete points

1 Select a path, using one of the selection tools. Select the Pen tool. Position your cursor on a curve or straight line segment. The cursor changes to the Add-anchor point cursor. Click to add an anchor point.

2 Alternatively, position your cursor on an existing anchor point. The cursor changes to the Delete-anchor point cursor. Click to delete the anchor point. The path is redrawn accordingly.

Selecting Anchor Points

A selected point is represented by a solid square; an anchor point that is not selected is represented as a hollow square.

To achieve the exact path you want you will typically need to edit the path. To do this you must select and manipulate anchor points and direction points. Use the Direct-selection tool to select and manipulate points.

You can use the Direct-selection tool or the Direct-lasso tool to marquee-select multiple points. Position the Direct-selection tool cursor outside the path, then press and drag to define the selection marquee (dotted rectangle).

Points included in the marquee area are selected when you release the mouse button. You can create a more freeform, irregular selection of points using the Direct-lasso tool.

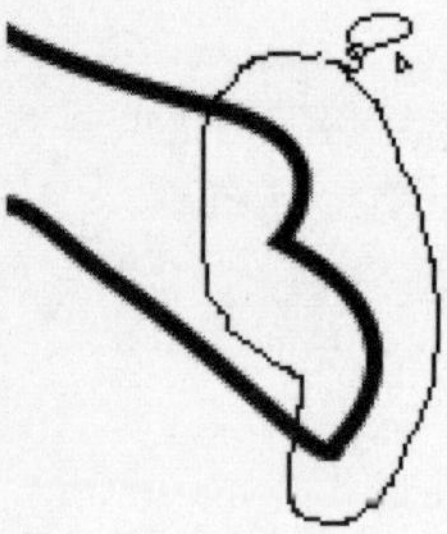

1. To select anchor points, select the Direct-selection tool. If the path you want to edit is already selected, click away from the object to deselect the shape. Click back on the path. The path is selected and anchor points should appear as hollow squares. If you click on a curve segment, direction lines may also appear. (If you use the Direct-selection tool and click in the fill area of a filled path you will select the object as if you are using the Selection tool. This means you will not be able to click on individual anchor points to select them.)

2. Click on an anchor point to select it. If the anchor point has associated direction points they will appear when you select the anchor point. A selected point is represented by a solid square.

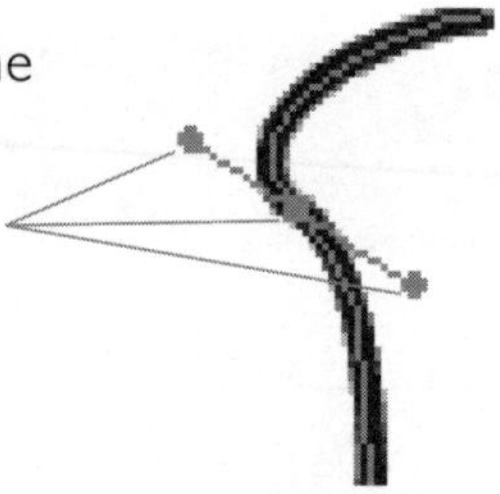

3. To select more than one anchor point, select the first point, then hold down Shift and click on the other points you want to add to the selection. Direction points disappear when you select more than one anchor point.

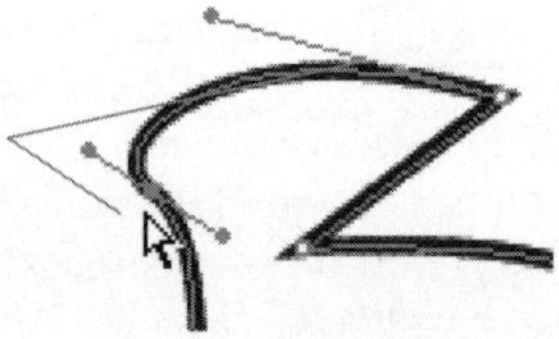

Editing Anchor Points and Segments

Once you have selected the anchor point(s) you want to work on, you can then make changes to the shape by repositioning the anchor points. You edit anchor points using the Direct-selection tool.

1. To edit anchor points, first select the anchor point(s) you want to work on. Still using the Direct-selection tool, position your cursor on the point then press and drag to reposition the point(s). The path is redrawn accordingly.

If all the anchor points are solid, dragging an anchor point will move the entire path, not individual points. If this happens, click away from the object to deselect it, then click back on the path (not the fill).

2. Start to drag the point, then hold down the Shift key to constrain the movement of the point(s) vertically, horizontally or at increments of 45 degrees.

3. Or, with the point(s) selected, press the arrow keys on the key board to nudge the points in 1 point increments.

4. Alternatively, position your cursor on a curve or straight line segment, then press and drag to edit the shape of the path.

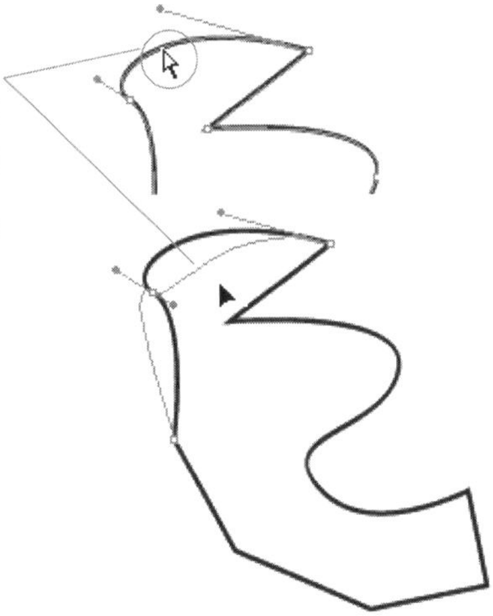

Using the Reshape Tool

The Reshape tool enables you to select sections of a path consisting of more than one anchor point and adjust them globally, maintaining the overall shape of the path.

1. To adjust a path using the Reshape Tool, use the Direct-selection tool to select the points you want to edit.

2. Select the Reshape tool.

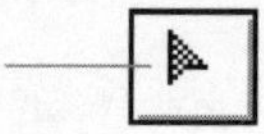

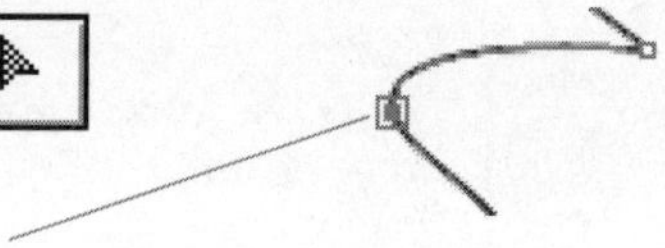

3. Position your cursor on one of the selected points, then click. This becomes the focal point for the changes you make.

4. Drag the focal point to adjust the path, maintaining the overall shape for the selected portion of the path.

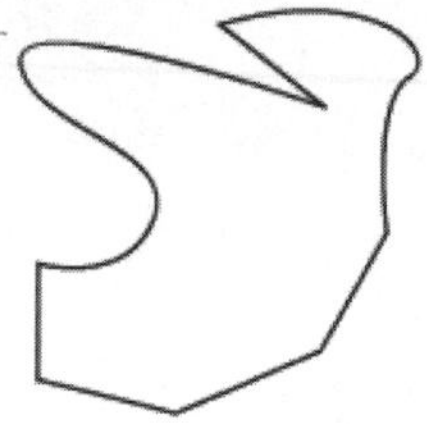

5. You can hold down Shift, then click on additional points if you want to create several focal points for the reshape operation.

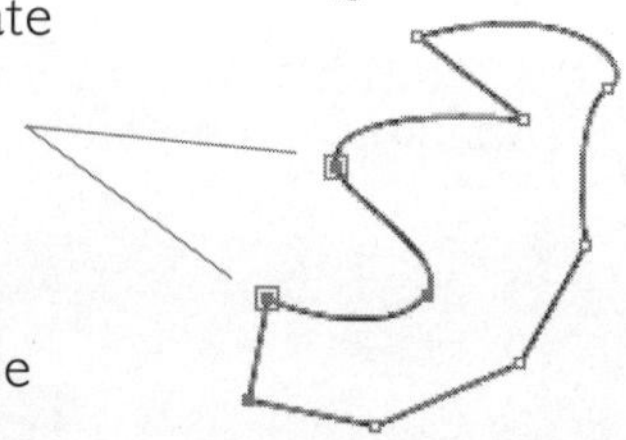

6. If you click on a curve or straight line segment with the Reshape tool, a new anchor point is added to the path.

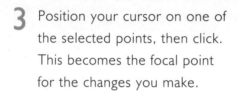

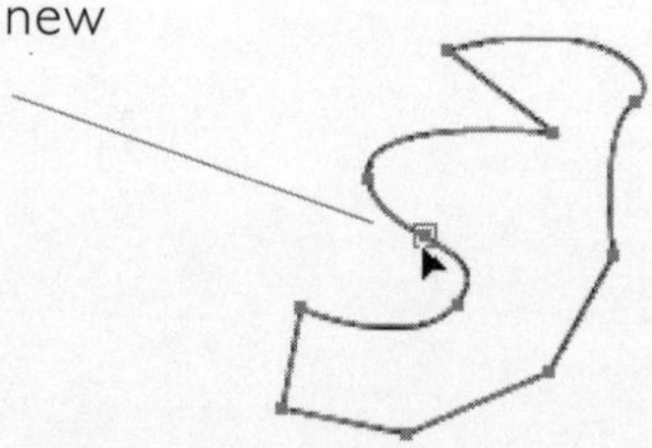

Editing Direction Points

When you click on an anchor point with a curve segment entering or leaving the point, you will also see one or two direction points associated with the anchor point. These control the length and shape of the curve segments.

Use the Direct-selection tool to edit direction points.

As you drag to reposition a direction point you will see a preview of the new shape of the path, indicated as a blue preview line.

1 To edit direction points, first select the curve point on which you want to work. When you click on an anchor point on a curve, direction points appear. Direction points control the length and shape of a curve segment.

Hold down Shift, then drag a direction point to constrain the movement of the point to vertical, horizontal or 45 degree increments.

2 Drag a direction point further away from the anchor point to increase the length of the curve segment. Drag the direction point closer to the anchor point to make the curve segment shorter.

3 Drag a direction point in a circular direction to change the angle at which the curve leaves or enters the point. This changes the shape of the curve segment.

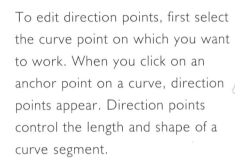

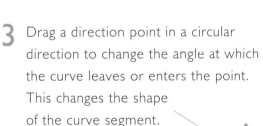

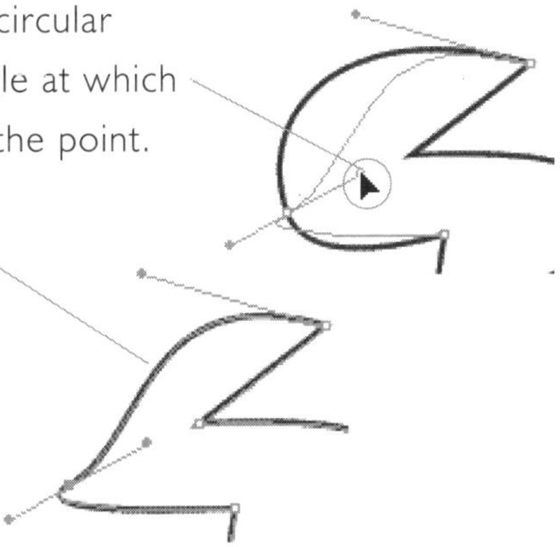

Smooth and Corner Points

Use the Direct-selection tool to edit Anchor points and Direction Points.

It is important to be able to identify and work with two kinds of anchor points – Smooth and Corner. You can identify each type by the way in which the associated direction points work.

Smooth Points

1. Select the point. Two direction points appear, connected to the anchor point by direction lines. Position your cursor on a direction point. Press and drag in a circular direction around the anchor point. The opposite direction point balances the move you make to the point, maintaining the precise alignment of both direction points in a straight line and guaranteeing the smooth transition of the curve through the anchor point.

Smooth points guarantee a smooth, continuous transition of the curve segments through the point.

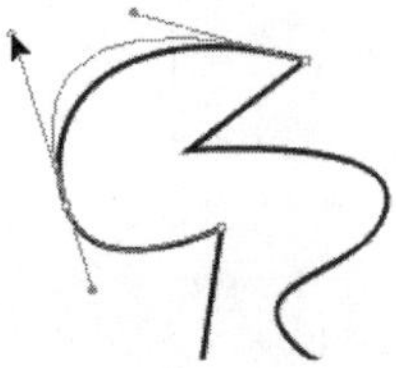

2. If you drag a direction point further away from or closer to the anchor point, the distance of the opposing direction point from the anchor point does not change.

Corner points are essential when you want to create a sharp change in direction at the anchor point.

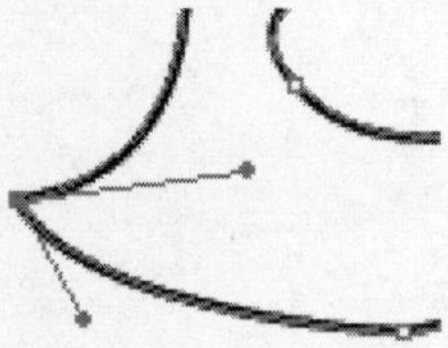

Corner Points

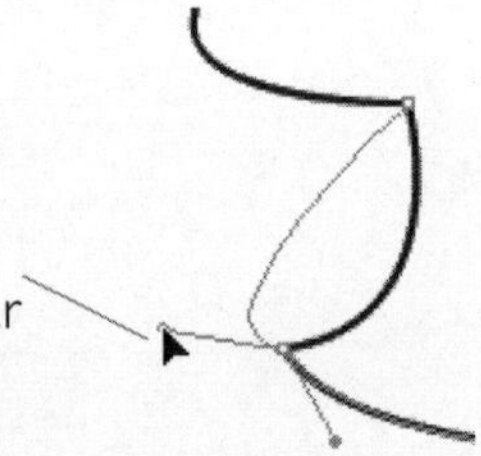

1. Select the point. Two direction points appear, connected to the anchor point by direction lines. Position your cursor on a direction point. Press and drag in a circular direction around the anchor point. The opposite direction point does not move. When you edit the direction points of a Corner point each direction point works completely independently of the other. This is what enables the sharp change in direction at the point.

Converting Points

Use the Convert-direction-point tool to convert points from smooth to corner and vice versa. You can also use the Convert-direction point tool to retract direction points for smooth or corner points and also to convert a retracted anchor point to a smooth point.

It is a good idea to get into the habit of selecting the Direct-selection tool immediately after converting a point if you want to make further edits to either the anchor point itself or its direction points. If you don't do this, you run the risk of undoing the conversion unintentionally.

Converting Smooth to Corner

1. To convert a smooth point to a corner point, use the Direct-selection tool to select a smooth point. Select the Convert-direction-point tool.

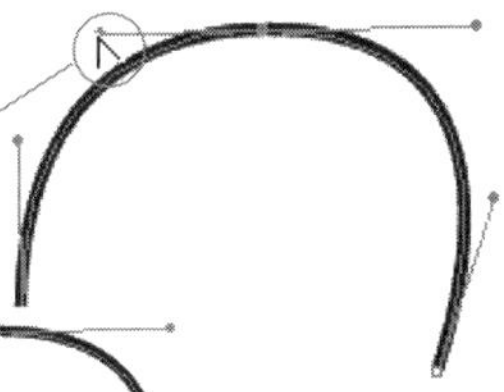

2. Position your cursor on a direction point. Drag the direction point to convert the point to a corner point.

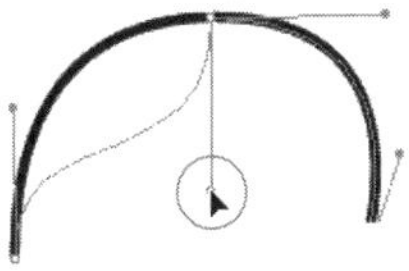

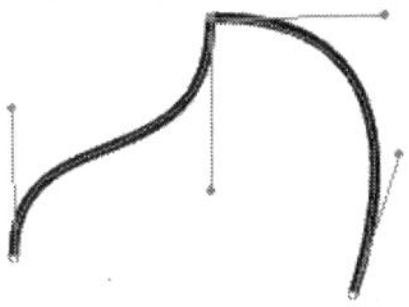

Converting Corner to Smooth

1. To convert a corner point to a smooth point, use the Direct-selection tool to select a corner point.

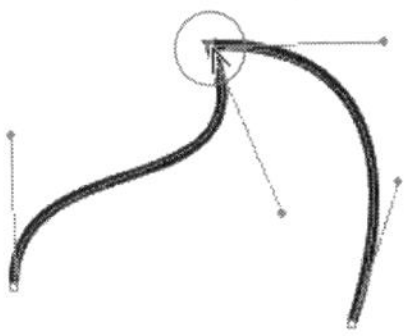

2. Select the Convert-direction-point tool. Position the cursor on the selected anchor point. Drag off the anchor point to define the shape of the smooth curve.

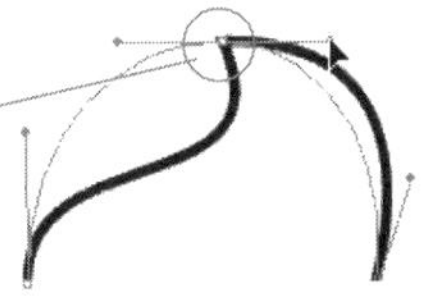

3 Select the Direct-selection tool if you want to make further changes to the anchor point or its direction points. If you continue to use the convert-direction-point tool you may re-convert the point back to a corner point.

Retracting Direction Points

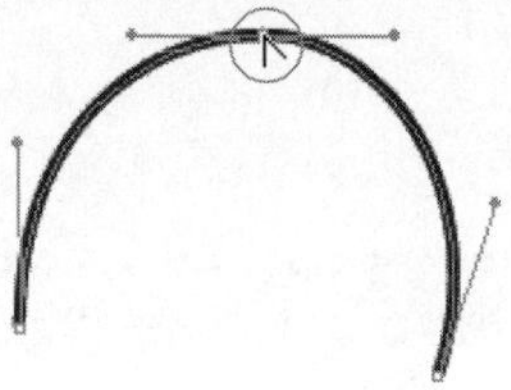

1 To retract direction points, select a smooth or corner point using the Direct-selection tool.

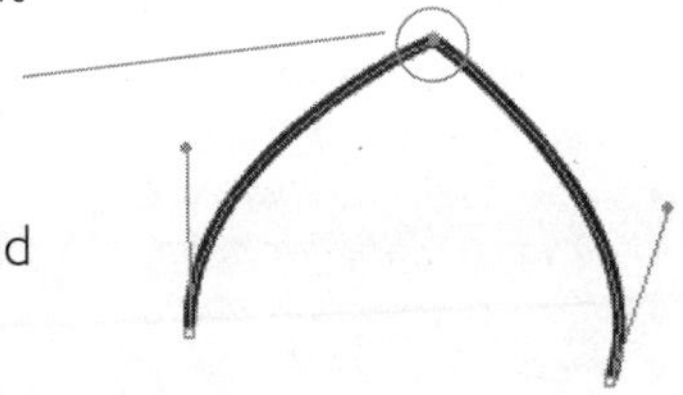

2 Select the Convert-direction-point tool. Position your cursor on the anchor point. Click to retract the direction points. The incoming and outgoing curve segments are redrawn accordingly.

Creating a Smooth Point from a Retracted Point

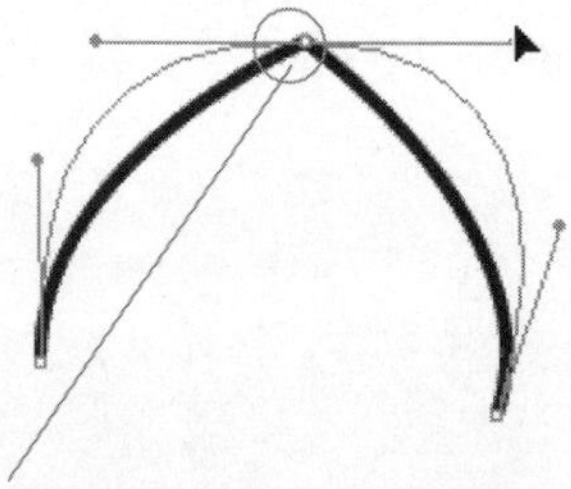

1 To convert a retracted point into a smooth point, select the retracted point using the Direct Selection tool.

2 Select the Convert-direction-point tool. Position your cursor on the retracted anchor point (one with no direction points). Drag off the point to create a smooth point.

Gradients and Gradient Meshes

A gradient fill is a gradual colour transition from one colour to another. You can also create multi-colour gradients. Use the Gradient palette to create custom gradients and the Gradient tool to control the length and direction of the gradient.

A gradient mesh allows you to fill an object with multiple colours that blend into one another in smooth gradients.

Covers

Chapter Twelve

Applying a Gradient Fill

A gradient fill is a gradual colour transition from one colour to another. You can also create and apply multi-colour gradients. Use the Gradient palette to create custom gradients and the Gradient tool to control the length and direction of the gradient.

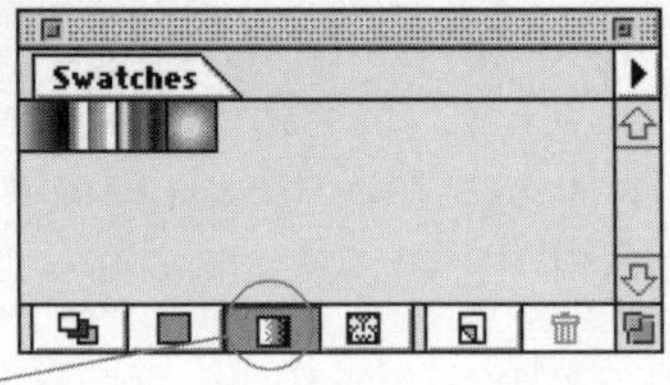

The default Adobe Illustrator start-up file contains sample of gradient fills. Click the Show Gradients button in the Swatches palette to see only available gradients in the Swatches palette.

You cannot apply a gradient fill to text until you have converted the text to outlines.

1 To apply a gradient, select an object via the Selection tool.

2 Click the Fill box in the Toolbox to make it active. Then, click on an existing gradient fill in the Swatches palette.

3 Or, click the Gradient button (>), below the Fill/Stroke boxes in the Toolbox. This shows the Gradient palette and applies the current gradient to the selected object.

Using the Gradient Tool

Hold down Shift as you drag the gradient tool to constrain it to multiples of 45 degrees.

1 Make sure the object remains selected. Select the Gradient tool. Position your cursor on the object. Press and drag. As you do so you will see a line. This line determines the direction and length of the gradient. For a linear gradient, the start and end colours fill any part of the object you do not drag the line over. For radial gradients, the end colour fills the remaining area of the object.

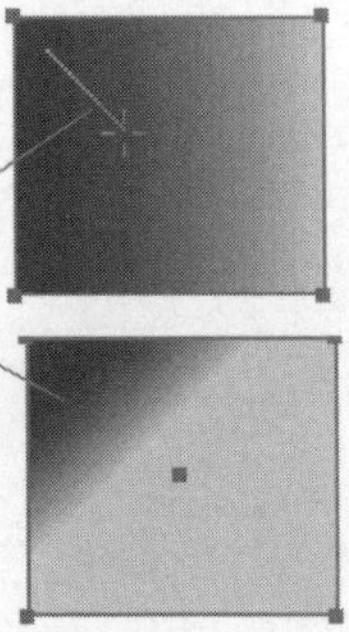

Creating a Gradient Fill

Use the Gradient palette to create custom/multicolour gradients. Save custom gradients in the Swatches palette.

1 To create a gradient, select an object using the Selection tool. Click the Fill box in the Toolbox.

If the Start and End colour icons do not appear in the palette below the Gradient Ramp, click on the ramp. The colour icons will appear.

2 Choose Window > Show Gradient, then Show Options from the pop-up in the Gradient palette. Choose Linear or Radial from the Type pop-up.

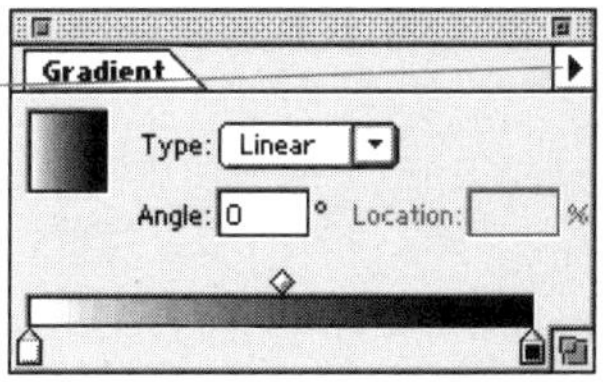

3 Click the Start colour icon – the 'roof' highlights. Mix a colour using the colour palette. The colour is applied to the gradient immediately.

Hold down Alt, then click on a colour in the Swatches palette to apply a colour to a selected Start/End colour icon.

4 Or, you can drag an existing colour swatch from the Swatches palette onto the Start colour icon.

5 Repeat the process for the End colour icon.

6 Choose Radial or Linear from the Type pop-up. A Radial gradient uses the start colour at the centre of the gradient.

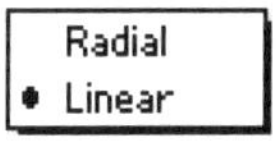

7 Specify an angle for a Linear gradient. Press Return/Enter to apply the change.

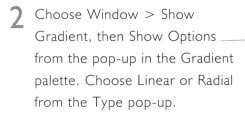

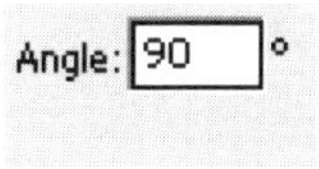

8 You can drag the Start/End colour icons to new positions on the Gradient Ramp to control the way the gradient works.

9 Drag the Mid-point slider to change the mid-point of the gradient – where both colours are at 50%.

10 Alternatively, click on one of the Start/End or Midpoint icons, then enter a value in the location field to specify an exact location for the icon.

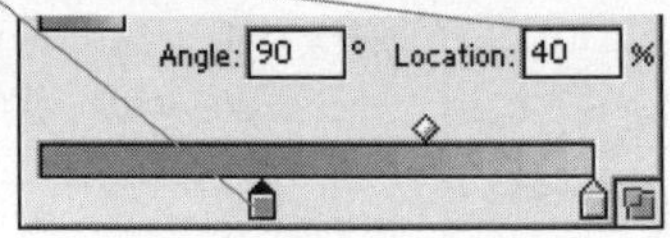

11 To save the gradient for future use, either drag the gradient fill box from the Gradient palette into the Swatches palette, or as long as the gradient currently appears in the Fill box, click the New Swatch button in the Swatches palette.

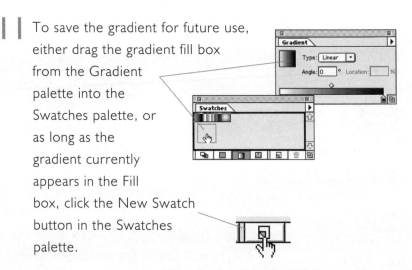

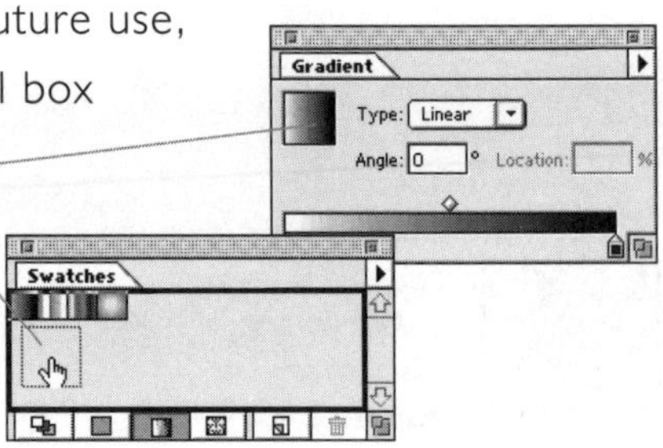

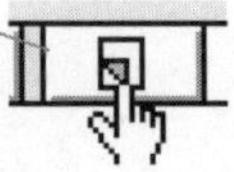

BEWARE

You can create gradients between different colour modes, e.g. a Process colour to a Spot colour, but mixed-mode gradients are converted to CMYK Process colours when printed or separated.

Creating a Gradient Mesh Object

Mesh objects cannot be converted back into standard paths. Make a copy of an object before converting it to a Mesh object so that you can return to the original path if required.

The Gradient Mesh tool provides a precise method for creating subtle colour transitions within an object. In a mesh object you can have multiple colours flowing in different directions with smooth colour transitions. You can easily and precisely adjust and manipulate multiple colour shifts using the mesh which defines areas of colour.

1 To create a Mesh object, select an object. Click on the Gradient Mesh tool:

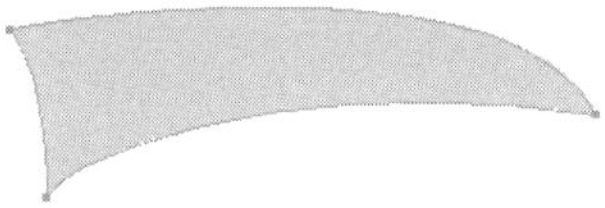

2 Place your cursor in the object. The cursor changes to the Gradient Mesh cursor.

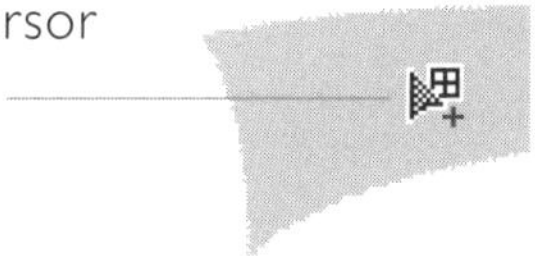

3 Click. A Mesh point is added together with mesh lines which divide the original path into areas referred to as patches. The curvature of the mesh lines depends on the shape of the path of the original object.

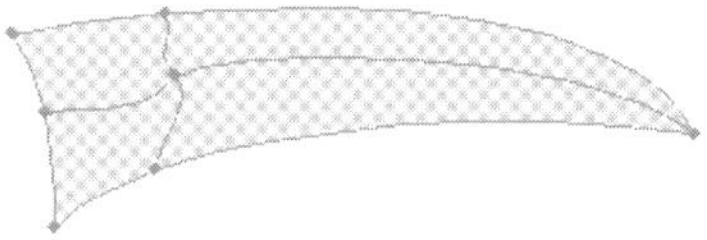

Keep mesh objects as simple as possible. Complex gradient mesh objects can slow performance, especially screen redraw. To maintain adequate performance it is better to create a number of mesh objects, rather than one large, complex mesh object.

4 To add further mesh points, select the Mesh tool, then, either click on a mesh line to create another mesh point on the line, or click elsewhere within the object to create a new series of mesh line divisions.

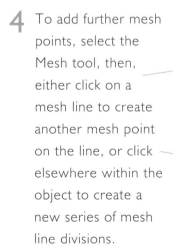

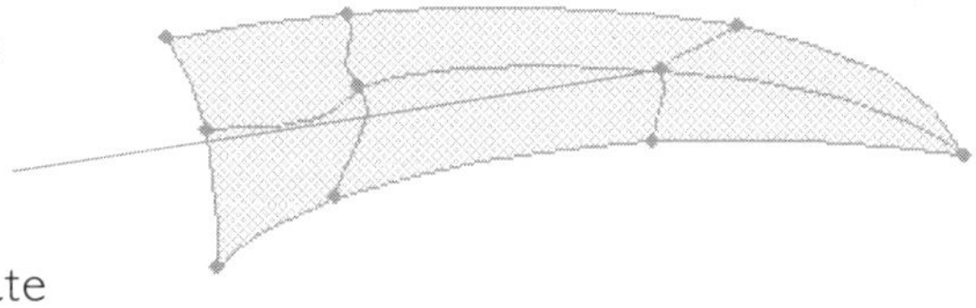

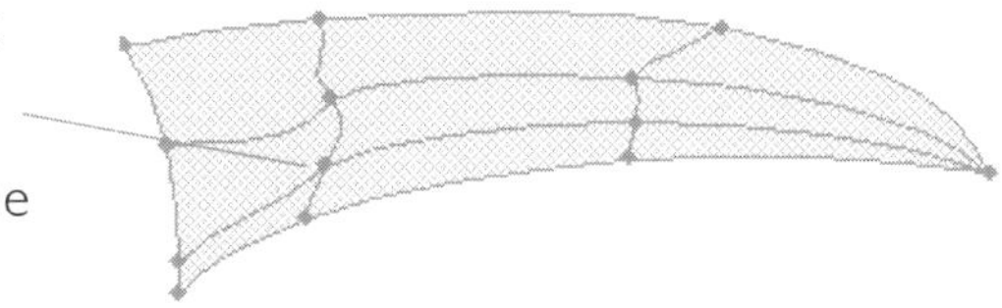

You cannot create gradient mesh objects from compound paths, text or placed EPS files.

Adding Colour to a Gradient Mesh

There is a variety of techniques for adding colour to a gradient mesh. You can select a mesh point, then apply colour using the Swatches or Color palette; you can drag and drop colour swatches onto a mesh point or into a mesh patch; and you can also use the Paintbucket tool.

Edit mesh points and mesh lines to change how the mesh gradients flow across the object.

Adding Colour to a Mesh point

1. To add colour to a mesh point, select the Direct-selection or the Gradient Mesh tool.

2. Click on a mesh point to select it. (Make sure that only one mesh point is selected.)

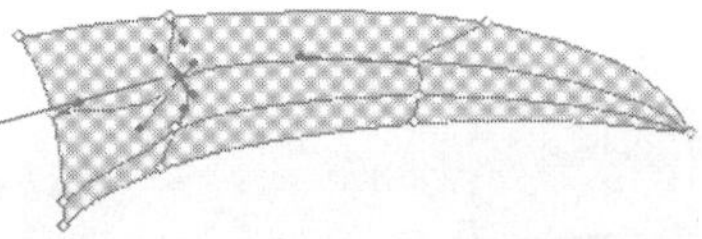

3. Click on a colour swatch in the Swatches palette.

4. To drag and drop colour onto a mesh point, select the mesh object using the Direct selection tool. Drag and drop a colour swatch onto one of the mesh points. Colour is applied to the point and radiates out from the point.

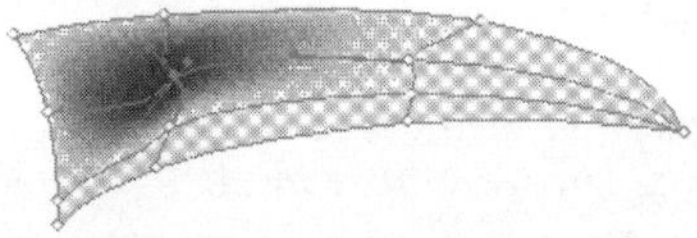

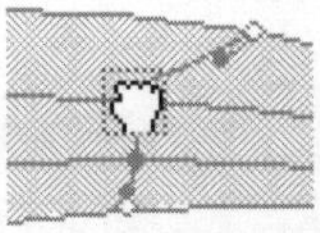

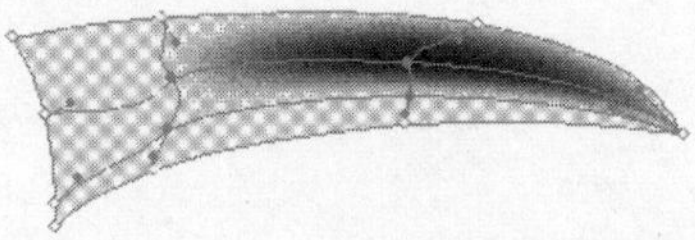

Adding colour to a mesh patch

1 Select the Direct-selection tool, then click on a mesh patch to select it.

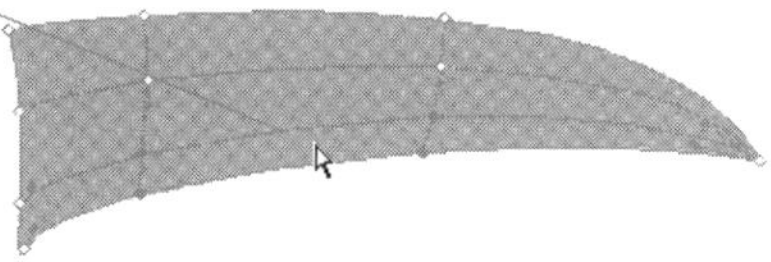

Use Outline view (Command/ Ctrl+Y) if you want to click precisely on a mesh point.

2 Click on a colour swatch in the Swatches palette.

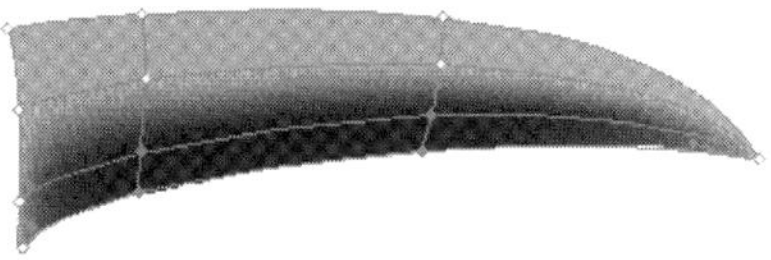

3 To drag and drop colour into a mesh patch, select the mesh object using the Selection or Direct-selection tool. Drag and drop a colour swatch into one of the mesh patches. The new colour fills the mesh patch and forms a colour transition into the neighbouring patches.

Adding colour using the Paintbucket tool

1 Make sure no objects are selected. Click the Foreground colour box, then click on a swatch in the Swatches palette, or use the Color palette to create the colour you want to use.

2 Select the Gradient Mesh object with the Selection or Direct-selection tool. Select the Paint Bucket tool. Click on a mesh patch or mesh point to apply the colour.

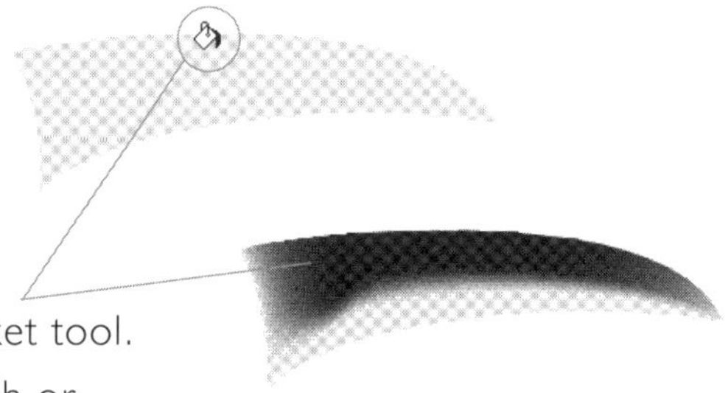

Editing a Gradient Mesh

Once you have created a mesh object you can edit mesh points to control the spread of colour in the shape.

It is best not to select a gradient mesh object with the Gradient Mesh tool as, in doing so, you will add new mesh lines.

1 To edit a mesh point, select a single mesh point using the Direct-selection tool. Four direction lines appear at the mesh point (see pages 153 for editing direction lines).

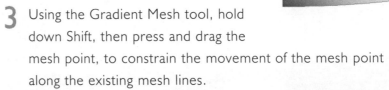

2 Select the Gradient Mesh tool for further editing of the mesh point, or continue to use the Direct-selection tool. Position your cursor on the selected mesh point, then press and drag to reposition the mesh point. The mesh lines are reshaped accordingly.

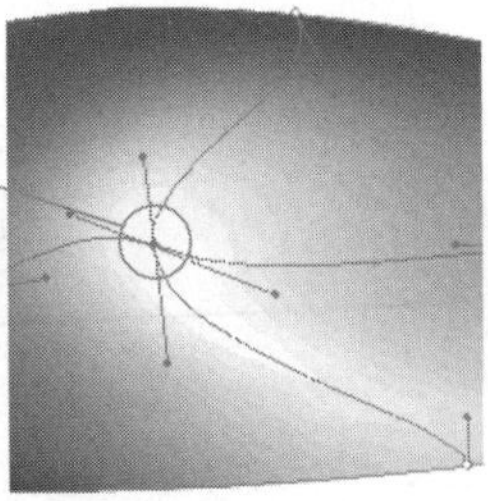

Editing mesh points and mesh lines follows the same basic principles as editing anchor points and direction lines. (See page 153.) You can edit mesh points using the Gradient Mesh tool, but be careful not to inadvertently create additional mesh lines.

3 Using the Gradient Mesh tool, hold down Shift, then press and drag the mesh point, to constrain the movement of the mesh point along the existing mesh lines.

4 Place the cursor on direction points, then drag to edit the shape of the mesh lines. Or hold down Shift then drag a direction point to rotate all direction lines uniformly at the same time.

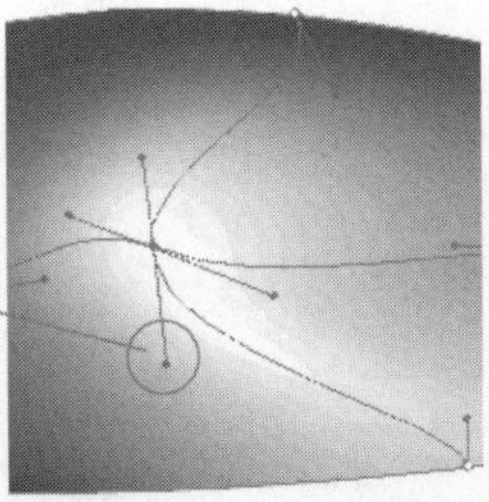

You can also use the Direct-selection tool and Convert-selection point tool to edit mesh points.

Deleting a Mesh Point

1 Select a mesh object using the Selection or Direct-selection tool. Select the Gradient Mesh tool. Hold down Alt, then click on the mesh point you want to delete.

Graphs

There are nine graph types to choose from in Adobe Illustrator. They are: Column, Stacked column, Bar, Stacked bar, Line, Area, Scatter, Pie and Radar graphs.

This chapter uses the example of a simple Column graph to demonstrate the principles of creating graphs in Adobe Illustrator.

Covers

Chapter Thirteen

Creating a Column Graph

The initial procedure for creating graphs is the same for all graph types available in Illustrator. Once created, each graph type can be manipulated and customised using a variety of options dependent on the graph type. The following example shows you how to create a simple Column Graph.

1 To create a column graph, select the Column Graph tool. Position your cursor on the page then click. The Graph dialogue appears. Enter Width/Height values for the graph then click OK.

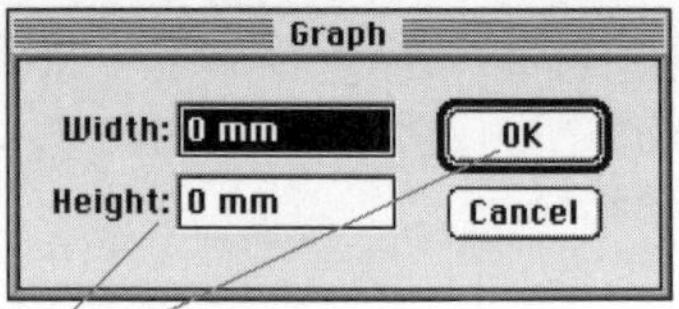

2 Alternatively, select the Column Graph tool, position your cursor, then press and drag to define visually the size for your graph.

3 Enter data for the graph in the Graph Data palette. (See page 167 for information on entering and manipulating data in the Graph Data palette.)

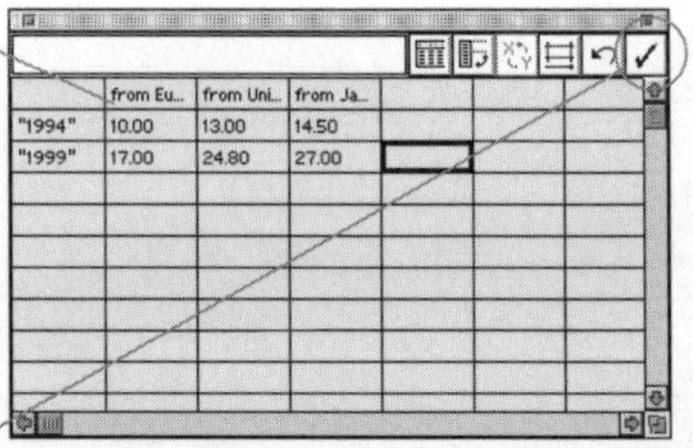

4 Click the Apply button to see the data plotted in the graph. Move the Graph Data palette if necessary to preview the graph in the Illustrator window. Click the Close box (Mac)/Close button (Windows) when you have finished entering data.

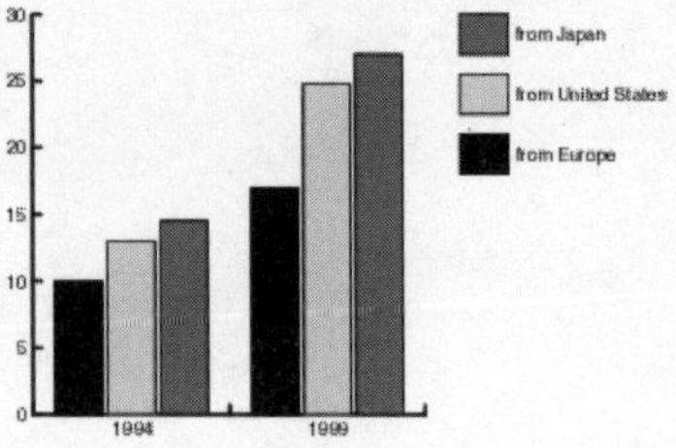

The Graph Data Palette

If you want to use numbers, as in this example, as the category labels, you must enclose the figures within quotation marks, otherwise Illustrator will plot the figures as values in the graph, giving unintended results.

The Graph Data palette offers a spreadsheet-like environment for entering the numerical data and labels used to plot the graph.

1. To enter data, click in a cell to activate it. A thick black border indicates a selected cell.

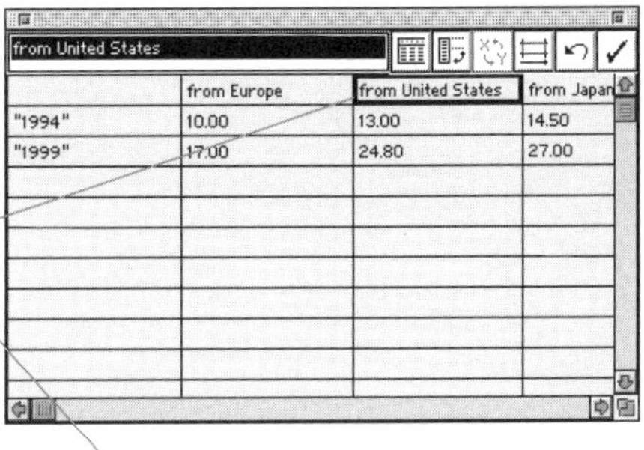

2. Enter numeric data or text labels using the keyboard. Characters or numbers you type appear in the data entry line at the top of the window.

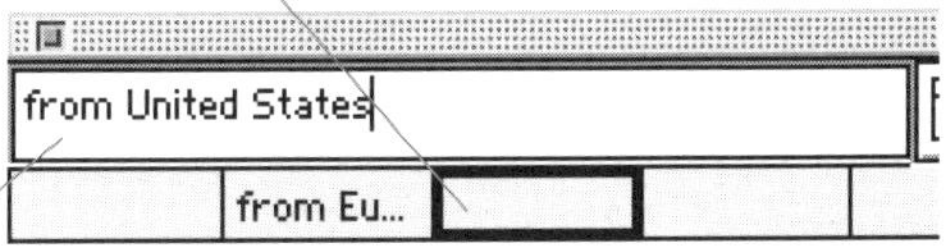

When you first create a new graph, the first cell in the Graph Data palette is highlighted and has a default value of 1. With the cell highlighted, press the Delete key to remove this value.

3. Press the Tab key to accept the entry. The data is entered in to the active cell and the highlight moves to the next cell to the right.

4. Press Return/Enter to move the highlight to the next cell down. Press the arrow keys on your keyboard to move the highlight one cell up/down/left/right.

5. To edit an existing entry, move to the cell so that it is selected, then use the data entry line to make changes as required. Press Return/Enter, Tab or an arrow key to accept the changes and move the highlight to another cell.

Controlling the width of cells

1. To make cells wider, so that long data entries are fully visible, click the Cell Style button. Enter a value for the column Width (up to 20 characters). This has no effect on the proportions of the graph – only how data is displayed in the Graph Data palette.

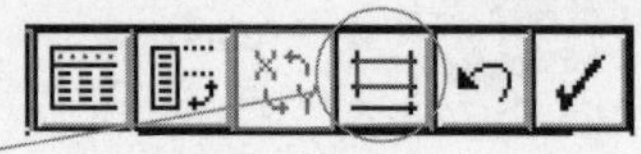

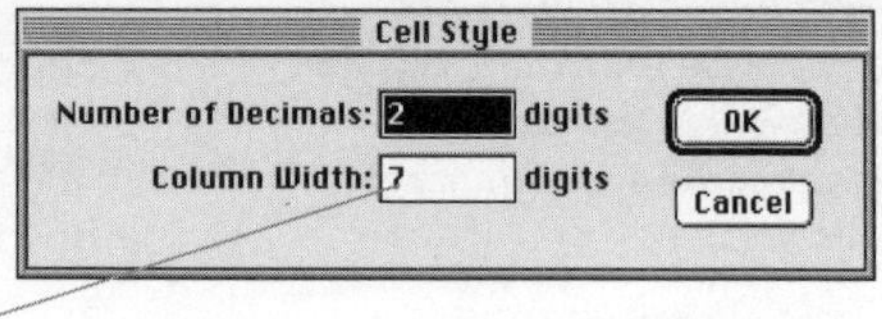

2. Alternatively, position your cursor on a column dividing line. The cursor will change to a bidirectional arrow. Press and drag to change the width of the cell manually.

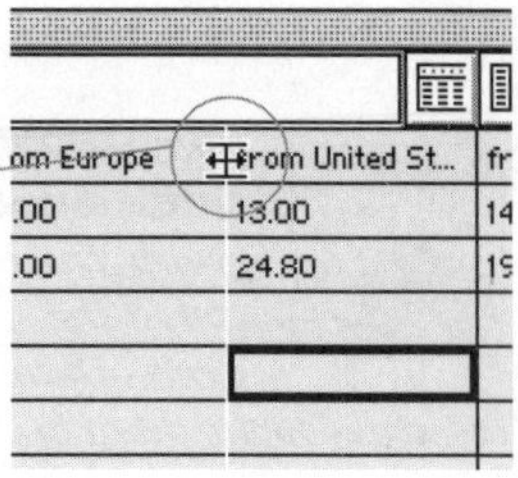

The Graph Type Dialogue Box

The following instructions refer to a Column Graph. Each graph type has options specific to that type of graph.

For each graph type, there is a range of options in the Graph Type dialogue box for customising its appearance. You can also use the Graph Type dialogue box to change the graph type used to plot the data entered in the Graph Data palette. For example, you might decide to change a Column Graph into a Line Graph.

Changing graph types

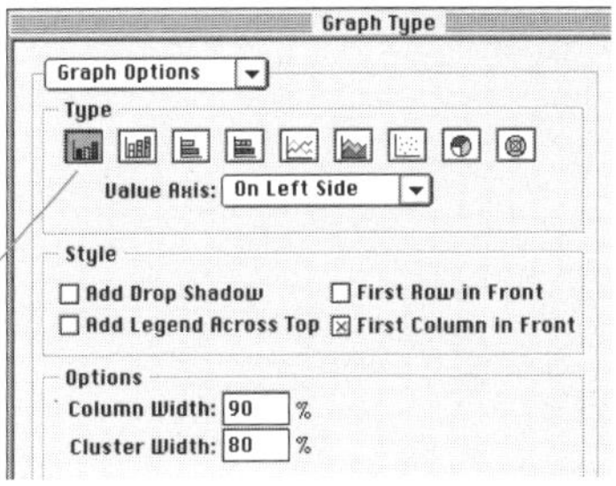

1. Use the Selection tool to select the graph, choose Object > Graph > Type. Click one of the graph type buttons to change the graph to another type.

The type of data and the way you have entered it in the Graph Data palette may mean that when you choose a different graph type you get unexpected or unintended results. For example, changing a Column Graph into a Pie Graph will not produce an acceptable result as the initial presentation of the data for each of these two graph types needs to be different.

Changing Graph Options

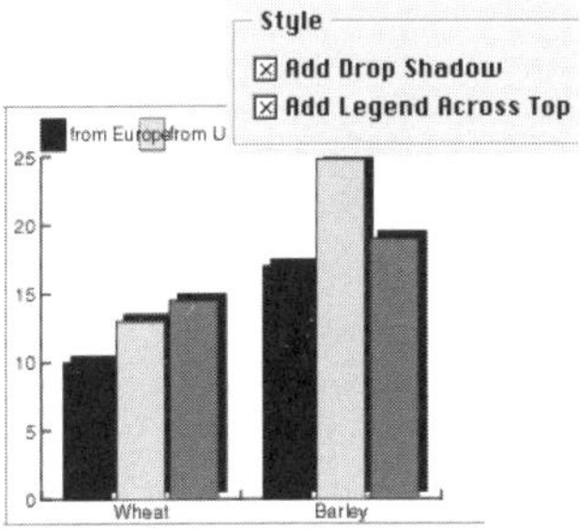

1. Select a chart using the Selection tool. Choose Object > Graph > Type. Make sure the Options pop-up is set to Graph Options.

2. Use Style options to add a standard drop shadow and/or to position the legend across the top of the graph.

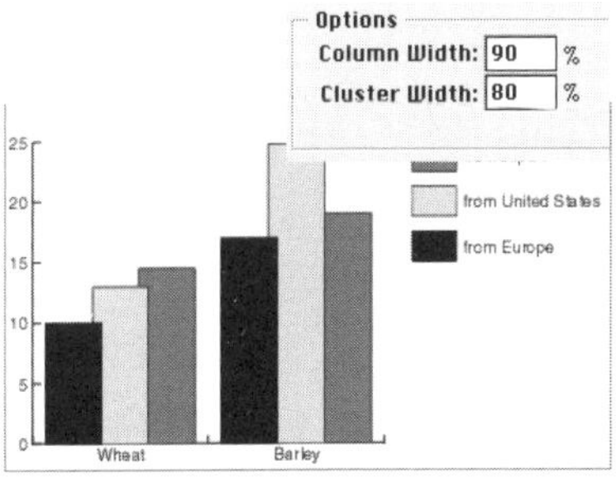

3. Change the Column Width value to change the width of the columns in the graph. Change the Cluster Width value to specify the width taken up by each series of columns.

Changing Value Axis Options

1 Select a chart using the Selection tool. Choose Object > Graph > Type. Set the Options pop-up to Value Axis.

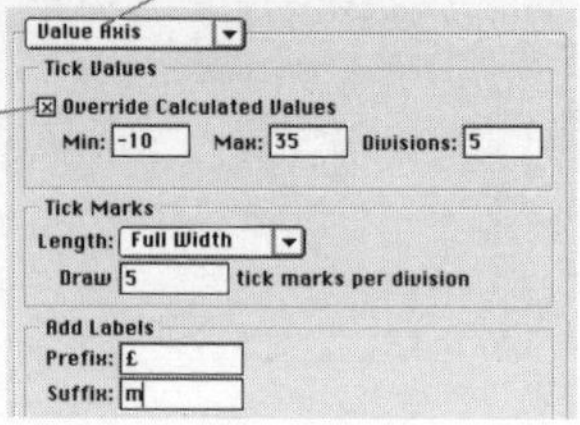

2 Select the Override Calculated Values option. Enter Minimum and Maximum values for the graph. By default, Illustrator calculates the minimum and maximum values from the data entered in the Graph Data palette. Enter a value for divisions to specify the increment used for the value axis.

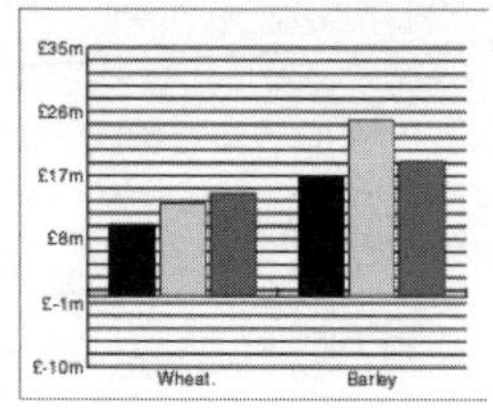

3 Use the Length pop-up to set tick marks to the desired length and specify how many are drawn per increment along the Value axis. Enter Prefix and Suffix labels for the Value axis labels if necessary.

Changing Category Axis Options

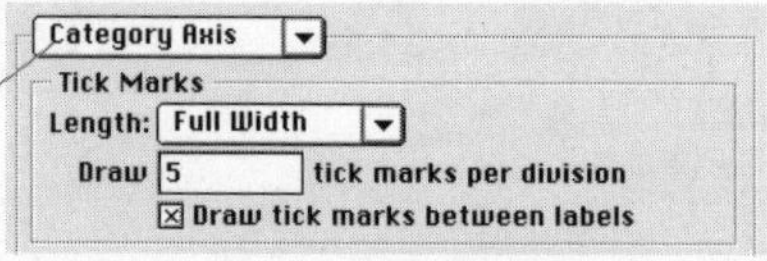

1 Select a chart. Choose Object > Graph > Type. Set the Options pop-up to Category Axis. Use the Length pop-up to set tick marks to the desired length and specify how many are drawn per increment along the axis.

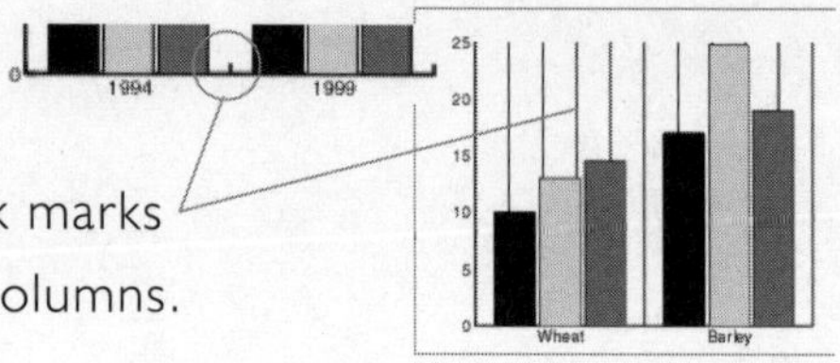

2 Select the Draw Tick Marks between labels option to place tick marks between each series of columns.

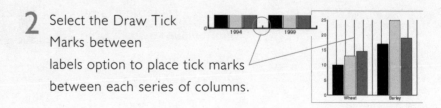

Editing Graph Data

Once you have created a graph you can edit the data and labels entered in the Graph Data palette, and you can change aspects of the graph such as the fill colour of the columns or the stroke colour and weight of lines, as well as the character attributes of text and value labels.

An essential point to understand about the way in which Illustrator creates graphs is that the initial graph consists of a series of grouped objects. As long as the graph remains grouped you can go back into the Graph Data palette (and the Graph Type palette) and edit the data from which the graph is plotted. Any changes you make automatically update the graph when you click on the apply button, or close the Graph Data palette.

However, if you opt to ungroup the graph, the dynamic link between data in the Graph Data palette and the graph is lost.

If you need to ungroup a graph in order to make additional changes to its appearance, as a precaution in case you need to make changes to the data from which the graph is plotted, make a copy of the graph first. The copy will retain a link to the original data and you can make changes to the original.

1. To edit graph data, select the graph using the Selection tool.

2. Choose Object > Graph > Data to show the Graph Data palette.

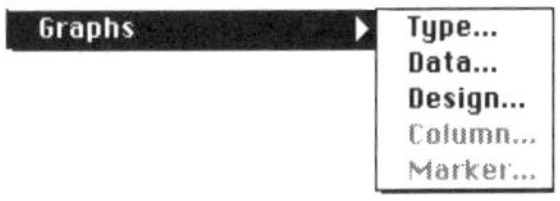

3. Make changes to the data/labels. Click the Apply button to preview changes in the Illustrator window.

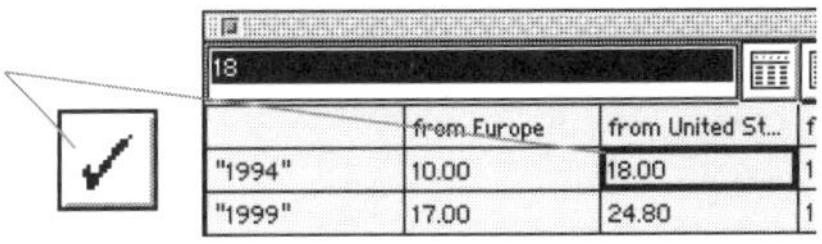

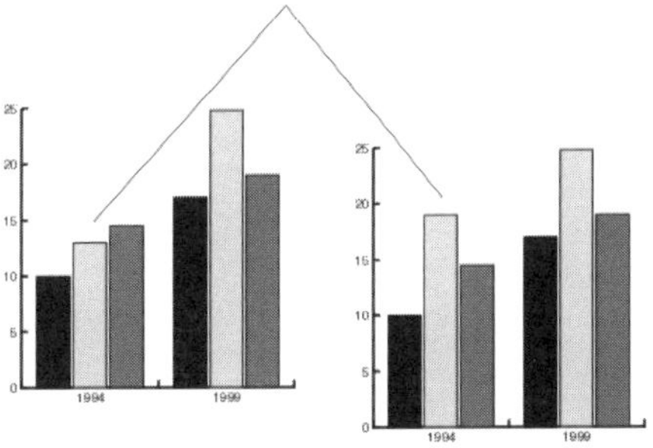

Some graph options such as font size and column markers may revert to their defaults if you make changes to the graph data.

4. Click the Close Box (Mac)/Close button (Windows) to accept the changes. Click the Save button in the Warning dialogue box if you closed the Graph Data palette without first clicking on the Apply button.

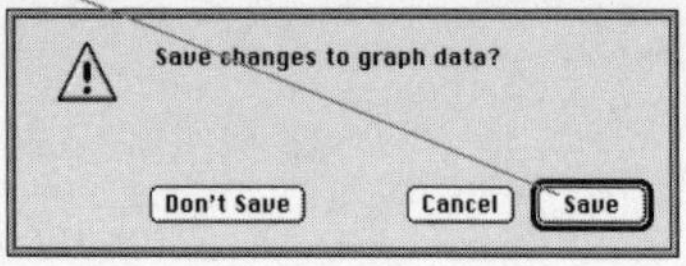

Reverting

1. Click the Revert button – – to return the data in the Graph Data palette to the stage it was at when you last clicked the Apply button.

Changing Graph Attributes

As well as editing the graph data and using the standard options available in the Graph Type dialogue box, you can change aspects of the graph such as the fill colour of the columns or the stroke colour and weight of lines, as well as the character attributes of text and value labels.

Illustrator creates a graph as a series of grouped objects. Use the Group-Selection tool to select related aspects of the graph, e.g. all the value labels or all the columns in a series, before making changes to their position or appearance.

Each time you click on the same object using the Group-selection tool you select upwards through any grouping hierarchy.

1 To change the colour of columns, select the Group-selection tool.

2 Click on the legend box of the series you want to change. The legend box is selected. Click the same legend box again. The columns that are grouped to the legend box are selected.

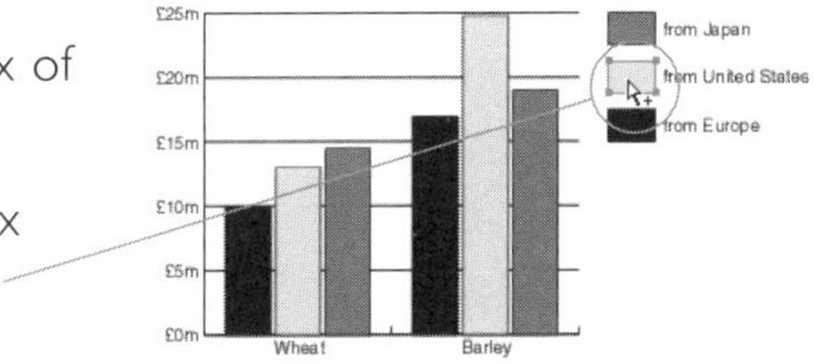

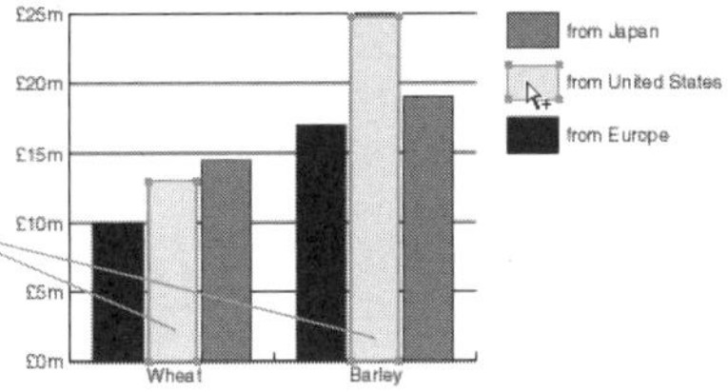

Do not click a third time unless you want to select the entire graph.

3 Make sure the Fill box is selected in the Toolbox. Click on a colour swatch in the Swatches palette to change the colour of the legend box and related columns.

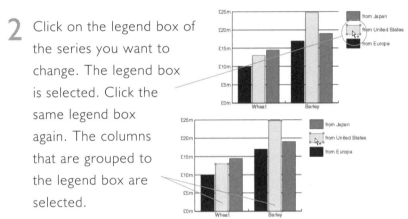

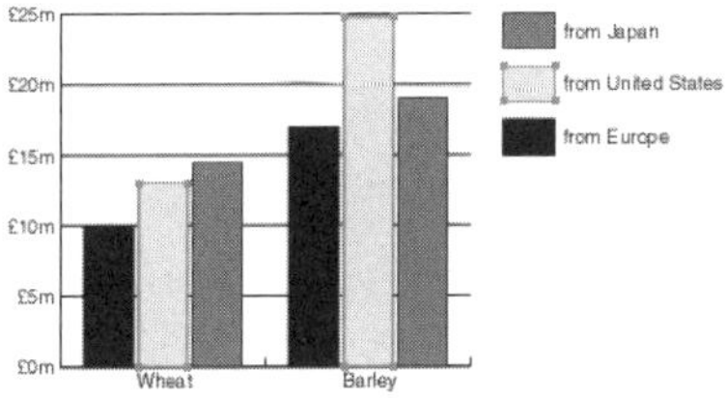

Changing the formatting of category labels

1. Select the Group-selection tool. Click twice on one of the Category labels.

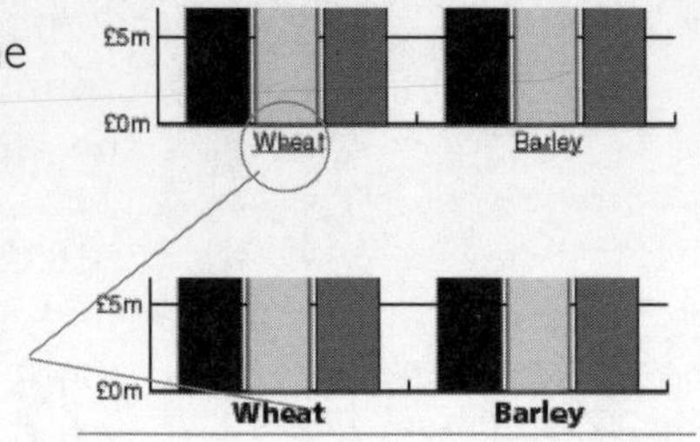

2. Use the Character palette to change the formatting of the labels.

Deleting a set of labels

1. Select the Group-selection tool.

2. Click twice on one of the Category or Value labels.

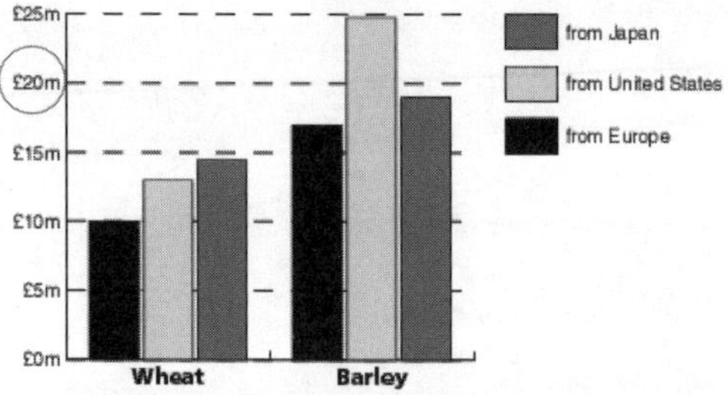

3. Press the delete key.

4. The labels no longer exist

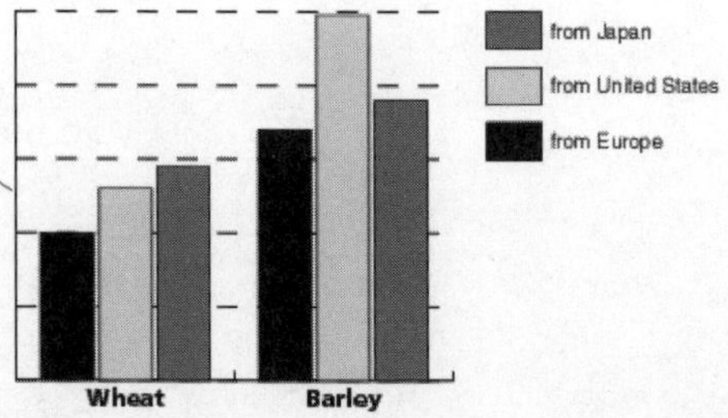

Printing

When you have completed an illustration, or at various stages as you build it, you will need to print a copy of the artwork for basic proofing purposes. This chapter covers the features necessary for printing composite proof copies to a laser printer.

Covers

Chapter Fourteen

Printing Composites – Mac

To create a colour or black and white composite proof of your Illustrator artwork, first use the Page Setup dialogue box to choose from a standard set of printing options, then use the Print dialogue box to print.

When you print a composite, all colours or shades in the file are printed on one sheet of paper.

1 To print a composite proof, choose File > Page Setup.

2 Choose the actual physical size of the paper in your printer onto which you want to print from the Paper Size pop-up.

3 You can enter a value in the Reduce or Enlarge % entry box to increase or decrease the size of the artwork that prints.

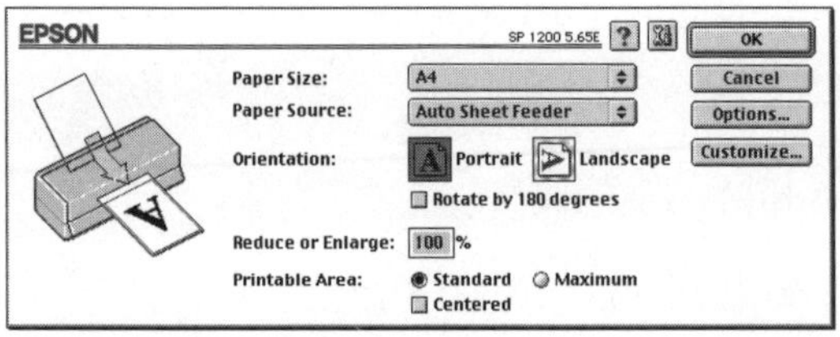

4 Use the Orientation buttons to set the orientation of the page to Portrait or Landscape as necessary.

5 Click the Options button to set further options for your printer as required. Refer to your printer manual for information on the options available. OK the dialogue box.

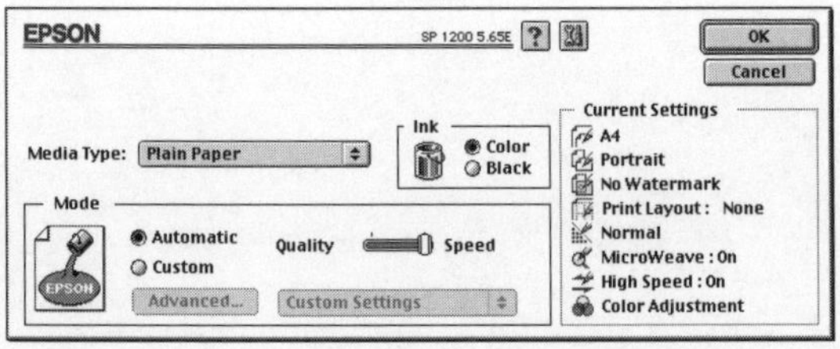

Printing the file

1 Choose File > Print.

2 Specify the number of copies you want to print. If you have more than one page in the document, specify the page range you want to print.

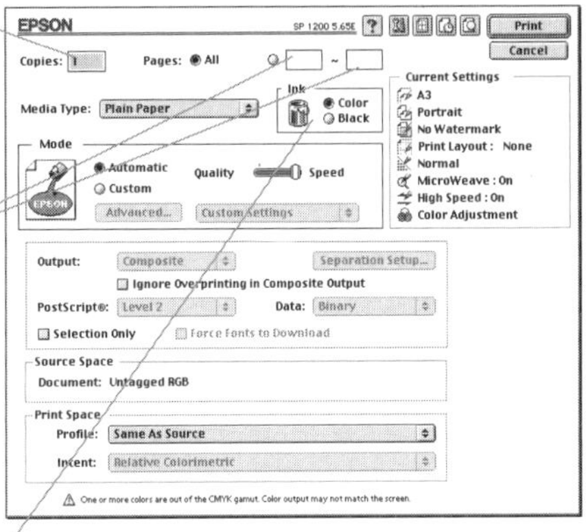

Illustrator prints all visible layers by default (unless the Print option in the Layer Options dialogue box is switched off). Invisible layers do not print. Use the Layer Options dialogue box to make a layer non-printing. When the Print option in the Layer Options dialogue box is off, even if the layer is visible, it will not print.

3 If you are using a colour printer choose whether you want to print in colour or black and white. Choosing Black is useful when you are doing initial proof copies and you want to conserve coloured inks.

4 For colour printers, choose a Media type to indicate the quality of paper on which you want to print.

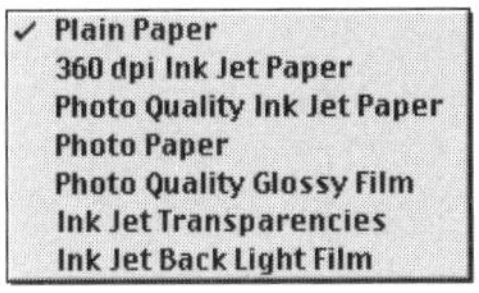

PostScript options are only available if you are printing to a PostScript printer.

5 Set Mode options, if available, for your printer.

6 Leave the Ignore Overprinting in Composite Output deselected if you want to print the artwork and simulate the results of any overprint settings in the file.

Printing Composites – Windows

To create a colour or black and white composite proof of your Illustrator artwork, first use the Print Setup dialogue box to choose from a standard set of printing options, then use the Print dialogue box to print.

When you print a composite, all colours or shades in the file are printed on one sheet of paper.

The effect of overprinting colours does not show on a composite.

1 To print a composite proof, choose File > Print Setup.

2 Make sure the correct printer is selected from the Printer Name pop-up. Choose the actual physical size of the paper in your printer onto which you want to print from the Paper pop-up.

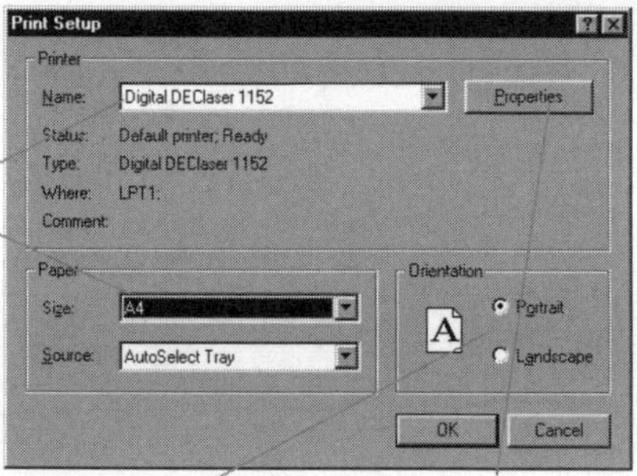

3 Use the Orientation buttons to set the orientation of the page to Portrait or Landscape as necessary.

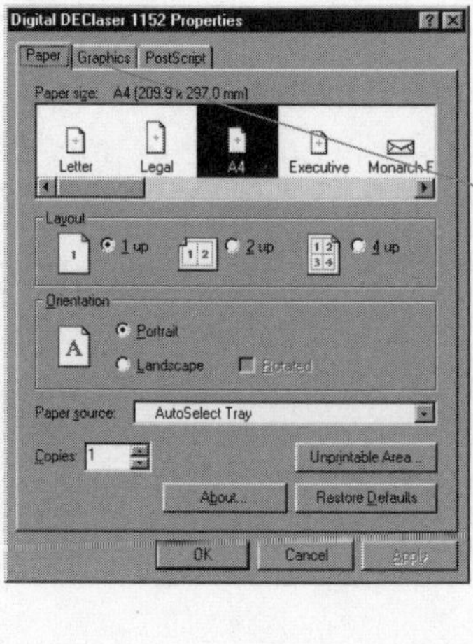

4 Click the Properties button to choose further PostScript options if required (e.g. click the Graphics tab, then set the Scaling % to increase or decrease the size of the artwork that prints).

Printing the file

Illustrator prints all visible layers by default (unless the Print option in the Layer Options dialogue box is switched off). Invisible layers do not print. Use the Layer Options dialogue box to make a layer non-printing. When the Print option in the Layer Options dialogue box is off, even if the layer is visible, it will not print.

1. Choose File > Print. Make sure you have the correct printer chosen from the Printer Name pop-up.

2. If you have more than one page in the document, specify the page range you want to print.

3. Leave the Output pop-up on Composite. Separations is only available if you have already set separation options using File > Separation Setup dialogue box.

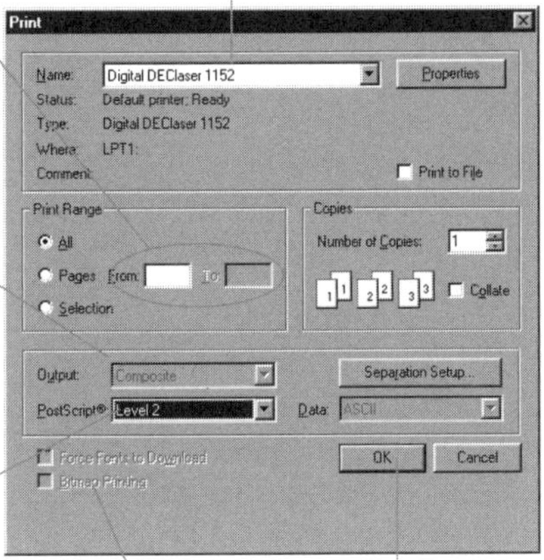

4. Use the PostScript pop-up if your printer is a PostScript printer or supports PostScript printing. Choosing the correct option optimises the printing of objects, especially complex artwork.

5. Bitmap (Windows only). Use this option when you are printing to a non-PostScript printer. The image is sent as a bitmap instead of vectors or curves. This can be a slower but more reliable method of printing.

6. Click OK.

Crop Marks

Crop Marks are small lines placed at the corners of a page to indicate where the page is to be trimmed. Illustrator can only create one set of crop marks for an illustration. You can create crop marks for an entire page, or you can create a rectangle to define the position of the crop marks.

1. To create crop marks for an entire page, choose Object > Crop Marks > Make. Crop marks appear around the corners of the page.

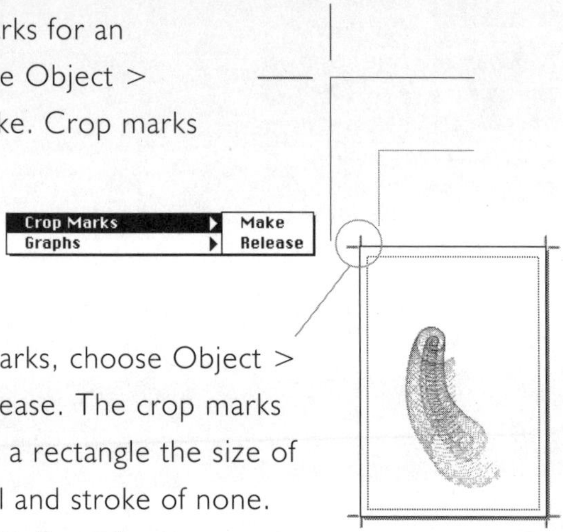

2. To release crop marks, choose Object > Crop Marks > Release. The crop marks are converted into a rectangle the size of the page, with a fill and stroke of none. Delete the rectangle if you have no further use for it.

Creating crop marks based on a rectangle

1. Create a rectangle to define an area of the page.

2. Choose Object > Crop Marks > Make. The original rectangle disappears and is replaced by crop marks which can be used to trim the page to the size of the rectangle you drew.

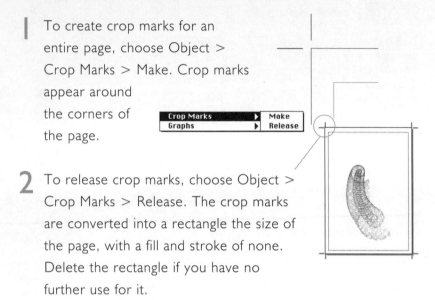

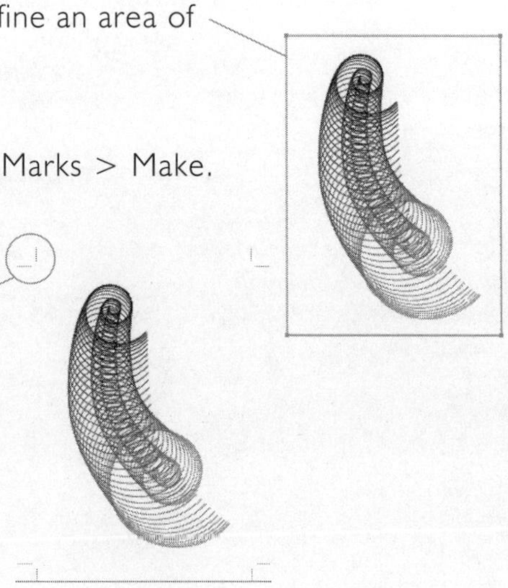

Trim Marks

Trim marks serve the same purpose as crop marks, but you can create more than one set of trim marks in an illustration.

1. To create trim marks, select an object or objects.

2. Choose Filter > Create > Trim Marks. Eight lines – the trim marks – are placed around the selected object(s).

3. To delete trim marks, use the Selection tool to select the trim marks then press the Backspace/Delete key.

Unlike crop marks, you can select, move and delete trim marks.

Group trim marks with the object(s) you originally selected to prevent accidentally moving or otherwise editing the trim marks.

Registration is the colour applied automatically to trim marks to ensure that they will appear on all plates if you make separations.

Printing Problems

In files consisting of multiple, complex paths, you can sometimes get problems printing your artwork. Use the following suggestions to attempt to get the file to print.

1. Patterns can sometimes cause printing problems. Choose Object > Expand to 'expand' or break the pattern into separate filled objects.

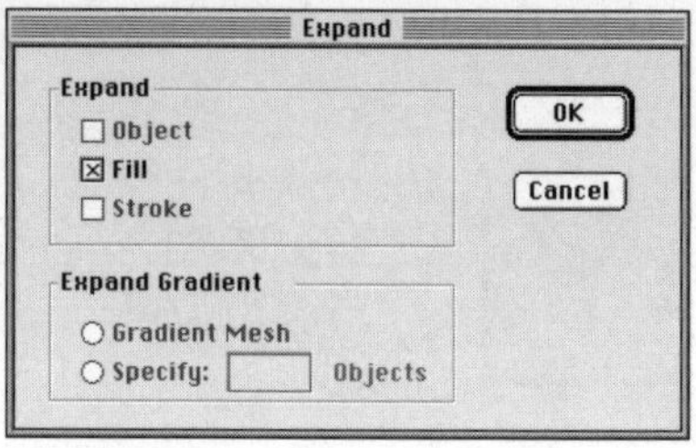

2. If the file is very complex and has a great many long, complex paths, you can also encounter printing problems. Try to simplify complex paths by reducing the number of points used in the path, using the Delete-anchor point tool.

Lines through paths indicating where paths are split can be seen in Outline View (Command/Ctrl+Y). These lines do not print or preview.

3. Alternatively, choose File > Document Setup. Select Printing and Export from the pop-up menu, then select the Split long paths option. Illustrator will then divide up or split any closed path that is too long to print. It's a good idea to make a copy of the file before you choose the Split long paths option so that you can return to the unsplit version if necessary. Otherwise, once paths are split, to make changes you either have to work with the separate shapes created by the command, or rejoin the paths using the Unite Pathfinder command.

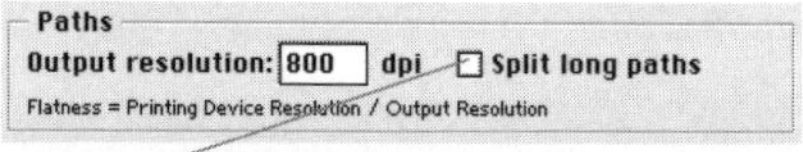

4. Compound Paths/Masks can cause problems when printing. Try printing a file copy without any suspect compounds/ masks to eliminate or confirm the object as the problem.

Filters and Effects

Chapter Fifteen

Adobe Illustrator ships with an extensive range of filters that you can use to change your artwork in various ways. The first group of filters alter, enhance or distort either the paths from which objects are created or their fills. The second group only work on placed bitmap images or objects created in Illustrator and then rasterised (made into a bitmap).

As the primary function of Adobe Illustrator is to create vector based artwork, this chapter aims to give you a feel for some of the initial group of filters. Take time to experiment with the various filters as they offer a great number of creative possibilities.

Use Effects to change the appearance of an object without changing the underlying shape of the object itself.

Covers

Punk and Bloat

Punk and Bloat, depending on the values you choose, can produce dramatic or subtle results – often the subtler results are more useable.

Punk creates sharp, spiked shapes by curving paths inward from the anchor points and moving anchor points outward. Bloat creates the opposite effect – rounded, bloated shapes, by curving paths outward from the anchor point and moving anchor points inward.

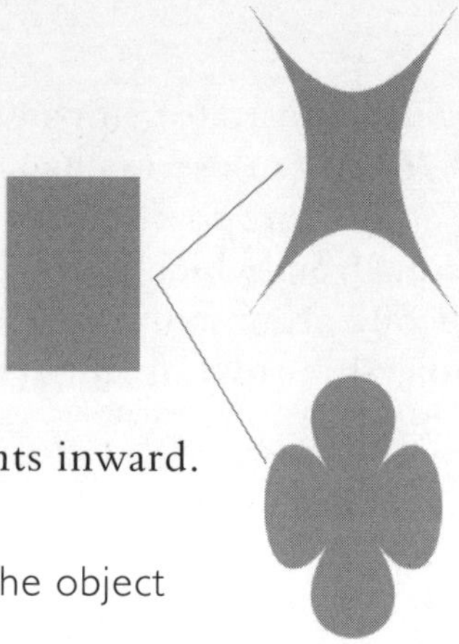

1 To Punk or Bloat an object, select the object using the Selection tool.

2 Choose Filter > Distort > Punk & Bloat.

3 Drag the slider toward Punk or Bloat to create the effect. Or, enter a value in the % entry field from 200 to -200.

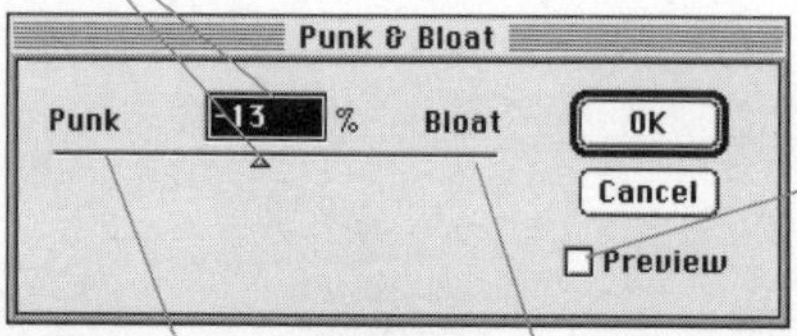

4 Select the Preview option to see the results of the effect before you OK the dialogue box.

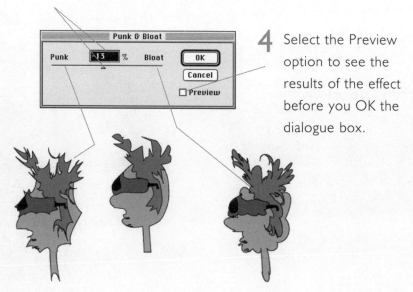

Roughen

The Roughen filter adds points to a path and moves them randomly inward and outward to roughen, or distort the original shape of the path.

1 To roughen an object, select an object using any of the selection tools. Choose Filter > Distort > Roughen.

2 Use the Size slider or enter a % value (0–100%) to specify how far from the original path anchor points can be moved.

3 Use the Details per Inch slider or enter a value (0–100) to determine how many extra points can be added per inch along the path.

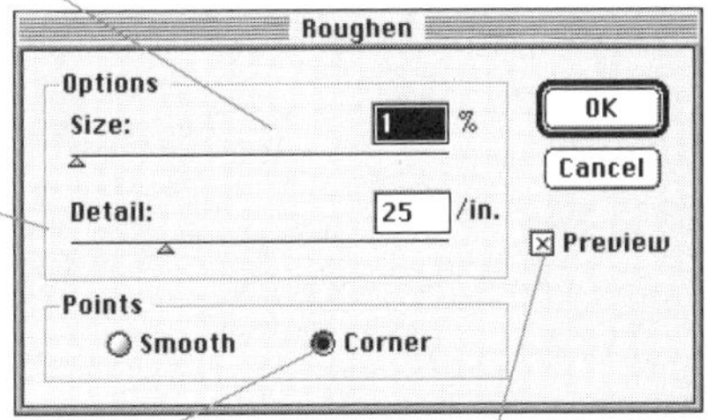

4 Select the Corner points option to create a sharp, jagged edge. Select the Smooth points option to create a smoother, softer edge effect.

5 Select the Preview option to preview the result before you OK the dialogue box.

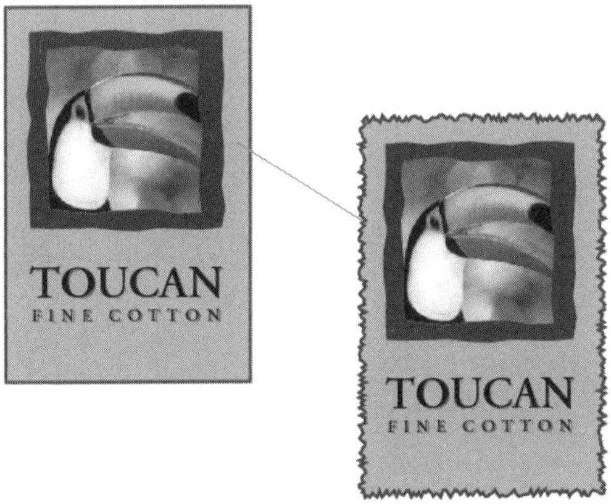

Stylize Filters

Use the Selection tool to select an object(s) before choosing Filter > Stylize.

Use Stylize filters to add a drop shadow to objects, to round corners and to add arrowheads to the ends of open paths.

1. To create a drop shadow, choose Drop Shadow from the Stylize submenu. Enter an 'X' value to move the shadow horizontally away from the original object. Enter a 'Y' value to move the shadow vertically away from the original. Enter a Darkness value to control the colour of the shadow. Select the Group Shadow option to automatically group the drop shadow with the original object.

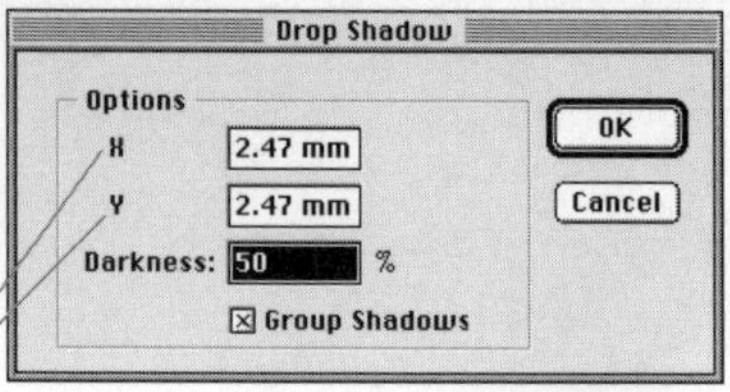

2. Choose Round Corners to create rounded corners on an object. Enter a Radius value to determine how rounded the corners become.

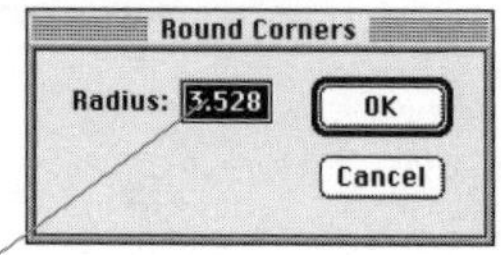

3. With an open path selected, choose Add Arrowheads. Click the Left/Right arrows to choose from the available styles. Use the 'Arrowhead at' pop-up to specify on which end of the path the arrowheads are placed. Use the Scale % pop-up to specify the size.

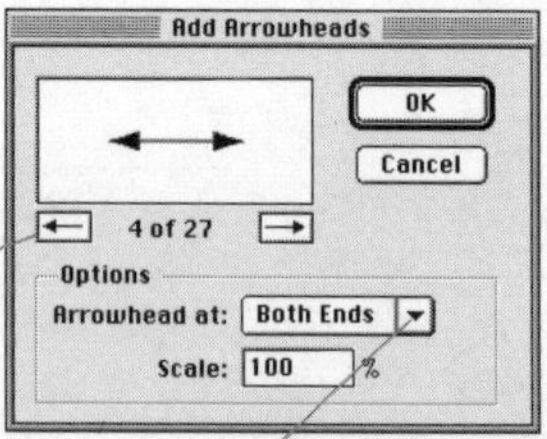

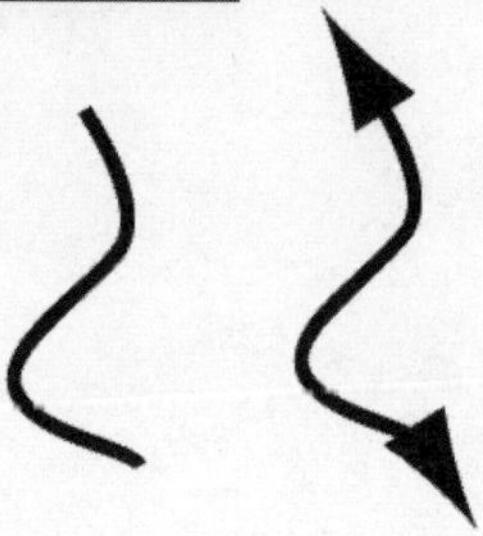

Effects

An Effect is one type of appearance attribute (see pages 90–91). When you apply an effect to an object, it changes the appearance of the object, not the original shape of the object itself. There is no limit to the number of effects you can apply to an object. The effects you apply to an object are listed in the Appearance palette. Use the Appearance palette to modify or delete effects.

Most of the effects available in the Effects menu also exist as commands or functions elsewhere in Adobe Illustrator.

1 To apply an effect to a selected object or group, choose Effect in the menu bar. Choose an effect from the list of effects.

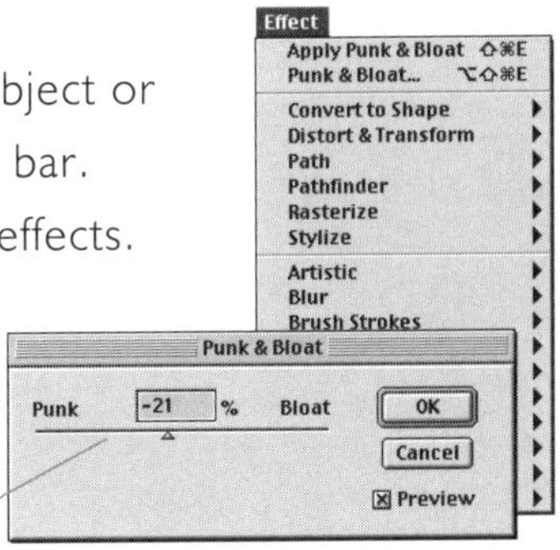

2 Create settings, depending on the effect chosen, as required. The effect changes the appearance of the object. The object itself is not changed.

An effect allows you to change the appearance of an object whilst preserving its underlying shape.

3 To edit the effect, make sure the Appearance palette is showing, then double-click the effect.

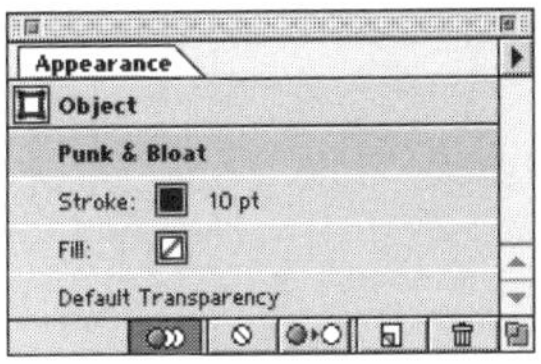

4 To apply an effect to a fill or stroke of a selected object, first click the Fill or Stroke entry in the Appearance palette, then apply the effect. For example, you can Scribble and Tweak (from the Distort sub-menu) the stroke of an object, without affecting the fill.

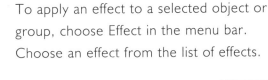

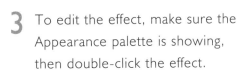

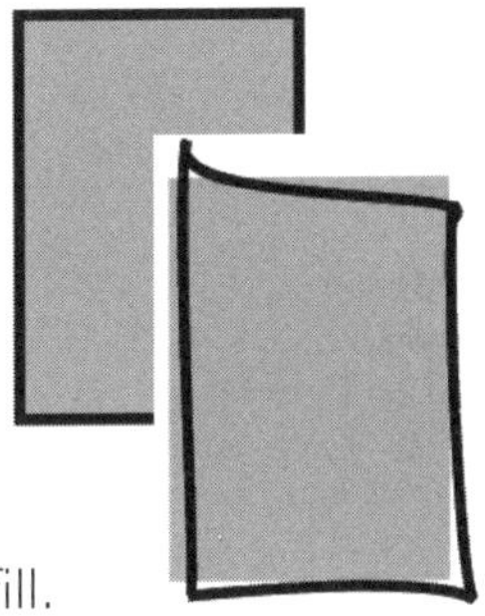

To apply an effect to a layer you must target the layer first (see page 72).

5 To remove an effect from a selected object, make sure the Appearance palette is showing, click on the effect entry then click the Wastebasket. Or drag the entry into it.

Index

a

b

c

d

e

q

r

s

t

U

V

W

Z